D1526821

# From Dissident to Party Politics:

# The Struggle for Democracy in

# Post-Communist Hungary, 1989-1994

Bernard Ivan Tamas

WITHDRAWN

East European Monographs, Boulder, Colorado
Distributed by Columbia University Press, New York
2007

East European Monographs, No. DCCVII

Printed in the United States of America

# Table of Contents

# Acknowledgements

The research that led to this book was conducted over two years in East-Central Europe with the help of three generous grants: A Fulbright Fellowship funded by both the Institute of International Education and the Hungarian government; a Robert F. Kennedy Fellowship from the American Hungarian Foundation; and a Port Fund Grant from Rutgers University. Far more people contributed than can be realistically mentioned here, but a few deserve special recognition. First and foremost, Gerald Pomper was central to the success of this project. He brought a critical eye to the work, read multiple drafts, and helped refine various aspects of the argument. Jan Kubik also helped considerably, as did P. Dennis Bathory and Joseph Borocz. My colleagues and friends Matt Reed and Manfred Steger gave critical feedback at various stages. Susan Craig, Jonathan McFall, Melina Patterson, Jamal Nassar, and Lane Crothers also contributed in meaningful ways.

I would also like to thank the many members of the Hungarian–American community in New Brunswick, NJ who helped the project in various ways. Two people who deserve special mention are August Molnár of the American Hungarian Foundation and Miklós Ruszcsák of the Hungarian Alumni Association.

In Hungary, Mária, Béla, and Mari Péterfia were an unending source of personal support, and Csilla Bartha, Tamás Kis, and Agnes Bankó helped push the research forward through their time and technical knowledge. The Central European University was extremely supportive, and I am especially thankful to the experts in Hungarian politics that I met there, including Gábor Tóka, András Bozóki, Zsolt Enyedi, and László Bruszt. Other scholars, including Attila Ágh, Gabriella Ilonszki, György Csepeli and Diane Morlang, similarly helped to make this book possible.

I also wish to thank the current or former politicians who gave me interviews or aided the research in other was. I am grateful to Tamás Beck, András Bozóki, Iván Csaba, Sándor Csoóri, József Gulyás, Gábor Fodor, Miklós Haraszti, István Hegedüs, Sándor Holbok, Géza Jeszenszky, János Kis, Béla Légár, Dan Odelscalchi, and László Vass, some of whom met with me multiple times to answer what must have seemed like unending questions about their respective parties. I am especially grateful to Miklós Haraszti, who gave me fifteen to twenty hours of taped interviews on the democratic opposition and the Alliance of Free Democrats.

My greatest thanks goes to my family, including my siblings, Peter, Mick, and Sophie, and especially my parents, who have always given me unwavering support. I therefore dedicate this book to my parents, Tamas and Marie Tamas, with my deepest love.

Introduction:

# Party Competence
# and the Struggle for Democracy

**Political Competence and Opposition:**

> *Private citizens who become princes purely by good fortune do so
> with little exertion on their own part; but subsequently they
> maintain their position only by considerable exertion. They make
> the journey as if they had wings; their problems start when they
> are alight... They do not know how to maintain their position,
> and they cannot do so... So they are destroyed in the first bad
> spell. This is inevitable unless those who have suddenly become
> princes are of such prowess that overnight they can learn how to
> preserve what fortune has tossed into their laps... (Niccolò
> Machiavelli, The Prince)[1]*

Around 1510, Niccolò Machiavelli begot modern political thought by
writing the first major treatise on political competence: *The Prince*. Machiavelli
made the critical transformation to seeing politics as a harsh and often brutal
struggle for power. Political ethics was relegated to a secondary position (and the
"sociology of government"—to the degree that one can claim any sociology before
the nineteenth century—remained no more than a means to his analytical end.)
But there was a second aspect of this transformation. The good prince for
Machiavelli was not the godly ruler or the philosopher king but the competent and
cold politician. Success at that struggle, he argued, is only half determined by
fortune. The skills and ruthlessness of the prince are equally important, especially
when fortune moves against him. Indeed, the structure of his book demonstrates
the centrality of competence and learning in Machiavelli's thoughts: *The Prince* is
a primer on the ignoble art of politics, a forceful guide on how to win and preserve
power over an Italian principality.

There are probably good historical reasons why Machiavelli is one of the
first to discuss competencies of politicians. Political competence and the
professionalization of politics are closely related topics, and professional
politicians began to rise in Europe around the period Machiavelli lived.[2] Indeed,
as a diplomat for the brief period when the Medici family was out of power in
Florence, Machiavelli seemed to fall into this group. Political professionals rose
in importance when princes began finding use for trained or well-educated
advisors. As feudal political systems were gradually replaced by representative
democracies, and as the courts of royalty were replaced by legislatures and
bureaucratic political organization, the professional politician became the central

player. Moreover, as the western world modernized, the expertise needed from professional politicians became more specialized. More accurately, modern politics became a group of specializations—the diplomat's expertise are different from that of the party politician or the policy advisor—and each specialization requires its own set of competencies.

Yet, political competence is hardly studied by political scientists. While a minority treat it as a factor, few treat it as a central issue and most ignore it completely. The reasons seem to be simple. Until relatively recently, most of political science research had a bias towards advanced, industrialized liberal democracies. In most of these countries, the government is run by a strata of political professionals with extensive backgrounds in politics. Political leaders mostly got to their positions through a gradual, incremental climb up a party ladder. Since competencies are built through experience, the main groups competing against each other for power would enter each political battle with roughly equal political competence. If one compares the political competencies of the major factions within most developed democracies, there is likely to be little difference overall, which in turn implies that political competencies have little impact on the system.

However, even in stable democracies, political competence can be ignored only with broad strokes. Oddities in institutional structures or variations in circumstances can produces situations in which people are lifted into positions for which they have limited background. In the United States, for example, politicians often climb up the party ranks through an odd obstacle course of primary and general elections. While the American system also produces a government filled mostly with political professionals having extensive political backgrounds, sometimes a politician can jump to a political positions for which she or he has limited relevant training. In 1992, for example, Bill Clinton's leap from governor of a small, rural state to president was aided by odd circumstances. President Bush's popularity after the first Gulf War scared off the most formidable Democratic challengers, producing an otherwise unlikely party nomination victory for Clinton. Then a deep recession helped lead to a Clinton electoral victory. In the process, someone with no serious experience in Washington politics was suddenly in charge, and then an administration led by someone thought to have exceptional native political abilities spent its first two years making significant, costly strategic mistakes.

But the issue goes beyond the question of which group already within the circles of power in a stable democracy benefits the most from relative political competence. Instead, the issue of political competencies becomes more important when one considers two other political situations. The first is when an opposition group is challenging an established political elite. The problem is conceptually simple: *The level of a person's political competencies tends to be positively related to that person's proximity to state power.* While some may be born with native skills that can be applied to politics, generally speaking competencies at politics must be developed through experience. For example, there is no training for running national level campaigns, or handling a mass media, or leading a party with branches across a country quite like actual involvement in these activities. Not only do professional politicians, political staff, career lobbyists and the like gain on-the-job experience. Major political parties and other governing organizations have the infrastructure through which aspiring politicians can climb gradually and, in the process, develop skills critical to political battle. In sharp contrast, opposition groups, citizen organizations, and minor parties rarely have the resources to build teams of politicians with the competence to effectively challenge those already in power.

Since relative political competencies influence the outcome of political struggle, generally speaking, *the political impact of varying political competencies in periods of political stability is to reinforced the established political order.* Those in power usually have an experience and therefore a competence advantage over opposition groups, even when circumstances shift against them. And in the uncommon situation in which an opposition group wins power, that group has a higher likelihood of making serious strategic errors and losing that quickly gained political positions.

A good example is the problems of minor parties. By definition, a minor or third party (as opposed to simply a smaller party in a legislature) is external to or at the fringes of state power. They face a fundamental dilemma: A minor party is unlikely to gain power or any serious role in the political struggle unless circumstances, usually widespread dissatisfaction with the established order, propels them rapidly into a position of contention. However, this rapid success and the speed of this move into an unfamiliar political realm, including competition against seasoned professionals and a higher level of public scrutiny, increases the chances of that party making strategic blunders or self-destructive maneuvers, undermining its attempt to gain power and influence the political system.

The issue of political competencies also becomes important whenever one considers political change. Because competencies are built largely through extended experience, rapid change almost by definition throws people into situations at which they have limited background.[3] There are two main ways this can occur. Rapid change can throw those already in power into unfamiliar political battles. For example, when a country shifts quickly from a dictatorship to a democracy, those in power during the previous regime can be put into an exceptionally difficult position. Not only are they normally hated and denigrated for their roles in the previous regime; they are also thrust into a new arena of political competition at which they have little experience. Strategies honed and habits engrained during the previous regime can overnight become passé at best and self-destructive at worst. In terms of the political survival of the previous elite, then, one question is how much the regime had already liberalized before the formal transition. In other words, how different is the post-transition politics from the pre-transition politics?

Rapid political change also tends to catapult people lower in the political ranks or completely outside the system into positions of power and therefore into unfamiliar political terrain. Part of the issue is that political change is often driven by people who were outside the centers of state power. Those in charge often have a vested interest in the status quo, and their replacement becomes critical to substantive change. Moreover, significant change can undermine the legitimacy of the institutional structures that had slowed politicians' climb to power. Other,

3

faster avenues for political advancement can emerge, and these avenues can open the door for people with little related political experience to gain significant power.

Dissidents during a democratic transition often face all of these problems. Having worked as the political opposition, usually for a decade or more, dissidents often become masters at the art of political subversion and of de-legitimating a regime. But when they are successful and the government democratizes, they are often pushed into new, unfamiliar roles. At this stage, they are transformed from outsiders attacking the regime to players helping build a regime. This leap into a new role can be critical for the health of the new, democratic regime. Representative democracy is dependent on competition among groups, especially political parties competing for seats, and these new organizations have to be built by somebody. Their roles as the opponents of the previous regime and especially the notoriety they gained through their brave work makes them excellent candidates for the new politics. Moreover, it is important that the previous elite does not simply maintain its old positions of power in the guise of a new system. The elite of the previous regime normally have an interest in keeping significant aspects of the previous system intact, and therefore a new government run by the old guard can undermine critical aspects of the democratic transformation.

But, these former dissidents often have little experience in the politics they are now thrust into. Having been the political opposition and therefore having lived on the fringes of society and possibly in prison, these individuals have no opportunity to develop competencies at national level politics. Following the transition, they not only have to handle new, unfamiliar responsibilities that have fallen into their laps. They also have to do so in a rapidly changing and often contentious situation. Even seasoned political professionals would likely have difficulty maintaining their positions in the midst of the political turmoil that often accompanies democratic transitions. For the former dissidents, it is an especially difficult task.

This book is about this Catch-22. Democratization requires new people, usually dissidents, to take critical roles in the new political system. But, the very fact that they are new to political competition at that level makes them unprepared for the tasks at hand. It is a situation very similar to one described by Machiavelli, quoted above. Moreover, this problem produces a danger. When this new group of political leaders fail, they can open the door for more extreme parties or parties of the previous regime coming to power. As the former opponents of the regime as well as longstanding proponents of democratization, their failure not only undermines their own public credibility; it can also hurt the legitimacy of the new political order.

The question then becomes, what type of political competence do these dissidents lack that is so essential for a new democratic state? One answer is, competence at party politics.

**From Dissident to Party Politics:**

Political parties are arguably the most important non-government institutions in modern democracy. They are a critical, pragmatic bridge between the few in office and the masses of citizens. All modern, representative democracies have competing political parties. There seems to be several reasons why. Parties give voters an easy way to select among politicians. Instead of having to absorb the stands of countless individual candidates, citizens can learn a few overarching differences among a handful of parties. Similarly, parties help make accountability simpler. If the public is unhappy with the government's performance at a given time, the party in power can be voted out of office in the hope that its replacement will achieve better. With no parties, the public could be easily confused over who to blame, eliminating a fundamental control over politicians' behavior.[4]

Parties also play a critical role during democratization, or the transition from a non-democratic state to one with representation based on regular, competitive elections. Political scientists have found a number of factors that drive a political system towards democratization, like economic modernization or when an economic crisis forces the government to shift its legitimacy to representation. Dissidents also play a role. Those in power virtually never give up authority willingly. Instead, dissident groups attempt to topple the regime, and then they try to either seize power completely from the previous rulers or share power with that established elite in a way that reduces the latter's role significantly.

These are two distinct steps. In the first step, loose groups of dissidents attempt various subversive strategies. Sometimes these groups lead large-scale protest movements, such as challenging the regime through mass demonstrations of opposition. Other times, notably when the first option is not realistic, small bands of dissidents living semi-underground attempt to undermine the legitimacy of the regime, calculating step by step how to coax it towards self-destruction while simultaneously trying to avoid extended imprisonment.

If the state does democratize—if the government accepts free elections or has those elections forced upon it—the role of these dissident groups takes a second step. Many of these groups now have to transform themselves into political parties and run candidates for elected office. One must assume that those in power would fight to retain their privileges positions every step of the way. Given the chance, they would work to hold onto their old positions under a new guise of representative democracy. By forming parties and running for office, dissident groups could hopefully wrestle state power from the previous rulers. More importantly, by successfully winning power and establishing a viable alternative to the political elite of the former regime, the opposition forces groups to compete for that power through developing mass appeal. The mechanics of representative democracy require multiple parties competing for public support, and during democratization the dissident groups are among the few places other than the former ruling party from which leaders of new parties can realistically emerge.

But there is a problem. *Dissident and party politics are two fundamentally different types of politics.* Since party politics is a specialized form of politics requiring skills developed through experience or training, the most capable people in dissident politics would enter party politics as virtual amateurs. Not only would the heroes as well as the unknown activists of the underground have to learn a completely new form of politics. They would effectively have to

5

unlearn dissident politics. To make matters worse, barely trained protesters aside, party politics requires far more manpower than oppositional politics, especially if the democratic opposition was a small, loose group of dissidents and is now heading a party or several parties running candidates for hundreds of elected offices. Former dissidents normally have only a few months to build political parties with organizations that reach all parts of the country. They have to construct their organizations so fast that they effectively have no time to learn this new politics, and they usually have to fill important positions with virtually anyone available, almost regardless of their backgrounds.

This produces a danger. The new, pro-democracy parties would enter national-level politics with low party competence. Since low party competence increases the chances that these parties would fail and become insignificant players in the new regime, the probability of the previous elite retaining or quickly regaining power also increases. It also increases the chances that more extreme parties could emerge, not only because the failure of parties built by dissidents opens room for these extreme parties but also because the behavior of the former dissidents influences the level of confidence in the new political system.

**Party Competence:**

The notion of party competence, as the term is used in this book, is rooted in the political sociology of Max Weber. For Weber, political parties in modern, mass democracies are large, bureaucratic organizations necessary to woo and organize the mass public. The goal of parties, he argues, is patronage, broadly understood. By winning elections, they place their politicians into elected offices. Since those elected officials need assistants, the party also provides government paid jobs for more party members. The government also needs judges, agency heads and a wide variety of other jobs that fall outside a civil service system, and the winning parties can determine who fills those positions. In this way, party politics is a career in which individuals join an organization and help it fight for control over government, and in return the party hands these individuals government paid jobs or positions paid for directly by the party.[5]

There is another reason why party politics has evolved into a career. Like other specialized areas of modern life, party competition requires specialized training. As Weber put it,

> *The development of politics into an organization which demanded training in the struggle for power, and in the methods of this struggle as developed by modern party policies, determined the separation of public functionaries into two categories, which, however, are my no means rigidly but nevertheless distinctly separated. These categories are 'administrative' officials on the one hand, and 'political' officials on the other.*[6]

Put simply, the training needed to run the administrative end of government is different from that needed in the political end, or the end held by party politicians. A primary skill needed for the party politician, Weber argues, is that of the demagogue. Weber is quick to caution that the "distasteful flavor" of the term should not cloud the critical point: A key area of competence in modern party politics is oratory. This, according to him, is a primary reason why lawyers play such a significant role in party politics:

> *The significance of lawyers in Occidental politics since the rise of parties is not accidental... To an outstanding degree, politics today is in fact conducted in public by means of the spoken or written word. To weigh the effect of the word properly falls within the range of the lawyers' task; but not at all into that of the civil servant. The latter is no demagogue, nor is it his purpose to be one.*[7]

This particular specialized training is necessary in party politics because party politics in liberal democracies is based on building support. Parties need more than the support of the mass public to be successful. Building off of a widely used framework developed by V.O. Key,[8] party politics can be seen as a synthesis of three areas of politics at once: There is a mass politics arena, a governmental or elite politics field, and there is intra-party politics. Parties obviously need mass support because they need votes during elections. Parties also need the support of elite organizations, like interest groups, because those organizations can provide other valuable resources, like money. Similarly, a party leadership must maintain the support of its membership, both the professionals and the rank-and-file, because it needs manpower focused on winning state power.

Intra-party politics is a good example of why support is so important to parties. Running a political party is quite different than running other bureaucratic organizations, like corporations. Unlike corporate heads, who can hire and fire largely at will, party leaders must maintain support of party members. There are several reasons why. Parties cannot afford to pay everyone, and even the professional politicians are paid more with promises of an interesting job than a significant salary. Similarly, party leaders do not own their parties, or at least they cannot treat their party as if it was their property. Unlike businesses, party leaders have to legitimate their leadership positions, usually through democratic procedures that could potentially open the door for internal challenge. Finally, party politicians can develop other resources, including positions handed to them by the party, to challenge the leadership. If the rank-and-file becomes disenchanted, it simply won't work for the party, which translates into a competitive disadvantage. Similarly, if party members are unhappy with the leadership, an intra-party struggle for power can break out that saps energy and other resources and potentially paralyzes the party's ability to focus on competing against other parties.

There is another reason why generally united support of the leadership is important. Since parties win power by convincing others to support them, including by justifying their quest for power, parties need to remain consistent and united in their presentation to the public. This point was developed by the rational choice school,[9] but the point is general enough that it is accepted by many party scholar. When a party is inconsistent about what policies it would support, the public becomes confused and potentially distrustful of what policies the party would actually legislate. This does not mean that, for example, economically conservative parties cannot support welfare policies. But, they have to couch that support within their justification for power. The same is true for social democratic parties, which can call for government cuts but must explain them within the framework of their larger goals of promoting the working class. Similarly, if the party is not generally united on its policy goals, the public can become confused about or distrustful of what policies it would actually implement.

Of course, parties in liberal democracies virtually always have competing factions with ideological differences. The public is unlikely to care about party politicians having an internal debate or jostling within the organization for power. But when the party slips into disarray or its behavior becomes unpredictable, it becomes questionable if that organization can govern, and public support will likely dive.

This need for consistency and unity in a multifaceted political struggle is a critical reason why party competence is so important, and also why it is such a serious problem for dissidents building parties. In the wake of a collapsing regime, dissidents could be smart enough to build a party organization off the optimistic excitement of finally ending a dictatorship and clever enough to create a colorful and convincing electoral campaign. But over time, and not all that much time, circumstances can shift rapidly. Party leaders can be pressed by various and often conflicting forces. The rank-and-file may have wants that would hurt public support, for example, or if the party has become part of a governing coalition, it can be pressed by coalition partners and other interests, including foreign governments and international organizations, to take steps that its public constituency would disapprove of. Under these conditions, these rapidly built parties must present a united front to an often uncertain public, and the party must remain largely consistent in its justifications even as the political environment changes rapidly. For the novices, it can be a trying task. They are more likely than the veterans of party politics to overreact to these pressures or to developing problems, or these neophytes to party politics might revert to more familiar strategies from their dissident days. Either way, the party will struggle and in the process potentially threaten the democratic transition.

**Dissidents Building Parties in Post-Communist Hungary:**

Hungary was one example of a nation that had a democratic transition pushed partially by a democratic opposition switching from dissident to party politics. These dissidents went through a period of rapidly building party organizations right before the elections of 1990. During those first competitive parliamentary elections since the 1940s, the Socialists were soundly defeated by these new parties. It was a devastating defeat. The Socialist party was discredited for its relationship with the Soviet occupation as well as its role in producing the economic crisis Hungary was facing. There was no sign that the party would recover anytime soon.

Indeed, the long-term disempowerment of the Socialists was a primary goal of many Hungarian dissidents. Hard-core dissidents often spoke of a need to stop *hatalomátmentés*, or the Socialists retaining control over Hungary with simply a new system to legitimate their positions of power. These dissidents believed that preventing *hatalomátmentés* required two critical steps. First, the Socialists had to be removed from critical positions of government. Not only did the dissidents need to defeat the Socialists in the election, but Socialists had to be removed from important positions in the government administration. Second, the Socialists had to be kept out of power for an extended period.[10] János Kis, the most prominent of the hard-core dissidents, argued that the Socialist party should not head the Hungarian government for at least twenty years after Hungary became a democracy.

But then something surprising happened. In 1994, just four years after Hungary became a democracy, the Socialists won an overwhelming electoral victory and regained governmental power. Despite being vilified as the collaborators of the hated Soviet occupation and the culprits behind Hungary's economic ills, Hungarians voted the Socialists back into power by a landslide. With six parties in Parliament, Hungarian voters handed the Socialists a majority of seats, producing no mathematical need for a coalition. The Socialists chose to go into a coalition with another party anyway. Combined, they held a supermajority large enough to change the Hungarian constitution at will. From that point on, the Socialists remained a dominant party in Hungary, barely losing the 1998 election—though they actually got the most party list votes—and then winning again in 2002.

Hungarian pundits and political scientists at the time attributed the Socialist resurrection of 1994 to a number of factors. Many argued that Hungarians became "nostalgic" for the security of state socialism. Others claimed that the Hungarian media had a Socialist bias and had actively promoted the Hungarian Socialist Party.[11] But, there was a fundamental problem with most of these explanations. Most made sense only if one examined the period from a distance. For example, the nostalgia theory, probably the most widely supported by political scientists, was based on looking at the two elections as snapshots. According to this theory, in 1990, economic ills and other factors led Hungarians to kick out the Socialists. By 1994, the economic conditions got much worse for most Hungarian, and surveys showed that Hungarians were dissatisfied with the new democracy. Since the economic situation for most Hungarians was better under state socialism, and since most were dissatisfied with democracy, they voted for a return to the economic security socialism used to provide them.

However, the nostalgia theory falls apart once one examines Hungarian party support between the two elections. Put simply, the rise of Socialist support did not correspondent with the economic decline or the drop in satisfaction with the new system. Unemployment rose rapidly after the transition but stabilized in 1992. Similarly, it was around 1992 that satisfaction with democracy was at its lowest point. Yet, at the time, an overwhelming plurality of around 45% of Hungarians supported a party from the dissident movement, the Federation of Young Democrats. The Young Democrats held three times the support of any other party, including the Socialists, until around March 1993, a year before the election. Then, suddenly, support for that party of former dissidents evaporated. As 80% to 85% of Young Democrat supporters deserted the party, support for the Socialists rose, leading to their victory and a political resurrection that put the Socialists back into the center of Hungarian politics.

In other words, the nostalgia theory cannot explain why during the height of economic distress Hungarians overwhelmingly supported the party built by the dissident group that had argued most adamantly for dismantling the socialist economic system, including the economic safety net. It also cannot explain why support for the Hungarian Socialist Party rose at the same time that unemployment stabilized and satisfaction with democracy increased.

In this book, a different explanation is given for that rapid turnaround. The leaders of the parties that came from the Hungarian dissident movement lacked the specialized competencies of running political parties. The rapid transformation catapulted them from one type of politics to another, giving them no time to develop skills in this new political arena. Faced with unfamiliar circumstances, they often reverted to inappropriate strategies from their pre-party days and rarely maintained any consistency in how they presented themselves. Each party from the dissident movement also experienced an intra-party crisis, and most flirted with disaster. Making repeated strategic blunders and unable to maintain party unity, these parties undermined their own public credibility as well as public trust in the new government. In sharp contrast, the Socialist party had reformed itself significantly since the 1960s in ways that produced Socialist politicians who were better prepared for multiparty politics. Maintaining a consistent, professional air, the Socialists eventually capitalized on missteps by the other parties.

*Political Backgrounds of Party Politicians:*

Other than those that were offshoots of the Socialist party, there were two main types of new parties formed in Hungary during its democratic transition. One type were parties that took a name of a pre-Stalin era party, like the Christian Democratic People's Party. These parties sometimes included members who had been politicians in the pre-1948 party of the same name. But there were few of these politicians, and while they brought some legitimacy to using the old party name, these senior citizens could not bring many skills applicable to party politics in Hungary of the 1990s. Other than these politicians with political experiences from the 1940s, the people who ran these parties had little background that could be applied to competitive party politics.[12]

The second type were dissident groups that transformed themselves itself into political parties during the regime change. There were three of these parties that played a major role in Hungarian politics. The first was the Alliance of Free Democrats, which was built by the hard-core opposition. This group of dissidents began forming in the 1970s after several of its members had been thrown out of the university system. While these dissidents were overtly political, their backgrounds were that of intellectual subversives. Their main leader, János Kis, was a philosopher, and many of these dissidents were writers. They were well versed in developing thoughtful and analytically consistent arguments about topics like why civil society is a necessary step for Hungary or why Hungary was heading into an economic crisis. They were also adept at attacking and undermining a regime. But while a few had been Socialist party members before the early 1970s—they had become disillusioned after the invasion of Prague in 1968—they had no political experience related to party politics.[13]

The second dissident organization that became a political party was the Hungarian Democratic Forum. The Democratic Forum founders were cultural intellectuals, mostly writers or literary historians connected to the populist writers movement. Early Democratic Forum leaders reached prominence in this organization based on their positions within the populist writers' movement, which was often related to their skills at Hungarian prose and the writing awards they had won. Recognizing their own limitations in this area, the Democratic Forum brought in an outsider, József Antall, to head the organization and lead the negotiations for a new democratic state. A museum director, Antall was also a historian who had studied constitutional law and the negotiations between Viennese and Budapest diplomats that led to the compromise behind the Austo-Hungarian Empire in 1867. Antall was fit for the role as chief negotiator for the opposition at the Trilateral Negotiations, which designed Hungary's democratic system. However, these political skills did not translate well into party politics, especially when it came to maintaining support within the populist dominated party apparatus.[14]

The dissident group that appeared to be most prepared for party politics was the Federation of Young Democrats. FIDESZ, as it was called (which is pronounced, "FEE-dess") was formed and run primarily by a group of law students who lived in special dormitories for excellent students from the countryside. Being trained primarily as lawyers instead of writers, historians or philosophers, the FIDESZ leadership was able to develop a direct rhetorical style that would fit party competition better than the longwinded style of other dissidents. Moreover, being mostly in their early to mid-twenties and having joined the democratic opposition just as the Socialist regime was coming to an end, they did not have to unlearn habits developed over a decade of political opposition. Nonetheless, while the FIDESZ leaders had a background more applicable to party politics than those of the other dissident organizations, they too were novices at this type of politics.[15]

Just as the backgrounds of these dissidents influenced their competencies at building and running parties, the evolution of the Socialist party since the Hungarian Revolution of 1956 led to a generation of Socialist politicians who were relatively well prepared for multi-party competition. In reaction to the revolution, the Socialist party began attempting to maintain domination by placating the public instead of terrorizing it. The Socialists opened relations with the West in order to gain loans and increase trade that would fuel an economy now focused on consumerism. Besides exposing many of these politicians to West European politics, Socialist politicians now had to function in a more complex elite environment, including trying to balance between Moscow and the West. At the same time, promotion within the party became based more on technical competence than ideological zeal, and with terror eliminated as a technique for maintaining party unity, intra-party politics became relatively more complex and nuanced. And while the Socialists had no more experience in electioneering than before, this new politics of placating the public did force them to develop greater skills at building public support. Over time, all of these changes would help prepare the generation of Socialist politicians who won power over the party in the late 1980s for multiparty politics in the early 1990s.[16]

These changes made the Socialists no better at electioneering than any other party. In fact, the three parties from the dissident movement probably ran

11

better campaigns in 1990. The difference became clear when each party ran into problems, internal conflicts or contradictory demands. The new parties tended to overreact and mishandle their problems, causing downward spirals of support and internal crises. The Socialists remained steady, despite the tremendous pressure put on the party after the collapse of state socialism.

*The Fall and Rise of the Hungarian Socialist Party, 1989-1994:*

Single-party, state socialism ended in Hungary in late 1989, and the first parliamentary elections of the new government were held in early 1990. The Hungarian Democratic Forum was the clear winner with 25% of the proportional representation vote; it became the head of a three party governing coalition. The Alliance of Free Democrats, which received just over 21% of that vote, became the main opposition party. The Federation of Young Democrats exceeded all expectations and received 9% of the proportional representation vote; it became a small opposition party in Parliament. The Hungarian Socialist Party received only 11% of the vote and less than 10% of the seats in Parliament.

In 1990, nobody expected a quick Socialist recovery from this devastating defeat. The Socialist party dealt with this crisis in two steps. First, it shuffled its leadership, removing several key figures, and then it remaining a unified party focused on rebuilding its legitimacy. Bill Lomax gave this description of the Socialists: "Following these changes, the new leadership of the party remained stable and united, and has not had to face any direct challenges... [The Hungarian Socialist Party], however, probably more than any other Hungarian party, has come to behave much like modern democratic parties in the West, so that debates over policy and ideology have not so far caused it irretrievable damage or served to tear it apart."[17] Béla Király, an American sociologist who left Hungary after the 1956 revolution and then returned to Hungary to become a member of Parliament, described the Socialists as follows:

> *The professionalism and moderation of the left-of-center policies of the [Hungarian Socialist Party] leadership was impressive to watch. Never during the four years of the first post-communist parliament were they demagogic obstructionists; they rather behaved as a Western-type loyal opposition. In parliamentary committees as well as during plenary sessions of the legislature, they presented professionally prepared, moderate, practical, constructive proposals. Their parliamentary fraction operated in unison, representing a disciplined, well-informed, dignified body of statesmen, rather than unruly politicians. General appreciation and respect followed, contributing with this earned prestige to the political standing of [the Hungarian Socialist Party].[18]*

The parties built by former dissidents faired much worse right after the transition. The Hungarian Democratic Forum began its slide towards internal collapse before even forming its government. As the lead governing party during a political and economic transition, the Democratic Forum faced serious problems. The party handled the political pressure by virtually imploding. The Prime

Minister attempted to exclude the party's main faction from the government. After the Prime Minister ran into difficulties in late 1990, the leaders of that faction began retaliating. In this instability, one of the founding populist writers who had been denied a choice position published a tract that accused the Prime Minister of botching the democratic transition.[19] Instead of distancing itself from this enormous political blunder, a highly public intra-party war broke out, with Democratic Forum members accusing each other in the press of being "fascists" and "Bolsheviks" and using various party forums to vote for each others' expulsion. Two warring factions emerged, each determined to push the other out. The internal war raged on through the 1994 election, crippling the Democratic Forum's campaign, even though a large number of Democratic Forum politicians had already quit or been thrown out.

While the problems for the Democratic Forum were partially bad reactions to external pressures, the Free Democrats problems stemmed purely from intra-party factors. As the main opposition party, the Free Democrats were in the best position to take advantage of the Democratic Forum's problems. However, by early 1991, there was a sense inside the party that the Free Democrats were not successful enough, even though they maintained consistent public support.[20] In response to this perceived crisis, the Free Democrat leadership set off a real crisis by abruptly reverting to strategies of its dissident period. Implicitly rejecting the role of loyal opposition, the Free Democrat leadership announced that the party would return to its radical roots and become adversary instead of simply the opponent of the Democratic Forum government, which it claimed had dictatorial tendencies. The Free Democrats then formed a social movement to fight this perceived attempt to undermine democracy; the Democratic Charter explicitly echoed strategies from the dissident period. Within two months, the dissident leadership of the Alliance of Free Democrats fell from power, with an outsider voted as party president. The party then slipped into an internal struggle for control over the organization. Eventually, allies of the dissidents regained power over the party, and in the process most of the hard-core dissidents were removed, but not before support for the Free Democrats was cut in half, down to 11%.

The group that benefited most from the other parties' problems was the Federation of Young Democrats. In the beginning, FIDESZ gained support mostly among young people because of its bold and often audacious stand against the Socialist regime. When the new parliament convened, male and female FIDESZ MPs attended in blue jeans and sandals, and the men wore long hair and rarely shaved. But, FIDESZ politicians also had attributes that became appealing once Hungarians saw beyond their ages and attire. Lawyers by training, the Young Democrats' rhetoric was clear, direct and grounded, a refreshing change from the more wordy speech of other new parties. The Young Democrat politicians were also united—or more accurately, they appeared united—and they kept a clear focus on pragmatic issues and often acted as a voice of reason when fights between other parties became especially bitter or ideological. By early 1991 FIDESZ was the most supported party. By the end of 1992, it held three to four times the support of each of the other parties.

It was under these conditions that the Young Democrats' leadership suddenly and unexpected changed the party's public presentation. It switched from a liberal to a conservative ideology at the 1993 party congress; it dropped its overwhelmingly popular youth image; and it forced out one of its most popular and liberal politicians.  In the twelve months before the 1994 parliamentary election, nearly 85% of FIDESZ supporters deserted the party.  The FIDESZ drop was echoed by the Socialists' rise.  Half of these FIDESZ deserters decided to vote for the Socialists, and the rest were distributed among the other parties.  In the end, the Socialists received 33% of the list vote, or the vote that applied to the proportional representation aspect of Hungary's electoral system.  The Socialists also swept the single-member district elections, winning a total of 54% of the seats in Parliament.

In short, the public rejection of the dissident parties was a precondition for the reemergence of the Hungarian Socialist Party as the strongest party in Hungary.  The drop in support of these new parties (especially the two in opposition and therefore not responsible with the economic crisis) was a direct consequence of their low party competence.  Had the Democrat Forum and Free Democrats not run into serious problems, it is unlikely that in 1991 and 1992 Hungarians would have considered supporting the Young Democrats, a group of blunt, unkempt men and women in their twenties with little experience beyond university.  Similarly, the Socialist resurrection began only after significant strategic mistakes by the Young Democrats.  The Socialists were not popular or probably even liked by Hungarians in 1994.  But after the problems with all the new parties, Hungarians seemed willing to overlook that detail.

**Chapter Outline:**
The argument in this book is elaborated in seven chapters.  Chapter 1 outlines the theory of party competence and its relationship to democratization in more detail.  Chapter 2 demonstrates how the Socialist party's reaction to the 1956 revolution, widely considered a disaster for the regime, led to a generation of Socialist politicians who were relatively better prepared for multiparty politics than their opponents.  It also discusses how these politicians with higher party competence came to power in 1988 and 1989.  Chapter 3 explores the rise of the networks in the Hungarian dissident movement that formed three parties (the Hungarian Democratic Forum, the Alliance of Free Democrats, and the Federation of Young Democrats) and demonstrates why that movement promoted politicians with low party competence.  The fourth chapter discusses the transition from opposition groups to parties right before the first parliamentary elections and shows why this rapid party formation and explosive expansion in membership exacerbated their party competence problems.  Chapter 5 shows how the evolution of the Hungarian Democratic Forum from the populist writers' movement led to its near self-destruction after taking power in 1990, once the pressures of governing and competing against other parties before a mass public required these inexperienced party politicians to begin making difficult strategic decisions.  The sixth chapter discusses how the dissidents who ran the Alliance of Free Democrats reverted to strategies from the dissident movement and how this reversal as well as a number of other strategic mistakes led directly to them being ousted from leadership of the party they built.  It also shows how these mistakes helped make the Federation of Young Democrats the most widely supported party by 1992.

The crux of the argument is made in Chapter 7. It describes how strategic blunders by the Federation of Young Democrats right before the 1994 elections led to the evaporation of its public support and the revival of the Hungarian Socialist Party. The chapter begins by reviewing the main explanations Hungarian scholars and pundits gave for why Hungarians voted the Socialists back into power so soon after the fall of communism. It also demonstrates through quantitative tests why none of these arguments can explain the Socialist revival in 1993 and 1994. The chapter then describes how and why the Young Democrats chose to abruptly change from a liberal to a conservative ideology in 1993 as well as make several other unwise decisions just before more than 80% of its supporters deserted the party. It also discusses how the Hungarian Socialist Party differed in presentation from the other parties and how this difference made it possible for the Socialists to gain widespread public support in 1994 after all the other parties had lost public confidence.

This book does not argue that the party with the highest competence always wins. It argues instead that competence is one important factor in party competition, a factor that parties deal with partially through political professionalization. This leads to an important conclusion about modern democracy, a point made in more stark terms by Robert Michels nearly a century ago. Mass democracies face a fundamental dilemma. Democracy requires a rotation of leadership, and its leadership should be no different than the population that it is supposed to represent. Yet, because of the importance of competence at multiparty competition, that political leadership virtually always evolves into a stable strata of political professionals. This issue is elaborated in the Conclusion.

# Notes:

1  Translated and introduced by George Bull. (Penguin Classics: New York), pp. 20-1.
2  Max Weber (1946), "Politics as a Vocation" in *From Max Weber: Essays in Sociology*, Edited and Translated by H.H. Gerth and C. Wright Mills, (New York: Oxford), pp. 92-3.
3  This notion of a relationship between social experiences and social competencies, or socially learned habits, is influenced by the writing of Pierre Bourdieu. Pierre Bourdieu and Loïc J.D. Wacquant (1992), *An Invitation to Reflexive Sociology*, (Chicago: University of Chicago Press), pp. 115–40; Pierre Bourdieu, 1980, *The Logic of Practice*, Translated by Richard Nice, (Stanford University Press: Stanford), pp. 66–79.
4  Alan Ware (1987), *Citizens, Parties and the State: A Reappraisal*, (Princeton: Princeton University Press), pp. 1-29.
5  Max Weber (1968), *Economy and Society: An Outline of Interpretive Sociology*, Edited by Guenther Roth and Claus Wittich, (Berkeley: University of California Press), pp. 284-5, 984-5.
6  Weber, "Politics as a Vocation", p. 90.
7  Ibid, p. 94-5

15

[8] V. O. Key (1942), *Politics, Parties and Pressure Groups* (New York: Thomas Y. Crowell).

[9] Anthony Downs (), An Economic Theory of Democracy, (New York: Harper and Row), pp. 96-113. This line of reason was developed further by Melvin Hinich and Michael Munger (1994), *Ideology and the Theory of Public Choice.* (Ann Arbor: University of Michigan Press).

[10] Interview, Miklós Haraszti.

[11] Béla K. Király (1995), "Soft Dictatorship, Lawful Revolution, and the Socialists' Return to Power", in *Lawful Revolution in Hungary, 1989–94.* Edited by Béla Király. (Highland Lakes, NJ: Atlantic Research) pp. 3–14; András Körösényi (1995), "The Reasons for the Defeat of the Right in Hungary,", trans. by Eszter Nadin with Johnathan Sunley, *East European Politics and Society*, 9, no. 1, pp. 179-94.

[12] Based on data gathered from József Kiss, ed. (1992), *Az 1990-ben Megválasztott Országgyűlés Almanachja [The Almanac of the Parliament Elected in 1990.]* (Budapest: Jelenkutató Alapítvány).

[13] Ervin Csizmadia (1995), *A Magyar Demokratikus Ellenzék (1968–1988): Monográfia [The Hungarian Democratic Opposition, 1968–1988: Monograph.]* (Budapest: T-Twins Kiadó).

[14] Based on data gathered from Sándor Agócs, ed. (1991), *Lakitelek 1987, A Magyarság Esélyei; A Tanácskozás Hiteles Jegyzőkönyve. [Lakitelek 1987, The Chances for Hungarianism; The Authentic Minutes of the Conference.]* (Budapest: Püski) as well as *Almanac of the Parliament Elected in 1990.* Also interviews with Géza Jeszenszky and Sándor Csoóri.

[15] Based on data gathered from András Bozóki, ed. (1992), *Tiszta Lappal: A FIDESZ a Magyar politikában, 1988–1991 [With a Clean Slate: FIDESZ in Hungarian Politics, 1988–1991.]* (Budapest: FIDESZ Press).

[16] Rudolf L. Tőkés (1996), *Hungary's Negotiated Revolution; Economic Reform, Social Change, and Political Succession*, (Cambridge: Cambridge University Press).

[17] Bill Lomax (1994), "Obstacles to the Development of Democratic Politics," in *The Journal of Communist Studies and Transition Politics*, Vol 10, no. 3. Special edition: *Hungary: The Politics of Transition.* edited by Terry Cox and Andy Furlong, pp. 88-9.

[18] Király (1995) "Soft Dictatorship…", p. 10.

[19] István Csurka, "Néhány gondolat a rendszerváltozás két esztendeje és az MDF új programja kapcsán" ["A Few Thoughts on the Two Year Anniversary of the Regime Transformation in Regards to MDF's New Program."] *Margyar Fórum*, August 20, 1992

[20] Zoltán Ripp (1995), *Szabad Demokraták: Történeti Vázlat a Szabad Demokraták Szövetségének politikájáról. [Free Democrats: A Historic Sketch of the Politics of the Alliance of Free Democrats.]* (Budapest: Politikatörténeti Alapitvány), pp. 85–102

Chapter 1:

# The Competence Factor
# in Party Politics and Democratization

Dissidents, those courageous people who confront dictatorial regimes and attempt to push them towards democracy, face exceptionally difficult tasks.  If they succeed, democracy is often the culmination of an extended, strategic struggle against an overwhelmingly powerful adversary.  But this struggle for democracy continues after a legal transformation.  Democratization requires two distinct steps for these activists.  First, they have to work to de-legitimate the regime and cajole it into a democratic transition, or force it to collapse.  Second, they need to form political parties and run for office in free elections.  They need to compete successfully against the survivors of the old regime as well as any anti-democrats who see the momentary instability as an opportunity to seize power.  The problem, in sum, is that dissident and party politics require different competencies, and the rapid change effectively flings the dissidents from one political arena into another.

This book is about this difficult transition.  More generally, it is about the relationship between political competence and fundamental change.  Those who push for change face a dilemma.  On the one hand, rapid change is often the only method for producing a real impact on a political system.  This is because change that rearranges the political dynamics comes mostly at odd moments when those in power have their backs to the wall, or when they are so internally divided that one faction is willing to make significant concessions in order to beat another faction.  On the other hand, rapid change almost always thrusts new people into positions of power.  This translates into people being tossed into situations that they have little background in and therefore are unlikely to have developed competencies.

In the case of democratization, the problem is particularly significant.  Competence is relevant in all areas of politics, but it is especially important to the politics of representative democracy, including the running of one of its key organizations, the political party.  There are reasons why there is a close relationship between the spread of democratic governments and the rise of political professionals.  As Robert Michels explained so well, modern, democratic politics requires political professionals.  Heavily influenced by his mentor, Max Weber, Michels argues that direct, mass democracy is impossible.  Democratic politics requires large organizations, like political parties.  To be effective at fighting for power, these organizations must be hierarchical, with a stable leadership at the top.  The organization is best served if these individuals, regardless of their original social class, become well-trained, career politicians.  However, because of the resources they secure, including the competencies they develop, these professional politicians become a political strata, and their interests become separate from the people they are supposed to represent.  In other words, the very skills that help these politicians put their respective organizations into political contention also help reinforce their own positions of power.[1]

While he does not spell it out this way, Michels argument leads to the conclusion that the competencies of professional politicians help them secure their positions of power in two ways. The first is the political competence difference between them and the mass public. Few people have the background to judge the merits of policy directly, which gives the professionals a significant advantage over the public, especially when other career politicians are not challenging them. Moreover, these politicians are specialists in the art of advocating these policies in overly simplistic terms, including transforming the policy impact into unrelated frameworks that fits the views of the public. Second, there is a political competence difference between the politicians in power and any activists attempting to oust them. Modern, democratic politics requires politicians with particular competencies, which helps lead to democratic governments being run by a strata of professional politicians with skills to guide the public and ward off external challenge.

This central importance of professional politicians in democratic politics is probably the reason why the eminent sociologist Max Weber focused one of his two most important and famous lectures on politics as a vocation. While arguing that they originally arose in the service of princes, Weber argued further that professional politicians eventually became closely linked to the modern political parties. To Weber, the professional politician lives for as well as lives off politics, it seems, because the primary reward of this career is not money but power. This need for party politicians to be capable of sustaining themselves without retaining their seats is one reason that lawyers have become such central players in modern politics. But, there are others, including particular competencies they bring to parties. Besides their understanding of the law, lawyers are also trained at the spoken word and at advocating positions, Weber argues. Weber also argues that parties need the "demagogue"—which he emphasizes is a term referring to skills, not necessarily with negative connotation—as well as the operatives who work in the background.[2]

This relationship between professional politicians and political parties can be understood within the larger framework of Weber's thinking. Weber could be considered a sociologist of modernity. While Karl Marx would likely see capitalism as the primary characteristic of the modern world, for Weber it is rationality. While his notion of rationality has a number of components, it includes instrumental rationality, or when a person or group selects a clearly defined end and then finds the most efficient means towards those ends. A bureaucracy is an example of a rational organization, and for Weber it is the organization that most typifies modernity. Bureaucracies not only have clearly defined rules and are organized by formal positions. They are also instrumentally rational, geared towards achieving particular ends. Indeed, a bureaucracy is very much like a social machine, and the individuals who work in these organizations are like the cogs. The person is hired to perform some task, and once that person is no longer useful or leaves the organization, he or she is simply replaced by another human cog.[3]

Most modern organizations are bureaucracies. Capitalist organizations bureaucratize so that they can more efficiently seek financial profit, and military organizations become bureaucracies so that they can be more effective killing machines. In the same way, political parties (or at least those in a position to win power within or over the government) are bureaucracies. They organize the individuals by function, and they are focused on a particular set of goals: Winning elected positions, creating patronage for their members, and securing power within or over the state.[4]

Most bureaucratic organizations require people with specific competencies. A military organization needs trained infantry, but at a higher level it also needs varying types of analysts and strategists. Certain corporations need varying types of skilled and unskilled labor to work on assembly lines and other lower ranked positions, but they also need people with specialized backgrounds in finance, management, marketing, an a range of other areas. Similarly, political parties need individuals to perform tasks like putting up posters or calling potential voters, but they also need people who perform complicated background work or who play the front role as candidates and "leaders." It would be dangerous for a military organization to have its strategic plans developed by novices, as it would be a corporation to have important decisions made by untrained neophytes. In the same way, as bureaucratic organizations driving to win power, political parties need people with particular competencies and therefore training and experience to be successful.[5]

In other words, mass democracy requires political parties—they simplify the voting decision and perform other useful tasks—and political parties need politicians with specialized competencies. But, this leads to two questions. One, what is party competence? Two, why is party competence so difficult to attain for people with unrelated backgrounds, like dissidents? While both answers are rooted in the sociology of Max Weber, they are given greater theoretical foundation by Pierre Bourdieu.

**Party Competence and the Social Politics of Pierre Bourdieu:**

Pierre Bourdieu is one of the few political thinkers for whom competence is a central theoretical component. Bourdieu's sociology is built on what he considers a contradiction in social thought. On the one hand, many sociologists assume that social structures guide and limit individuals' thoughts and behavior. (For example, many political scientists begin with the assumption that institutional structures guide individuals' perspectives and actions.) On the other hand, many make the exact opposite claim: Individuals' thoughts and actions produce and change social structures. (For example, rational choice theory assumes that the actions of self-interested and rational decision-makers create and change economic markets and other social institutions.) He then asks, how can social institutions drive individual thinking at the same time that individual thinking drives social institutions? He attempts to resolve this contradiction by arguing that social behavior occurs through the interaction between his two key terms: *field* and *habitus*.[6]

While ruthless in his attacks against rational choice theory, which he calls "RAT" for rational action theory, Bourdieu's theory does have significant similarities with both rational choice and game theory. He argues that people are constantly involved in loosely defined games in which players are strategic, have stakes, and can gain "capital," like money, status, or power. Also showing significant influence by Ervin Goffman, Bourdieu argues that these social games are mostly theatrical in nature. People play roles, which they use to gain capital within the social setting. However, one's success is partially influenced by one's competence, or whether one has developed strategies appropriate for the particular game. The loosely defined game is what Bourdieu calls a "field;" the socially learned strategies for fields are what Bourdieu calls the "habitus."

For Bourdieu, the terms "game" and "field" are not synonymous. A game is simply one type of field; it is a field organized through well-defined rules. While in games the rules are spelled out beforehand, the boundaries of fields evolve through the interaction itself. These boundaries will rarely be clear and, in fact, will be in a constant state of flux. A field of interaction is always defined partially by the larger social setting and partially by the relationship of the individual players. Games will usually have clear guidelines that determine winners and losers. In fields, a player's gain is often determined by less tangible or clearly definable factors, like status. Players always position themselves to gain some form of "capital": possibly monetary, often status. Fields can therefore be understood as loosely defined and fluctuating games in which players are always attempting to make gains relative to other players.[7]

Bourdieu also argues that fields are usually defined symbolically. Because symbolic frameworks disguise self-interest, they help people who benefit from a social or economic system to legitimate those benefits by making them seem natural. These frames usually cannot be invented out of thin air. Nonetheless, the players themselves choose the frames through which they understand their relationships. According to Bourdieu, this is how fields (and potential roles in these theatrical games) are defined. The moment of legitimacy is reached when the players accept the same frames from which to interpret their interaction. For Bourdieu, those defined as better in this legitimated framework are considered to have greater "symbolic capital;" they are the winners in this fluid game. Those who are defined as being lower in the pecking order are considered victims of "symbolic violence;" they are pushed down and harmed by symbols that define them in negative, undesirable ways.[8]

For Bourdieu, competence and success are closely related. He argues that one's ability to play a role convincingly is determined by one's habitus. The habitus is one's socially learned strategies for playing within particular fields. It can be equated with socially learned habits, provided that one understands habits in terms of strategies. The habitus does not drive individuals in the way that commands dictate computer behavior. The person is always working toward some end, usually toward maintaining or improving his or her position in the field. The habitus determines what strategies that person can choose and how skilled he or she is at them.[9]

Bourdieu's habitus has several implications. First, it implies that individuals will tend to perform better in fields at which they have greater experience. Second, human behavior is durable but changeable. A person who enters a new field will often have great difficulty performing convincingly. However, over time, that person may in fact learn new strategies for performing in this setting. The old habits will nonetheless remain. An immigrant may learn to function well in the new culture, but he or she may make social faux pas for many years. The working class kid may climb into high society, but there is a good chance that he or she will look clumsy in this setting and be branded "nouveau riche" by those with more practice. Similarly, the dissident may learn party politics, but she or he may never play it as well as the professional with decades of experience.

*Bourdieu's Parties: Grand Struggle on the Small Stage:*

Bourdieu's framework is best known for its application to pre-industrial societies in the second half of *The Logic of Practice*, the artistic field in *The Field of Cultural Production*,[10] the academic field in *Homo Academicus*,[11] and mass culture in *Distinction*.[12] But, he clearly intended this relationship between habitus and field to be a general social theory applicable to a wide variety of situations. For example, he outlines a theory of party politics in his essay: "Political Representation: Elements for a Theory of the Political Field."[13]

It is not difficult to see that Bourdieu's party theory is a synthesis of his analysis of the artistic field with the political writings of Max Weber. Bourdieu sees parties as teams of political professionals who compete for the votes of the politically non-professional. Politics is the realm of professionals, Bourdieu argues, because it requires a particular competence that comes from a specialized background. He writes that in

> politics as in art, the dispossession of the majority of the people is a correlate, or even a consequence, of the concentration of the specifically political means of production in the hands of professionals, who can enter into the distinctive political game with some chance of success only on condition that they possess a specific competence. Indeed, nothing is less natural than the mode of thought and action demanded by participation in the political field: like the religious, artistic or scientific habitus, the habitus of the politician depends on special training.[14]

For Bourdieu, the political game—he uses both "game" and "field" in this context—in a mass democracy is very much theater. The successful performance by a political actor is always "doubly determined;" it must always be understood in relation to the audience and, at the same time, in relation to the other performers on the political stage. Political actors must act as representatives of primary audience concerns in terms that the audience understands, that is, through the symbolic frames of the culture. But, at the same time, politicians must distinguish themselves in a positive way from the other actors on the political stage. They must give the audience reason to support them instead of their opponents. This need to distinguish themselves from each other before a mass audience is one reason why political conflict, no matter how complicated or technical, moves toward a simple us-versus-them, left-versus-right framework. It is also why the meaning of "left" and "right" changes over time and by region. Simplicity is critical for victory in this fight.[15]

This need for simplicity through symbolism is also why parties are necessary, Bourdieu continues. Parties simplify political struggle for the audience by grouping the professionals into teams. To accomplish this, the party must take on a symbolic stand, an "ideology," that defines itself and its opponents, unifying support for the team while distinguishing that team from others on the political stage. But, while promoting this simplification, parties also limit the politicians that can enter the political struggle. First, only a few parties can be on the political stage at the same time. Second, those teams largely determine which politicians can get on stage and which are entirely excluded. This is done through both selection and training.

This is the key to Bourdieu's link between political competence and the distribution of political power. Bourdieu argues that institutions, in their attempts to survive, follow criteria for selecting members and excluding others. They then tacitly or explicitly give those members specialized training that builds competence in the game that the institution plays—competence that would be difficult to attain outside the institutions directly involved in the game. Parties are therefore fundamental to the process of democratic politics becoming run by a small number of "political producers," that is, a strata of professionals.[16]

For Bourdieu, this doubly determined politics, with its big audience and small stage, is the primary reason that representative politics becomes the playground of a few professionals. On the one hand, the mass audience's need for simplicity creates a necessity for a few teams that can boil down conflicts and regulate entry. On the other hand, the high stakes of this game breeds a ferocity in which team success becomes partially dependent on competence at that specialized struggle.

**The Struggle for Party Resources:**
But what exactly is at stake in this theatrical struggle among professional party politicians? Parties are organizations driven to gain power within or over government. According to Max Weber, a government (or more accurately, a "state") is "a human community that (successfully) claims *the monopoly of the legitimate use of violence in a territory*."[17] It is the only institution that can legitimately imprison or kill people, and it is the only organization that can make "laws", or rules that are backed by the real threat of incarceration or death. He went on to define politics as "striving to share power or striving to influence the distribution of power, either among states or among groups within states."[18] Professional politicians, then, are people who make a career out of striving to share control over that legitimate use of violence. Political parties are means to this end; they are a way for individuals to move from the citizenry into the ranks of those who rule.

The characteristic that distinguishes parties from other political organizations in mass democracies (for example, interest groups and lobbying organizations) is that they run candidates for elected office.[19] The goal, it should be emphasized, is power, not elected seats. Seats are never ends in themselves. In a situation in which the elected seats are token positions, competition is usually minimal. When the seats are central to the running of government, parties and their allies struggle ferociously over winning these prized possessions.

More specifically, this struggle among parties is a struggle over *resources* needed for gaining power. Certainly, one of the key resources is elected positions, since they give the party much needed votes on the floor of parliament and voices in parliamentary committees. Another important resource is votes during elections; it is only with millions of votes each election that a party can gain those much-needed seats. Parties also need labor; they need a large network of professional staff as well as unskilled workers to run an organization with a legislative arm that also runs national campaigns on a regular cycle. Similarly, parties need money in order to run the large national campaigns that they need to build voter support as well as run national organizations.

Most of these resources are fluid and hard to control. These votes are important resources to parties in both concrete terms (i.e., they translate into elected positions) and symbolic terms (e.g., they can be used to legitimize a party's negotiating position.) But, there is no guarantee that the party will receive the same percent of votes the next election. In the same way, while having an army of campaign workers produces a great advantage, the choice of whether to work long hours for the party is entirely in the control of the workers. Similarly, while parties can spend money largely as they please, they usually have to raise that money from contributors. They cannot control whether others will donate to the party, nor can they be sure whether their previous level of income will continue.

For these reasons, the most important resource for a party is support, generally understood. If the party can build support among a significant fraction of voters, that party will gain the votes it needs to enter or reenter parliament after the next election and possibly win enough seats to head a government coalition. If the party can build support among organized interests, it can usually raise the money it needs to run expensive electoral campaigns and a party organization with branches throughout the country. Similarly, if a party can build loyalty among a large group of potential activists, it can gain a great deal of free labor. Generally speaking, support leads to other resources.

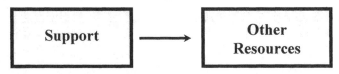

But, this relationship can also be reversed: Other resources can be used to build support. Money is an excellent example of this. It can be used for many parts of electoral campaigns, including polling and advertising, which can lead to greater mass support. Similarly, legislative staff can be used to work with lobbyists and construct legislation in a way that helps build support among elite groups as well as the masses. The free labor of activists can be used to run many parts of electoral campaigns. Even elected positions, usually considered the goals of party action, can be used to build support. Positions in parliament legitimize the party before the public and other groups, since positions mean that the party has at least some control over policy. Parties in parliament also usually gain a great deal more free media coverage. Therefore, in general, the causal relationship can be reversed.

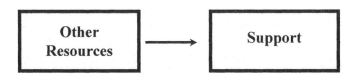

At first glance, these two arguments (i.e., that support leads to other resources and that other resources lead to support) may appear to be a theoretical dilemma. I would argue instead that this seeming contradiction is the key to understanding party competition as well as why a few parties dominate most representative democracies for extended periods. In sum, the struggle for resources functions like a spiral. Parties acquire resources (whether money, status, membership, or something else) and use them to compete for more resources. A party will raise money, use it to buy television and radio commercials, through which it hopes to build mass support. That mass support, it hopes, will translate into elected seats. Positions in government are then used to produce legislation, which it hopes can be used further to win the support within the mass public and among organized interests. That support among organized interests can then be used to raise money, which can then be used for campaigning before the mass public. The movement of party resource to party resource can therefore by visualized as follows:

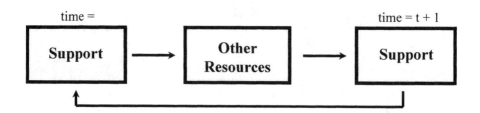

This circular relationship implies that parties can have upward or downward spirals of support. Let's say that a party gains a boost in public support. That party becomes a better investment for elite groups, whose aim is primarily to influence policy. Similarly, the party becomes more attractive to potential activists, most of whom would rather be involved with a party that is likely to win. It also becomes more attractive to potential staffers and others who might bring expertise to the party. In this way, a party can increase its amount money and labor simply because its public support has increased. Then, if that money and labor is wisely applied to building further public support, that mass support can increase further, which makes the party even more attractive to potential donors and activists.

But the spiral of support can move in the opposite direction as well. If a party's public support drops significantly, that party may well see the amount of donations it receives drop as well, which may make rebuilding that public support more difficult. Often more serious, the drop of public support can lead to intra-party dissatisfaction with the party leadership, regardless of whether the leadership is to blame for the decline. Besides often causing an exodus of members, this drop also opens the door for internal challenge. If a group begins a serious challenge against the leadership in a way that divides the party before the public, public support is almost guaranteed to decline further. Therefore, the drop in support can often trigger a downward spiral of support.

The critical distinction seems to be between the parties that win seats in parliament and those that hold no seats. A spot in parliament, whether as "government" or "opposition", is a critical resource for maintaining support. It is a vehicle for public exposure and legitimacy. It provides credibility for potential donors. And it gives the sense of victory that is necessary for attracting all but the most zealous activists and delusional careerists. So, if a party in parliament experiences a downward spiral of support that leads it to winning no seats in a parliamentary election, that party usually has lost the critical resource it would need to rebuild its basis of support.

Moreover, support is always a finite commodity. There are only so many organized interest groups with resources valuable to parties. There are only so many people willing to take on an active role in party politics for little or no money. And while almost any country has many voters, even the number of votes is not infinite. In other words, the tendency for support and other resources to spiral upward or downward has a tendency to lead to a few parties monopolizing the critical resources. Since the parties with the public support monopolize the money, labor, and other resources needed to build public support, they effectively become a multi-party oligarchy. This is especially true because of the critical role of winning parliamentary seats. If a political system has a large number of parties but only a few win elected positions, those few will gain a virtual monopoly of all available party resources, not the least being money and public exposure.

monopoly of all available party resources, not the least being money and public exposure. Moreover, if support for parties in parliament begins shifting dramatically, parties that experience downward spirals could fall far enough that they are effectively eliminated from political contention, making even smaller the number of parties that share among themselves virtually all the party resources.

**Party Struggle and the Debated Concepts of Parties:**

Even in the best circumstances, this struggle over support among multiple parties is difficult. On its surface, it is a daunting task. Besides trying to gain a resource it can never control (i.e., support) and beyond the fact that other parties and political actors are constantly trying to undermine their attempts to gain power, the tasks before party politicians are inherently contradictory.

This contradictory nature of party politics is reflected in the debates that political scientists have among themselves about parties. Gerald Pomper in *Passions and Interests: Political Party Concepts of American Democracy*[20] and Angelo Panebianco in *Political Parties: Organization and Power*[21] have each outlined contradictory claims party theories have presented. Five questions can be identified from these lists of rival theoretical frameworks:

1. Are parties (a) dependent on organized interests and other elite groups, or (b) slaves to a voting public that directly decides how many seats the party wins each election?

2. Do party leaders (a) run party organizations in order to pursue external goals like state power, or (b) pursue external goals in order to maintain control over the party?

3. To be successful, do parties need to promote (a) the selective interest of a coalition, or (b) the collective good of the country?

4. Do parties provide their supporters (a) concrete benefits or (b) a faith to believe in?

5. Are party organizations run (a) as oligarchies with a small group in power, or (b) through democratic procedures?

The correct answer is (a) *and* (b) for all five questions. Pomper argues that these different concepts are simply ideal frameworks. Actual political parties possess all of the characteristics that he described on an abstract level as polar opposites. Similarly, Panebianco dismisses these differences as academic prejudices and false dichotomies. Instead, I would argue that these contradictory frameworks reflect real and contradictory goals that parties must pursue. Parties are dependent on elite organizations at the same time that they are slaves to voters. They pursue the interests of select groups as well as a collective good. They are run like oligarchies and with democratic procedures. To be successful, parties must somehow accomplish these contradictory goals, which requires a particular form of political struggle as well as competence at that specialized politics.

*1. Mass versus Elite Support:*

Pomper's first distinction is between the elite focus and mass focus of party theories. This distinction reflects the most important duality in political parties. On the one hand, successful parties have factions within parliamentary bodies that attempt to gain control over policy and other aspects of state power. On the other hand, parties are

25

organizations that attempt to win support by the mass public and win elections. Maurice Duverger pointed out this duality in *Political Parties*. In fact, he argues, parties came into being when parliamentary groups and electoral committees (that is, members of parliament voting together and running for office together, respectively) combined:

> *The more the right to vote is extended and multiplied, the more necessary it becomes to organize the electors by means of committees capable of making the candidates known and of canalizing the votes in their direction. The rise of parties is thus bound up with the rise of parliamentary groups and electoral committees. Nonetheless, some deviate more or less from this general scheme. They originate outside the electoral and parliamentary cycle, and this fact is their most outstanding common characteristic.*"[22]

This duality is not merely conceptual, nor is it trivial. Parliamentary politics is the politics of constructing legislation, building support for that legislation, and then attempting to push the implementation of that policy. It is very detail oriented, and much of this politics is performed through face-to-face interaction. Building mass support for the party requires a different focus. While parliamentary politics requires politicians to be specific and clear, mass politics requires politicians to focus on generalities and indeed to oversimplify. Moreover, any close contact between party politicians and the mass public is brief and usually superficial.

There is another important characteristic of this duality. Each side of this struggle has its own audience. On the mass politics side, the audience is, of course, individual voters, who control a critical resource, the vote. On the elite politics side, the audience is made up of lobbyists and organized interests involved directly in the legislative and administrative process. More formally, in representative democracies, this audience is made up of "elite organizations," or organized groups with specific sets of interests in state policy, direct contact with party politicians and their staff, and some resources of value to parties. Certainly, this audience includes interest groups, or organizations external from the party or state with specific policy agendas, lobbyists, and some resources (e.g., money, information, the ability to influence potential voters) that they attempt to trade for favorable policy outcomes. Government agencies could fit this characteristic as well; they are organized groups with a vested interest in policy (e.g., funding to the agency) and resources that can help or hurt parties in a number of ways, including by whether they implement policy decisions. Foreign governments and international financial organizations also fit this characteristic. Moreover, in this definition, business groups and labor unions are both elite organizations if they attempt to directly influence policy, though the relative influence of these groups is influenced mostly by the resources that they can bring to parties and politicians.

A primary problem for parties is that they need support from both to succeed. They must perform before both at once. But, these audiences are fundamentally different. Often, but not always, the elite groups and mass audience have different interests. For example, a large portion of the public may want some form of policy reform, but that reform may either cost money or in some other way conflict with the interests of groups that elite organizations represent. Conversely, elite organizations may promote policy changes that benefit them or their clients but may produce greater costs for most of the public. Indeed, the predicament of the Iraq War for Tony Blair's Labour Party provides an excellent example of the dilemma: How does the party appease both a critical ally, the United States, wanting to attack Iraq and a public that is highly skeptical of war? Resolving these types of dilemmas while maintaining support in each audience is critical to party success—and Blair's maneuvering during and after the attack illustrates both the methods involved and their limitations.

There is another fundamental difference between these audiences. Elite organizations either hire or are run by political professionals. Because they spend considerable time on political issues, these representatives of elite organizations usually understand the political and policy dimension of each fight in detail. In comparison, the masses are (almost by definition) not political professionals. Having careers and lives separate from the political process, they understand politics in general terms, and they often translate political questions into non-political frameworks (e.g., "common sense.") This means that parties must at once communicate to two audiences that are looking for different types of information.

However, this difference is also a key to how parties can maintain support in both at once.

## 2. Intra-Party versus Extra-Party Politics:

The previous section made an implicit assumption that is hardly correct. It treated each party as if it was a single actor that attempts to win resources needed to gain power over the state. More accurately, parties are also organized networks of politicians with their own views and interests. This leads to struggles for power within the party networks as well. Furthermore, these internal and external struggles are interdependent. Panebianco expressed this interdependence by describing two opposite frameworks of party behavior: the "rational" and "natural" models. In the rational model, parties organize to pursue external goals, like government power. In the natural model, party goals are the outcome of struggles within the organization; the only aim party members have in common in the survival of the organization.

While the mass public provides votes and elite organizations provide money and other resources, the party network provides the party labor. This labor comes in a number of forms. Party politicians run for offices in electoral campaigns and, if victorious, perform legislative or administrative duties. Professional staff provides administrative or technical labor. Besides running the party apparatus, they also perform polling, advertising, and other work requiring high levels of specialized knowledge. Formally independent consultants connected to the network; they also provide specialized labor. Finally, the party rank-and-file provides largely unskilled labor, mostly for free.

There are two primary intra-party dangers that party leaders face. The first is a membership exodus. When party members at any level leave the party, the organization experiences a drop in manpower. Moreover, if politicians begin leaving the party, the party can seem disunited to the public and elite organizations. The second danger is an internal challenge to the leadership's position. A serious challenge will usually be made by a politician and followed by some fraction of the other three groups. It always produces a decentralization of power. It leads to party labor (and other resources) becoming spent on the internal struggle instead of on winning external resources. Moreover, if the intra-party conflict becomes public knowledge, the party can look disunited and lose credibility.

Just as with the mass audience and elite organizations, party politicians must perform before the external audience and internal network at the same time. The problem is that these are also not identical groups. To the contrary, the party network tends to be more coherent and zealous than the other audiences. There is often the very real danger that an appeal to a more diverse external audience can upset the internal audience and open the door to an intra-party challenge. Conversely, moves to appease the internal audience can easily cause a drop in support by the external audiences.

But there are usually ways around this problem as well. While the differences between the internal and external audiences cause party leaders problems, those differences also produce a solution.

*The Three-Sided Party Struggle:*

The discussion in the last two sections can be conceptualized another way. One can describe it instead as each party needing to build support in three audiences. First, the party must build support within a large fraction of the voting public. Second, the party needs to build support among elite organizations that can provide money and other resources or, conversely, can hurt the party's attempt to win power. Third, parties need to build loyalty among both the professionals and activists who can provide labor or, conversely, who can undermine the party's attempt to win state power.

This description echoes the framework presented by political scientist V.O. Key. Key distinguishes among "party as an organization," "party as an electorate," and "party in government."[23] This framework can be altered to define party politics as occurring within fields of struggle for support and other resources. The overall struggle for state power can be called the *party field*. Within the party field are three smaller fields. In a mass democracy, parties must compete for public support and votes; the struggle among parties for votes is the *mass politics field*. Once parties organize, the leadership needs to work to maintain the support of the membership and to fend off internal challenge to its control; the fight to maintain internal support is the *intra-party field*. Finally, in order to raise money and gain other resources, parties need to build support among organized interests; the struggle to win that support is the *elite politics field*.

These are interdependent arenas. Without mass support, a party will not make a good investment for elite organizations. Business groups may adore a pro-business party, but if that party has no mass support, it has no potential to influence policy. Similarly, a large party network is impossible to run without mass and elite support. Through votes the party wins seats that provide party members jobs, including as legislators, as legislative staff, as members of the government administration, or as bureaucrats. And, donations from elite groups help pay the salaries of professional staff and party consultants. In sum, to be successful and especially to govern, a party must have a large fraction of support in the mass and elite audiences and be loyally supported by the party network. [24] Gains in any audience can translate into gains in other audiences, but losses in any audience can also translate into losses in other audiences.

*3. Coalition Support versus Collective Good:*

The third question is whether parties promote the special interests of a select coalition or the collective good of the country. Both Pomper and Panebianco address this question. Pomper argues that some party concepts emphasize that parties have collective goals while others emphasize coalitional goals. In the same vein, Panebianco distinguishes between theories that argue that parties give incentives collectively to the whole membership or selectively to a few. These debates mirror each other: By "goals" Pomper is discussing the party's relationship to the surrounding society; by "incentives" Panebianco is explaining the internal workings of the party.

How do parties appear to be promoting their respective coalition's interest at the same time that they appear to be promoting the collective good? Parties can resolve this dilemma by defining the specific interests of its coalition as if they were in everyone's interest (except maybe some well-defined enemy.) Party politicians almost always present themselves as pursuing goals that are good for the entire country, not just a small group. "Libertarian" parties might promote cuts in the minimum wage that directly promote industries dependent on low wage labor, for example, but they will always justify those cuts as good for workers and the economy as a whole. "Social democratic" parties might support increases in the minimum wage, which is to the advantage of organized labor and certain industries, but it too will present that support as good for all workers and the entire economy. Similarly, "conservative" parties might support teaching Christianity in public schools, which is the direct interest of certain religious groups; but, they will always present this proposal as if it benefited everyone, such as by claiming that it promotes a general good like "ethics" or "values."

The well-defined enemy is not always necessary for this technique to work. But, it helps. Fat-cats who line their pockets, lazy bureaucrats who thrive on inefficiency, and homosexuals who are trying to undermine families and marriage: These are all caricatures that help make the argument of a collective good more believable. In other words, those who disagree don't have a different interest, since the proposal is in *everyone's* interest. Instead, those who disagree have bad intentions, or those with bad intentions have misled them.

Moreover, there is no reason that politicians cannot believe that they are pursuing the good of the nation while they promote the specific interests of groups that provide them money and other resources. The politician whose career is funded by small business may well believe that workers are better off with a lower minimum wage. Similarly, the politician who fights for prayer in school may well believe that saying Christian prayers would be the best thing for children with Jewish, Hindu, or atheist parents. Self-delusion may be irrational, but it is optimal to deluding others since the most convincing actor is the one who becomes the part.

Finally, this technique helps resolve the dilemma of elite groups and the mass public being different types of audiences. Parties can promote the specific interests of elite groups by defining those interests as good for "voters", "taxpayers", "workers", or "law-abiding citizens". In other words, they can define those interests as being good for virtually everyone. Since this is an issue of perception, since policy tends to be complex and technical, and since few members of the mass public are political professionals and have the background to judge the authenticity of policy claims, they can often be convinced that measures are in their interest even when they are not.

*Concrete Benefits versus a Symbolic Faith:*

This dilemma between coalition interests and a collective good is related to the fourth question: Do parties provide their supporters concrete benefits or a faith to believe in? Pomper defines this dilemma in more general term. He distinguishes party theories by their modes, or the "combination of the style, incentives, and system of membership compensation for the party."[25] These theories tend to claim that parties use either "instrumental" or "expressive" methods for achieving their goals. It is the difference, he says, between the party as a tool and the party as a faith. But, as Pomper points out, any party, to be competitive, must use some combination of instrumental and expressive modes. A party must provide its constituents both concrete goods (jobs, government contracts, and the like) and symbolic representations, and that party must be run as bureaucratic organizations at the same time that it acts as a faith for the membership.

It is worth noting that Pomper is using the term "instrumental" in two related ways. On the one hand, he is referring to parties being instrumentally rational; they are taking strategic steps that will maximize their chances of reaching well-defined and self-interested goals. So, if the party wants to win elections, the party must create the type of organization that maximizes its chances of winning those elections. On the other hand, the term "instrumental" also refers to giving constituents or party members concrete goods. In this second case, the constituents and members are being instrumentally rational. They see supporting the party as a means for reaching their own ends, like money, jobs, and government services that benefit them personally. In this way, Pomper is acknowledging the framework of party competition presented by Anthony Downs and developed further by the rational choice school.

And here lies the intellectual dilemma. If voters and others are being instrumentally rational (that is, if their primary motivation is self-interest), then why do parties need to present themselves as promoting a larger faith, or an "ideology?" Downs echoes this dilemma, though apparently by accident. Applying the self-interest axiom to voters, he writes, "This axiom implies that each citizen casts his vote for the party he believes will provide him with more benefits than any other."[26] But, oddly, after arguing that parties develop ideologies as weapons in the struggle for office, he writes, "We define an ideology as a verbal image of the good society and the chief means of constructing such a society."[27] Why would an economic model, driven entirely by the self-interest axiom, include a notion of the good society, an idealistic vision? A good society is clearly not a consequence of his self-interest framework. Instead, the tendency of politicians and parties to define themselves as being on a mission towards a greater good is a problem for theories built on assumptions of personal gain.

The solution to this dilemma echoes and expands the solution of the previous dilemma. Not only do parties define the interests of their coalitions in collective terms. They also express those instrumental interests as if they were a faith in a greater good. This faith has two critical advantages. It helps disguise the interests of the party and its coalition, thereby helping reinforce the illusion that the party is pursuing a collective good. It also helps produce a sense of purpose for party members who do not receive direct benefits from party victories.

Parties can accomplish this by expressing this self-interested faith through symbols. The power of symbols comes from the fact that they are both unified and fuzzy. They are unified by a central, tangible frame—be it an object, a word, or a characteristic—that is easily recognizable and retained. The Christian cross fits this requirement; so do terms like "liberal," "conservative", "nation", "Europe", and "freedom." The fuzziness comes from the application of the frame; people can use that object or word to interpret a wide variety of thoughts and feelings.[28] "Liberalism" is a good example of this. A self-proclaimed liberal party can associate the term with liberty, civil and human rights, progressiveness, and modernization—all of which seem to be larger goods that are positive for everyone. Similarly, opposing parties can try to use that fuzziness against the party. In some countries, they can associate liberalism with the most ruthless aspects of capitalism. In other countries, they can try to define liberals as "bleeding hearts" who are out to help disliked groups or people who would be better off helping themselves. Liberalism can also be equated with atheism or Judaism, and it can be defined as a threat to national traditions.

This fuzzy application of a simple frame makes symbols a powerful tool in political struggles. On the one hand, they provide economy to arguments. Virtually any political stand can be summarized as "liberal" or "illiberal", "conservative" or "not conservative", "pro-Europe" or "anti-Europe", and so on, especially when those making the arguments do not care about logical consistency but do care about winning. On the other hand, these political symbols help legitimate those arguments. By couching political stand in universal terms like "freedom", the debate becomes over not differences in self-interest but over fundamental principles. These uses of grand symbols disguise underlying interests. Couching debates of fiscal or monetary policy in terms like "freedom," "fairness," or "Founding Fathers," for example, helps hide the specific gains or losses groups would make with each policy change. In this way, parties can attract the support of special interest groups in the elite and mass audiences while maintaining a legitimate claim for support from those who do not benefit.

This duality also works within the party. Even when parties are victorious, there are never enough jobs and other benefits to pay off all party members. So, others are encouraged to continue working for the party by making that party into a faith. By presenting itself as pursuing some universal and fundamental good, it justifies a faith-like work by the rank-and-file to promote other people's political careers. The Conservatives *must* defeat Labour, the Democrats *must* stop those Republicans, each party must put its own candidate's into office, otherwise terrible, terrible things might happen to the nation. In other words, by presenting the particular interests of the party leaders, consultants, paid staff, allies, and coalition partners as if they were part of a greater good, they can "pay" the unpaid workers with an often delusional sense of purpose.

## 5. Internal Democracy versus Party Oligarchy:

This need for parties to be both a faith for its members and an instrument in the drive for power produces a new dilemma. In order for a party to be an effective "tool", it must be organized in a hierarchical structure with those on top controlling most decisions. Otherwise, its strategic decision-making would become slow and inconsistent, and the party may even become paralyzed by an inability to make decisions. Moreover, wide decision-making procedures create a wide distribution of power, which invite costly internal challenges against the leadership.

However, since the party also functions as a community driven by a faith, the party leadership must legitimate its leadership position to the membership. Not justifying that position also opens the leadership to internal challenge (in this case, on the grounds that the leaders have no legitimate reason for running the party and gaining benefits that come from their positions.) It also eliminates an excuse as to why the rank-and-file should be working without pay to advance the leaders' careers. As it turns out, the easiest way to justify their positions is through internal democracy. By having the leadership elected by some subset of the membership, party leaders can justify why they and not others are heading the party and receiving many of its benefits.

And so, here is another dilemma. On the one hand, party survival depends on intra-party power centralizing to the leaders. On the other hand, party leaders cannot legitimate their positions without intra-party democracy, which decentralizes power. As Panebianco pointed out, this dilemma has been reflected in scholarly debate on parties. There are those theories that assume that party leaders are largely autonomous in their actions, and there are theories that assume that party organizations significantly constrain leaders.

Robert Michels' "iron law of party oligarchy" has significantly influenced this debate. According to Michels, even the most democratic parties shift towards being controlled by a small group of professional politicians. Good or bad intentions are not the issue. Michels argues that running a party requires a high level of specialized competence. However, as the leaders gain that competence, they becomes indispensable to the organization at the same time that their relative level of knowledge makes them steadily more independent of the membership. In the conclusion of *Political Parties*, he writes:

> *Now, if we leave out of consideration the tendency of the leaders to organize themselves and to consolidate their interests, and if we leave also out of consideration the gratitude of the led toward the leaders, and the general immobility and passivity of the masses, we are led to conclude that the principal cause of oligarchy in the democratic parties is to be found in the technical indispensability of leadership.[29]*

Showing a clear influence by Michels, Maurice Duverger nonetheless argues that there is more to this issue. Party leaders face a serious conflict. On the one hand, parties need to appear internally democratic. On the other hand, the realities of political struggle require them to be controlled by a handful of leaders in an undemocratic manner. He writes:

> *[The] leadership of political parties—like that of most present-day social groups: Trade Unions, associations, business firms, and so on—present dual characteristics: it is democratic in appearance and oligarchic in reality... The almost universal reverence paid to democracy is explained by the fact that it appears legitimate in the eyes of contemporaries. In every age men formulate their own ideal of the organization and devotion of power within social groups: it is natural for them to offer obedience to the leaders who conform to this common ideal and to refuse obedience to others. The dominant belief determines the legitimacy of the leader, in the sociological sense of the term legitimacy... Democracy remains the dominant doctrine of the contemporary age, that which determines the legitimacy of power. The parties are the most compelled to take this into account in that their activity lies directly in the political field, in which there is constant reference to democratic doctrines.[30]*

He continues:

> *Practical efficiency, however, drives them hard in the opposite direction. Democratic principles demand that leadership at all levels be elective, that it be frequently renewed, collective in character, weak in authority. Organized in this fashion, a party is not well armed for the struggles of*

*politics... It has often been observed that a democratic state at war with a dictatorial state must progressively adopt the methods of its rival, if it is to defeat it. The same phenomenon occurs on the party level in political warfare: in order to safeguard their existence the parties of democratic structure must follow the pattern of the others. They do it the more easily because their leaders tend naturally to retain power and to increase it, because their members scarcely hinder this tendency and on the contrary even strengthen it by hero-worshipping the leaders: on all these points the analysis made by Roberto Michels continues to hold true.[31]*

Duverger outlines many techniques parties use to retain control while faking internal democracy: Parties use indirect representation; they rig nomination processes; they pack electoral bodies or manipulate votes; they have elected "titular" leaders and unelected people who really run the party. Indeed, Duverge's examples far from exhaust the issue. They show instead the centrality of achieving this duality if a party is to succeed in the political struggle.

## Party Struggle, Party Theater:

There is another issue that parties must face. On the one hand, voters and other audiences seem to judge parties on the policy stands they take. On the other hand, these same audiences also judge whether these party politicians have the right "character" to govern. In other words, picking the right policy stands and presenting the right rhetoric is not enough. The policy expert is often the worst party politician, and the great rhetorician can often turn off potential supporters. Instead, the most successful party politicians present themselves as the best people to run the state. They are the most capable politicians. They are the most ethical. They are more of "leaders", or their candidate is more "presidential". In sum, they have the best "character", with character being defined by whatever the audiences perceive to be the best for running the state.

So, parties have to present themselves as promoters of policy stands that would attract potential supporters, and they have to present themselves as having the "character" that potential supporters would want to see in their officeholders. In the former case, the party presents a vision of what the government should strive for. This vision promotes the special interests of its coalition through symbolism that disguises that self-interest by making it appear to be a collective good and even a principled stand. In the latter case, the party presents its political actors as the best people to accomplish this vision. In other words, the politicians become part of the party's symbolic presentation. If a party presents itself as "conservative", then its politicians had better look and talk "conservative", that is, conservative as it is defined symbolically by the party and understood by potential supporters. If a party instead presents itself as "radical", that party's politicians should probably look and act different than the "conservative" politicians. In this way, party politics is not fought simply by presenting different policy stands or visions of the country's future. It is instead a form of competitive, political theater.

This theatrical competition engulfs every part of party competition. Every change in the setting can be drawn into the performance, regardless of how far fetched. Unemployment has dropped over the last quarter? It must be because of the party's skill at "running" the (capitalist) economy, as well as its moral mettle. An escaped lunatic murdered a young child? It is clearly the fault of the other party and time for a moving speech. If being a "family man" is likely to improve a politician's chances of winning support, then that politician is likely to drag his alienated children and estranged wife into the performance. The atheist politician will lead prayer sessions. The elitist politician will tell heartwarming stories of how she grew up on a small farm. All will be professionally dressed—that is, unless a strategist directed them to wear blue jeans.

To make this performance believable, the party's politicians have to be largely consistent and united in the way they present themselves. Consistency over time is particularly important for the key elements of the party's presentation, like its ideology. A party is unlikely to be successful if it proclaims to hold conservative ideals one day and then suddenly changes to another justification for its quest for power. (This does not mean that a conservative party cannot support policies that are not, strictly speaking, conservative; they simply have to couch them in a conservative framework.) Similarly, a party needs to be largely united in the way it presents itself. There are almost always internal conflicts within parties, and sometimes those conflicts are played out in front of the public. However, those conflicts can undermine the party's credibility when there is public debate over the most basic tenants of the party or when party members challenge the credibility of other politicians from that party. It is much more damaging if a party member makes speeches about the party's prime minister candidate being unfit than if that same speech is given by a member of an opposing party.

In this way, parties are very much like theater companies. Their primary means of survival is through giving good performances. If a theater company attracts an audience, it can raise money, attract investors, maintain its staff and actors, and most important, stay on stage. Similarly, if a party can attract enough support, it can win votes, raise money, and gain a slew of other political resources. They are in an ongoing performance to attract support within three audiences (the mass public, elite groups, and the party membership) in an attempt to win power over the state. But, this form of political struggle requires a high level of competence.

*The Exclusive Multi-Party Stage:*

A number of factors make party theater extremely difficult. First, party politicians are in an ongoing performance in front of three different audiences: They act before a voting public, elite organizations, and the party network (in the last case, especially the rank-and-file.) Parties must be capable of building support within all three at once if they want even a chance to win state power. Second, there are usually multiple parties on the political stage, with each trying to outperform and undermine the other. Third, parties do not control the setting behind their actors. An economic downturn or international crisis can easily ruin an otherwise compelling performance, for example. Fourth, parties have little control over whether they can even get on stage. Most parties do not even have the opportunity to perform before larger audiences and attempt to win support from within them.

The main political stage in most representative systems is parliament. It provides a setting on which the party can give its performances to the largest audiences on a repeated, consistent manner. Those parties not on the main stage (i.e., not in the parliament or congress) can rarely find adequate alternative stages and get the audience attention needed to develop mass support, build elite connections, or maintain a rank-and-file. Those on the main stage, on the other hand, must work hard to stay there. They have to maintain public support to keep getting reelected, and they have to do anything possible to keep minor parties from stealing some of their limelight.

Indeed, getting on the main stage is the key to party success. Staying on stage is what we can refer to as political survival. The difference between being on the main stage and not is usually the difference between large support and virtually no support, real campaign money and virtually no money, an army of members and a handful of devoted volunteers. There is another important difference: It is often also the difference between attracting competent, professional politicians (or having the resources to train politicians) and having to push novices on stage. In political terms, it is the difference between those who eat and those who go hungry.

The difficulty of this ongoing performance is also influenced by the party's position on the main stage. One can distinguish among three primary positions on this stage: parties in government, parties in opposition, and parties off the stage. As a general rule, the closer the party is to governing, the more difficult multi-audience problems become.

A party entirely off stage—that is, a party completely without elected seats—rarely has more than a small, often homogenous group paying any attention to it. Its audience is usually either a small cluster of elite groups or a homogeneous faction in the mass public that is disenchanted with mainstream politics. This party can therefore tailor its performance for a homogeneous audience.

The party with elected seats but in opposition will usually have the opportunity to build larger support within the mass public and the elite. Since an opposition party tends not to be responsible for policy, it is not forced into taking concrete actions that might undermine its performance. Nonetheless, an opposition party's supporters tend to be more heterogeneous and have more conflicting interests than supporters of a minor party, making a successful performance more difficult.

Governing parties tend to play the central role in this competitive theater. Governing parties are more capable of defining the policy debate; they can make concrete policy decisions; and they choose the ministers and the holders of other government positions. In other words, they get to play the lead, and they have greater control over the setting. This produces many advantages, but it also has negative consequences. All parties act as if they were the group most capable of governing, but only governing parties have to demonstrate that capability through concrete action. Any change in the setting, like an economic shift, can be attributed to the governing party. Moreover, concrete decisions often mean choosing sides. An opposition party can make any set of claims, regardless of how unrealistic, as long as they appear realistic and relatively consistent by the audience; for example, it can often claim that it would reduce debt by eliminating "inefficiency", "fraud", and "loopholes." A party governing over a debt problem, on the other hand, often has no choice but to cut popular social programs and raise taxes in order to avoid an economic crisis. The governing party has to make concrete choices that directly affect organized interests as well as the mass public, choices that can undermine the performance and set off a downward spiral of support.

**Party Competence and Democratization:**

This categorization of parties by their proximity to state power (i.e., parties in parliament and governing, parties in parliament and in opposition, and parties external to parliament) sums up the party competence problems dissidents, activists and leaders of minor parties face. Competence at a particular field is primarily a matter of experience, or the degree to which the individual or group have experiences in fields analogous to the current field. Even if the dissidents or activists are running political organizations, even political parties, the experiences of running those organizations outside of parliament are hardly analogous to running a party with seats in parliament. Therefore, to the degree that rapid change flings them from the margins of the political system to the center of political struggle, they are being tossed, like career aliens, from one social realm into another.

But there is more to this issue. When looking at a party as a team of politicians, party competence is that team's collective skills at party politics. Since competence is primarily a product of experience, party competence is effectively the degree to which this team's background prepared it for its current challenge of running a party in a multiparty democracy. One issue is how previous experience might have prepared these individuals for the theatrical nature of party politics. Beyond that, since party politics occurs in three fields at once—the mass politics, elite politics and intra-party politics fields—the real questions become how much these politicians, as a group, had backgrounds analogous to each political arena. To what degree did they have experiences comparable to attempting to build support within a mass public? How did their backgrounds relate to working within an elite political environment, including building support among organizations like interest groups, government agencies, or international organizations? How much experience did these individuals have in running an organization like a successful political party?

In other words, one can analyze party competence by examining how the party team's background as a group relates to the various aspects of running a party in a mass democracy. While those with the most relevant backgrounds would have a distinct competence advantage, those with little related background would be more likely to make strategic mistakes. The latter might be clever enough to play a good performance at good moments, especially during the euphoria of political change. But as circumstances turn difficult, this group would be more likely to make mistakes that undermine its performance and cause its support and resources to decline. The party would be more likely to react to problems by making dramatic changes to its stands or ideology in ways that appear inconsistent. Its politicians would be more likely to revert to strategies they learned during their pre-party experiences. And this party would be more likely to have debilitating intra-party conflicts. Internal struggles for power, common in all parties, would be more likely to degenerate into intra-party wars that are visible to the public and cause the organization to shift towards implosion.

In terms of its impact on political success, party competence is mostly a relative factor. It is a question of how much better the background of one party is against its competitors. In this regard, the worst position to be in is a minor party in a stable representative democracy. The politicians within the major parties are normally experienced and trained career party politicians. They usually work within a stable party bureaucracy, which requires them to climb slowly, forcing them to gradually build valuable skills at party politics. Moreover, the party structure can play a gatekeeping role based partially on competence, thereby increasing the chances that the most skillful party politicians would rise to positions critical for the party's success. Because they are career politicians, those in positions of power would effectively continue to train in multiparty competition over extended periods, solidifying those skills.

In sharp contrast, minor party politicians in stable democracies are unlikely to gain any relevant experience. An unsuccessful party has neither the means nor the need for a large party organization, thereby effectively eliminating any background in intra-party politics. It is also unlikely to gain enough public support to give the party any experience in building and sustaining mass support. And since the party is unlikely to win any seats and impact any legislation, there is little reason for elite political organizations to interact with these politicians.

Of course, this is also impacted by the electoral system. In a system that tends to allow parties into government with little public support, such as a pure proportional representation system with a low minimum vote requirement, smaller parties can take limited steps onto the main political stage, and this can give them an opportunity to learn multiparty politics without the pressure of being a larger or especially a governing party. These parties would also be more capable of attracting candidates with relevant backgrounds, since in this setting winning an elected position is not unreasonable. On the other extreme, when the electoral system largely excludes minor parties, the party team has little chance to gain a background in real multiparty politics. If the rare, and unlikely, circumstance emerges that these politicians suddenly win a significant number of elected positions, their low party competence would likely become a serious liability that major parties can use against them to regain their hegemonic positions.

Because the political system itself changes, democratization produces a different set of dynamics. The elite from the previous regime does not necessarily have a significant party competence advantage. The critical issue is, how good of an analogy was the politics of the previous regime to that of the emerging democracy? This can be divided into three areas. First, to what degree were elite groups in the previous regime fractured in ways that echo dynamics in representative democracies? In practical terms, a critical question is how much civil society had developed before the transition. Are there economic groups that are semi-independent from the government, or are all economic decisions centrally controlled? Are there semi-independent organizations that function something like interest groups? Moreover, how complicated is the country's international relations? Is it an isolated regime or simply a satellite of an occupying power, or is that government playing a balancing act among a range of governments and international organizations? The more fractured the elite organizations the previous regime dealt with, the more likely its leaders built competencies analogous to elite politics in representative democracies.

Second, to what degree were these leaders engaged in internal party politics that was analogous to functioning within a party in a liberal state? The critical questions are whether the previous regime had a political party, and if so, how it promoted members and maintained party discipline. A single party regime could base promotion primarily on ideological zeal or an obedient submission to the central leadership, and it could maintain intra-party discipline through terror. But, a single party regime might also base promotion partially on competencies, and it could even create a bureaucratic structure that promotes the development of political skills. If party discipline is not maintained through terror, factionalism could emerge that is analogous to the dynamics that occur within parties within liberal democracies. If intra-party order was maintained through methods other than terror, promotion was based significantly on competencies, and intra-party politics was played out through factions attempting to build support, then the politicians who functioned and thrived in this system over decades would likely have built skills applicable to intra-party politics in a representative government.

Finally, to what degree did the previous regime placate the public? Did the government maintain control over the public by terrorizing it and demanding submission to an overstated ideology and a despotic ruler? Conversely, did the government actually work to maintain support by the public at large? The more the regime kept itself in power through techniques that required actually selling itself to the public, the more skills its leaders may have gained that would be applicable to multiparty competition.

Because party politics is multifaceted, many of the same questions can be raised about former dissidents and others who build parties quickly as a regime is being transformed into a representative democracy. If these emerging party politicians had a dissident or some other organization before the transition, how much did that re-party organization function like a party? Did the organization work to build mass support, and if so, did it use techniques that were analogous to the methods parties use to win electoral campaigns and battle other parties before the public? Did the organization work to gain the support of other political organizations, or did it remain largely isolated from these group? To what degree was that structure a good analogy to party organization? Was it a large organization with internal factions, for example, or maybe was it a loose network of activists?

There is another issue that technically applies to the former ruling party but is especially important for newly emerging parties. Because the democratic transition often transforms these groups from relatively small political networks to large, national operations virtually overnight, often the party rapidly expands in membership and puts completely new people into positions of power. A first question is what percent of the party's politicians were actually members of the pre-party organization before the regime change. For those politicians not involved in the pre-party organization, the functioning of that organization would have had no impact on their political competencies. A second question would be what background these individuals had that might be analogous to party politics. It is quite possible that many politicians in these new parties are political neophytes. Having no political experience whatever, they may nonetheless have backgrounds that build skills useful to a political party. For example, lawyers tend to have skills applicable to multiparty competitions, as do newscasters, journalists and to a lesser degree people with backgrounds in policy areas. On the other hand, accountants, writers, doctors and many other careers are unlikely to build competencies that are transferable to party politics.

In sum, competence is important in multi-party politics because of the fractured nature of representative democracy. Power in other regimes might come to those who are on top of a caste system defined by traditions and maybe religion, or it might come to those who are most ruthless in killing opponents and intimidating the public and government officials alike. In representative democracy, teams of politicians form political parties and win power by building support within an enormous and fractured mass public as well as among competing elite organizations. Liberal democracy is complicated, and therefore success in game demands significant competence.

Competence is not the only determinant of party success, for sure, but it is fundamental to the long-term success of any party. For dissidents building new parties during a democratic transition, the need for skilled party politicians in the midst of a political upheaval is a fundamental dilemma. They cannot acquire those competencies without time, which the speed of a transition rarely affords them. Since the experience needed to develop competencies at winning and sustaining power usually come to those already in positions of power, party competence tends to reinforce the established order, even during moments of rapid change.

# Notes:

[1] Roberto Michels (1962) *Political Parties; A Sociological Study of the Oligarchical Tendencies of Modern Democracy*, Trans. by Eden and Cedar Paul, (New York: The Free Press).

[2] Max Weber (1946), "Politics as a Vocation" in *From Max Weber: Essays in Sociology*, Edited and Translated by H.H. Gerth and C. Wright Mills, (New York: Oxford), pp. 77-128.

[3] Max Weber (1968), *Economy and Society: An Outline of Interpretive Sociology*, Edited by Guenther Roth and Claus Wittich, (Berkeley: University of California Press), pp. 956-1005.

[4] Ibid, pp. 223-6, 284-8, 1002-3.

[5] Ibid, pp. 958-63.

[6] Pierre Bourdieu, 1987, "Social Space and Symbolic Power", In *In Other Words; Essays Towards a Reflexive Sociology*, Translated by Matthew Adamson, (Stanford: Stanford University Press), pp. 122-39. See also John B. Thompson's introduction in Pierre Bourdieu, 1991, *Language and Symbolic Power*, Edited by John B. Thompson, (Cambridge: Harvard University Press), especially pp. 10–12.

[7] For Bourdieu's definition of fields and their relationship to games, see Pierre Bourdieu and Loïc J.D. Wacquant, 1992, *An Invitation to Reflexive Sociology*, (Chicago: University of Chicago Press), pp. 94–115 and *The Logic of Practice*, pp. 66–79.

[8] For Bourdieu on symbolic capital and violence, *An Invitation...* pp. 118-20 and 167-8, respectively.

[9] *An Invitation ...* pp. 115–40 and *The Logic of Practice*, pp. 66–79.

[10] Pierre Bourdieu, 1993, *The Field of Cultural Production; Essays on Art and Literature*, Edited by Randal Johnson, (New York: Columbia University Press).

[11] Pierre Bourdieu, 1988, *Homo Academicus*, Translated by Peter Collier, (Stanford: Stanford University Press).

[12] Pierre Bourdieu, 1984, *Distinction; A Social Critique of the Judgement of Taste*, Trans. by Richard Nice, (Harvard University Press: Cambridge).

[13] In *Language and Symbolic Power*, pp. 171–202.

[14] Ibid, 176.

[15] Ibid, 182–3.

[16] Ibid, 175–8. Also Bourdieu's "On Symbolic Power" in the same volume, pp. 164–8, and John Thompson's introduction, pp. 26–7.

[17] Weber, "Politics as a Vocation", p. 78. The italics are mine.

[18] Ibid.

[19] Anthony Downs (1957), *An Economic Theory of Democracy*, (Harper & Row: New York) p. 24-27. Downs defines parties as follows: "a political party is a team of men seeking to control the governing apparatus by gaining office in a duly constituted election." See also Leon Epstein (1986) *Political Parties in the American Mold*, (Madison: University of Wisconsin) pp. 18-23.

[20] 1992, (Lawrence, KS: University Press of Kansas), pp. 1–19.

[21] 1988, (Cambridge: Cambridge University Press), pp. 6–20.

[22] Maurice Duverger, (1954) *Political Parties; Their Organization and Activities in the Modern State*, Trans. by Barbara North and Robert North, (London: Lowe & Brydone), p. xxiv.

[23] V.O. Key (1964) *Politics, Parties, and Pressure Groups*, 5th ed. (New York: Crowell).

[24] The critical exception is when politicians choose to forfeit support from one audience in order to maintain support in the other two. This usually occurs when politicians, often in the fringes, choose to ignore the elite field. However, this strategy usually eliminates any chance for the party to enter government—how does one raise contributions from big donors, for example, when one is calling for the overthrow of capitalism?—and certainly makes effective governing impossible.

[25] Pomper, p. 9.

[26] Downs, p. 36.

[27] Downs, p. 96.

[28] Pierre Bourdieu, 1980, *The Logic of Practice,* Translated by Richard Nice, (Stanford: Stanford University Press), p. 86.

[29] Michels, p. 364.

[30] Duverger, pp. 133–4.

[31] Ibid, p. 134.

**Chapter 2:**

# Party Competence and the Rise of the Hungarian Socialist Party, 1956-1989

On October 1, 1956, Júlia Rajk was taken to the pit in which her husband's body had been dumped. László Rajk had been a prominent home Communist. Unlike the *Muscovites*, who spent the early 1940s as Stalin's guests in Moscow, the *home Communists* spent the war in Hungary trying to hold together the underground party and resist the Nazi occupation. A leader of the underground, László Rajk became the victim of one of Hungary's most famous show trials in 1949. In 1956, three years after Stalin's death, the party finally agreed to give him a funeral—it seems, in order to bury the matter once and for all. The surviving home Communists, many of whom were just released from prison, had other plans. They wanted to use Rajk as their key symbol of the Muscovites' corruption and illegitimacy.

It had been a spectacular show trial—and the main accuser was none other than Rajk's friend and confidant János Kádár. Like most prominent home Communists, Kádár was himself subsequently imprisoned by the Stalinist party leaders and set free following Stalin's death in 1953. During the power struggle in Moscow that followed, the Hungarian Stalinist dictator Mátyás Rákosi fell from grace but had regained his foothold by 1956. A power struggle inside the Hungarian Workers' Party was under way between two wings, which we could now call the "nativists" (mostly former home Communists as well as their social democratic and populist allies) and the "Stalinists" (the most powerful Muscovites and their allies.) A key player was Júlia Rajk. She had gone to a number of meetings among party member to demand that the Stalinist wing tell her where her husband's body had been deposited and to insist that the party give him a proper funeral. In the end, the Rákosi clan conceded.

The problem was that László Rajk was not the only former Communist in the pit. His remains were found with the bones of the other defendants in that trial. So, Júlia Rajk was asked to distinguish her husband's skull from the others just dug up. This procedure was then continued from body part to body part. The party official would pick up a bone, show it to Rajk, and ask: "Was this your husband's?"

Overwhelmed with emotion, in tears, Rajk informed the party as well as her friends in the nativist wing that her husband deserved a funeral fitting for a

41

minister. (He was the Minister of Interior at the time of his arrest.) She also insisted that it be open to the public; otherwise, she simply would not attend. After some haggling, the party partially conceded. The nativists, however, took this as their opportunity to completely discredit the Stalinist wing. While the party was following its usual policy of inviting select groups of workers to make the event look representative, the nativists organized the funeral into a mass protest against the regime. On October 6, the re-burial of László Rajk became a partially illegal, 200,000 person strong, mass protest against the dictatorship of Mátyás Rákosi and his Stalinist allies.[1]

Two weeks later, on October 23, a group of university students organized a march from the Technical University to the Statue of József Bem, a Polish general who had helped Hungary fight the Russian Army in the 1848 revolution. The protest swelled steadily, crossed the Danube River over the Margit Bridge, passed party headquarters, and took over the large square in front of parliament. This barely controlled mass expanded rapidly, then split into further demonstrations, including one that packed into the narrow street in front of the radio station. The protestors demanded that their sixteen points be read over national radio. The police inside opened fire on the crowd. Then, instead of defending the state, the soldiers called out to protect the radio station handed their weapons to protesters. The Hungarian Revolution of 1956 had begun.

The events leading up to the Hungarian Revolution began with an conflict within the Hungarian Workers' Party that was triggered by Stalin's death and the subsequent struggle for power in Moscow. In turn this intra-party conflict and the revolution it helped ignite produced the preconditions for the rise of a socialist party better prepared for multi-party competition. After the revolution, both the reform-oriented nativists and the orthodox Stalinists fell from power, and the centrist and pragmatic János Kádár was put in charge of the party by Moscow. A primary focus of Kádár's party was to avoid another uprising. After a half-decade of severe repression, by the mid-1960s this party instituted a wide range of reforms in order to placate the Hungarian public. It also created closer ties with the West and permitted semi-independent organizations to form. Furthermore, the Kádár group replaced intra-party terror with a reward system that promoted party careerism. In sum, the Hungarian Socialist Workers' Party developed many of the characteristics of a party in a pluralist society. The post-revolution party worked to maintain the support of three groups: a mass public it feared, elite groups that were far from homogeneous, and a party membership it could not control through terror. It was in this setting that Socialist politicians could develop many of the skills needed to succeed in a representative democracy.

This chapter will discuss the evolution of the Hungarian Socialist Workers' Party from 1956 to 1989 and demonstrate how it led to the rise of the Hungarian Socialist Party soon after the fall of the Berlin Wall. It will show how the Hungarian communist party gradually developed into an organization that promoted pragmatic, professional politicians with competencies applicable to multi-party politics. Specifically, it will show that the party politics that emerged after the 1956 revolution was in many ways analogous to multi-party politics and that the politicians who formed the Hungarian Socialist Party in 1989 had received the bulk of their party experience during this period of soft communism. They had been professional politicians who were climbing their way up the party hierarchy when the fall of Kádár and the Iron Curtain flung them into the party leadership.

## The Evolution to a Competent Party:

The Hungarian Communist Party—a party that had several names over the twentieth century—was formed in the late nineteenth century as a small band of radicals led by Béla Kun; it included the Marxist philosopher György Lukács. As the Austro-Hungarian Empire collapsed immediately after the First World War, this group spearheaded the second communist revolution and formed the short-lived Soviet Republic of Hungary. The republic collapsed in a few months, and this small group was forced underground.[2] The Communists became a small, loose network of radicals who seemed to spend their time either incarcerated or fearing arrest. By the end of World War II, the Hungarian communists were geographically separated into several groups. Some were still underground or in prison in Hungary. Some lived in Moscow. Some continued their work in other parts of Europe, like those who had fought in the Spanish Civil War. Following the war, these divided groups united again and, with the backing of the Soviet Union, took political control over Hungary.

During the Soviet occupation, the history of the Hungarian communist party fell roughly into two periods. First, the Stalinist or Rákosi period lasted from about 1948, when Rákosi finished eliminating other political parties and began purging enemies of the Communist movement, until the 1956 revolution. Second, the Kádár era lasted from 1956 until the party was officially turned into the Hungarian Socialist Party in 1989.

There is little reason to believe that competence at multi-party politics could have developed during the Stalinist period. While party politics in a Stalinist system is not entirely different from that of a multi-party, representative system, those differences are nonetheless significant. Elite politics during the Rákosi era was largely a submission to Moscow's wishes. In a multi-party system, there tends to be a plurality of elite groups, and the party must work to maintain support among them. Intra-party politics was largely a subservience enforced through violence and legitimated through overstated ideology. There was little room for building coalitions of support or gathering other party resources, a hallmark of intra-party politics in less brutal systems. Mass politics during the Stalinist era was mostly overstated ideology backed by the ever-present threat of punishment. There was little attempt to build coalitions of mass support, as parties must do in a representative system. Indeed, few skills at multi-party theater are developed when party leaders are obediently bowing to one small audience while terrorizing the other two.

However, this party politics, while closer to the stereotype of parties running satellite states, was not the party politics of János Kádár. In the latter period, Hungarian party politics became much more like (but certainly not identical to) party politics in a representative system. A primary goal of the Hungarian Socialist Workers' Party was to maintain support by Moscow while placating the seemingly volatile Hungarian public. In order to avoid public opposition to its domination, the party began a policy of state promoted consumerism and more open social policies. The economic expansion required trade and therefore better relations with the West, especially West Germany. The party now had a divided group of elites that it had to please. It had to appear "liberal" to the West at the same time that it appeared sufficiently communist to Moscow. Moreover, since it wanted to distance itself from Stalinism for both the mass public and the West, the more brutal approaches to maintaining intra-party unity became out of reach. Finesse became more important to both the party center and those members who hoped to climb the party hierarchy. Like in multi-party systems, party politics in Kádár's Hungary became more complex, forcing anyone who wanted political success to develop competencies at this politics.

In 1988, Kádár was ousted from power. While Rákosi had been in power for five years (from 1948 to 1953) and then again for fourteen months in 1955 and 1956, Kádár ruled Hungary for over thirty years. A year after Kádár's fall, a younger generation of reform communists took over the party and renamed it the Hungarian Socialist Party.

While some Socialist politicians were party members before 1956, virtually all of them had gained their most significant party experiences during the Kádár regime. Examining the parliamentary faction that entered the multi-party parliament in 1990 indicates this. Only two of these MP's had been members of a socialist party before the communist takeover; (Rezsô Nyers was a Social Democrat before the parties were combined in 1948, and Pál Demény headed a communist movement before being imprisoned for many years by Rákosi.) Five of these MP's joined the party during the Rákosi era and remained communist party members until 1989. This group included several key figures in the post-1989 party, like Imre Pozsgay (who joined in 1951,) Mátyás Szûrös (who joined in 1951,) and Gyula Horn (who joined in 1954.) Fourteen, or over 40%, had joined from 1961 to 1968, during the first part of Kádár's move towards reform. Nine, or 27%, joined or rejoined in the late 1960's or during the 1970's. One joined in the 1980's while Kádár was still in power, and only two had joined after the Hungarian Socialist Party was formed. In all, nearly three out of every four Socialist members of parliament in 1990 (or 73%) had joined the Socialist party during Kádár's reign.[3]

But even these statistics understate the point. With the exception of Demény and the two MP's that had not been party members, the critical pre-1989 party experience of every one of these politicians came during the Kádár years. While Nyers had begun his climb up the party ladder during the Rákosi years, he reached his most prominent positions early in the Kádár era. Pozsgay, Szûrös, and Horn had each spent five years or less in Rákosi's Hungarian Workers' Party and over thirty years in the post-1956 Hungarian Socialist Workers' Party. The critical moments of their careers—and the moments when they were winning positions through which they could learn party politics—all came long after Kádár took power. Therefore, whatever competencies at party politics Socialist politicians had before the 1989 regime change, they would have been developed by working in Kádár's party.

For these reasons, to understand the competencies that these politicians might have developed, one must examine the party during the Kádár era.

*The Political Crisis of János Kádár:*

Kádár's party, the Hungarian Socialist Workers' Party, was created not in a vacuum but in reaction to a popular revolution. The revolution broke out on October 23, 1956, and there was no functioning communist party to speak of in Hungary by November 1956. The rank-and-file was either hiding or supporting the rebels, and the sparse leadership that was left quickly abandoned its pro-Russian roots for a stance of national independence and Hungarian neutrality in the Cold War. Moreover, before its collapse, the former party had been deeply divided between the nativists and Stalinists. Kádár was made the new leader of a governing party that had just experienced a popular revolution—worse, a revolt against one wing of the party that was supported by another wing of the party. The legitimacy of the new leadership within this dispersed and divided organization would be shaky at best.

The public crisis was even greater. The Socialists' mass politics strategy had been completely undermined. The crux of this crisis was well summarized by Kádár in Moscow as he learned that a Russian attack was imminent: "The moral position of the communists will be nil."[4] The remotest possibility of legitimate party domination was destroyed at the very moment that rule by terror was also eliminated as a long-term option. The violence of 1956 demonstrated that mass revolution was both possible and costly. The Hungarian Communists had no choice: No longer able to depend on provoking fear—since now both the public and the party had good reason to fear each other—they would have to placate the public into submission.

The revolution changed the way that Moscow dealt with its Hungarian satellite as well. The Kremlin leadership concluded by the end of 1956 that political stability in Hungary would require a looser relationship between empire and colony; the latter would need more autonomy. Indeed, this seems to have been the consensus reached in the CPSU presidium within the first days of the revolution. The standard internal explanation for the revolt seems to be that the Rákosi group tried to keep order entirely through their relationship with the Soviet Union. After requesting suggestions from a number of people, including Rákosi, Khrushchev decided to place CPSU support behind the "centrist" János Kádár. (It is speculated that Rákosi's endorsement of another candidate turned into a critical plus for Kádár in Khrushchev's eyes.) Backed by Moscow and its tanks, Kádár was given the task of rebuilding communist party control and resolving the crises it faced.[5]

Kádár's long-term solution to this party crisis is a primary reason why politicians in Hungarian Socialist Workers' Party, including those who subsequently formed and ran the Hungarian Socialist Party, could develop competencies needed for multi-party politics. While there certainly were not going to be competitive elections in the coming years, and therefore Socialist politicians would not learn the art of campaigning, other aspects of multi-party politics would become key characteristics of Socialist politics in the coming years. Socialist party politicians would need to learn how to build public support for the party, how to develop support among multiple and often rival elite groups, and how to maintain intra-party control without resorting to violence.

*Kádár's Mass and Elite Politics Strategies:*

It took until 1962 for Kádár to secure his position in the party and the country. Once power was centralized into his own hands, the party changed the way that it related to the mass public. The party ideology, to the degree that it presented any ideology, became a form of socialism that was promoted by the nativist wing's key figure, Imre Nagy, who became Prime Minister in 1953 and again during the uprising. Purposely unlike the party of Miklós Rákosi, from which it wanted to distance itself, Kádár's party significantly downplayed its communist roots and relationship with the Soviet Union. Instead, it tended to refer to itself as "socialist" and was far more likely to use patriotic than communist rhetoric. With this symbolic shift away from Rákosi's hard communism also came the symbolism of openness. The most famous Kádár line from the early 1960s was a Jesus quote from the Gospels of Mark and Luke: "He who is not against us is with us." The party and the public would have a new relationship: As long as the public did not challenge the party's monopoly over political power, the public would be largely left alone.

Part of this symbolism of openness was a changed cultural policy by the party. The new cultural policies were directed by György Aczél, a close ally of Kádár's. Aczél was a home Communist who had fought in the underground resistance against the Nazi occupation. Like Kádár, he was imprisoned during the Rákosi era. Unlike Kádár and many of his other comrades, Aczél was knowledgeable in literature and art, though he had barely a secondary education. [6]

A key to this cultural policy was to build a mutually advantageous relationship between the party and the populist writers and artists. From the perspective of the party, the populist writers would make either useful allies or dangerous adversaries. On the one hand, they could be used to justify the regime's position and especially to promote the impression that this government was much more tolerant than its predecessor. On the other hand, these very people were among those who had spearheaded the revolution. Prominent populists were among those who gave stirring speeches against the Rákosi regime at Bem Square, and the populist writer Gyula Illyés had published his subsequently famous "A Sentence About Tyranny" during the uprising. [7] The party's strategy was to give them enough freedom to keep them passively loyal but not so much latitude that they might challenge the regime.

Luckily for the regime, the populists seemed open to this arrangement. The populists and the nativist wing of the communist party had ties since at least the period between the two world wars, and, in fairness to the populists, their opposition had been specifically against the Stalinism of Rákosi. They were, for example, strong supporters of Imre Nagy. [8] In June 1958—the same month that Nagy was executed—the party issued a report that spelled out what the new party leadership would encourage and tolerate from the populists. In 1962, the populist writer László Németh wrote an extended response to Aczél that called for subsidized mass education, flexible censorship, and the official encouragement of "local" patriotism. [9] Peaceful coexistence between the party and the populists developed during this period—to the point where prominent members of the latter group, including Illyés and the composer Zoltán Kodály, were honored guests at

46

the Socialists' party congresses. This mutually advantageous relationship lasted until at least 1973, when intra-party power shifted back towards the hard-liners.

By the mid-1960's, many of Németh's proposals became part of the party's cultural policies. The government opened the state-subsidized universities to all irrespective of class or party affiliation. (One unexpected effect was that the first few years of the more open universities produced the core group of young intellectuals that would later create the democratic opposition and then the Alliance of Free Democrats, another political party.) Censorship became more lax, with Hungarians being able to read, watch or hear a much wider variety of classical, traditional and popular art, though literature that directly challenged the government was strictly forbidden. Travel restrictions began to gradually drop, making it possible for Hungarians to do a small amount of traveling. Overall, the party developed what has been called a new "social contract" with the Hungarian mass public in which the public did not challenge the party's political hegemony and the party gave the public significant freedom in non-political arenas.

With these important symbolic changes to the party's mass politics strategy also came concrete changes: Part of this "social contract" was that the party would insure that the standard of living in Hungarian would increase steadily. Hungarians experienced a dramatic increase in their standard of living from 1960 to 1970. Already in 1957, the year after the revolution, Hungarian's standard of living improved even as Budapest was rebuilt and opposition was being eliminated. That standard of living improved *every year* of the 1960's and would continue to improve into the mid-1970's.[10]

However, this need to continually improve the standard of living produced economic problems for Kádár's party. By the mid-1960's, economic growth in this centrally planned economy could continue only if the standard of living was reduced—a move that the party considered dangerous—or foreign debt was increased further. Between 1959 and 1964, Hungary's foreign debt had already more than doubled.[11] The party attempted to solve this problem by creating a new, reformed version of centralized planning. This move towards economic reform began in 1962, after Kádár solidified intra-party power partially by removing potential opponents. Rezsô Nyers, the former Social Democrat who was Minister of Finance (and would become the first president of the Hungarian Socialist Party in 1989) was advanced to the Politburo and made secretary of the Central Committee. He became the primary architect of the planned economic changes, called the New Economic Mechanism.[12]

The New Economic Mechanism was a centralized, socialist attempt to mimic Adam Smith's invisible hand. Ministries still had administrative authority over companies, which was to be used only in exceptional circumstances, and the government continued to control investment, including who would be given credit. The government also retained its control over large-scale investments, and it continued to set the main national objectives. But, enterprises were instructed to maximize profits, and the government guided this profit orientation through taxation and subsidies. Prices of consumer goods and services became more closely linked to production costs, though the government continued to subsidies certain items, like milk, bread, and books. The government also instituted some level of profit sharing for employees, in which a percent of salaries were based on the profits the company earned. However, even with these market-oriented changes, one socialist ideal was maintained: Everyone was guaranteed a job.[13]

For our purposes, the most important characteristic of the New Economic Mechanism was that it changed elite politics for the Socialist party. First, by decentralizing economic power, it also created new centers of power, organizations with separate interests that lobbied the party for government subsidies and credit. This was not civil society, for sure, but it was more like civil society than when the economic decisions were planned centrally by the party bureaucracy. There was therefore some limited creation of elite groups that were semi-independent from the party. Second, the New Economic Mechanism required the party to build stronger relationships with western countries, which were to be its lenders and alternate trade partners. The party would now begin a balancing act between Moscow and the capitalist West. To maintain this economic dependence on both sides of the Cold War, it would present a front of "liberal communism." It presented itself at once as non-repressive and somewhat open to capitalism to the West at the same time that it maintained an image of communism (if "goulash communism") and loyalty to the Soviet Union.

*Kádárism and the Rise of Party Competence:*

Because the party was promoting a different strategy than its Stalinist predecessor, it needed to attract and train a different type of party politician. The need for ideological rigor was gone. Instead, people were needed who brought Kádár's party certain competencies. One, the New Economic Mechanism, and in general the more open administration, required a party leadership of much higher technical knowledge, especially about topics related to economics and foreign policy. "Technocrats" began to play a much greater role in the day-to-day running of the party and its government. Two, since the party was increasing its dealings with the West, the presentation of a professional image became far more important. Finally, an image of competence was critical to the mass politics strategy. Partially, this was a way to distinguish itself from the Stalinist period, when the communist party developed a general image of ineptitude. This image of expertise was also central to its basis of legitimacy: Its entire justification to the public for being in power was that it could produce a decent, secure life for most Hungarians.

The Kádár regime's emphasis on technocratic competence, coupled with the stability of this party network, produced a situation in which internal promotion required (and thereby produced) competence in two critical areas of party politics: intra-party and elite politics. With rare exception, stability is the first prerequisite of party competence, since stability leads to a network with extended experience in party politics. In the Rákosi era, the party expanded rapidly, bringing in people lacking party experience and indeed any political or administrative background. The Rákosi gang made this problem worse by purging, imprisoning, or executing a large portion of the upper level party members who had some political competencies. The situation was completely different during the Kádár era. The climb towards the center of this party was long and laborious. About a third (12 of 33, or 36%) of Hungarian Socialist Party MP's in 1989 had been Central Committee members. On average, it took them just under twenty years (19.75) to become members of this committee after joining the party. Of these politicians, the shortest time from joining the party to entering its Central Committee was ten years; the longest time, held respectively by Gyula Horn and Imre Pozsgay, was thirty-one and thirty years.[14]

Part of what made this climb arduous (though certainly much less dangerous) was the shift away from ideological rigor and terror. Advancement slows when one's superiors are not being imprisoned or executed. More important, with the elimination of intra-party violence, room for subtle maneuvering increased. The key to intra-party success was support, especially by Kádár. But while Kádár held a great deal of intra-party power, he was not omnipotent. Even Kádár was partially dependent on support within the organization; among other reasons, others in the party center and the membership in general were quite capable of hurting his credibility with Moscow and the mass public. Intra-party advancement therefore required support from a number of groups, not just the party center. Ambitious politicians needed people to promote them, and they needed to avoid opponents who might try to subvert those ambitions.

The climb towards the center of this expertise-oriented party also began to require policy skills. The first generation of Kádár leaders, few of whom had much formal education, went through exhausting study as they developed the new system. Those who wanted to join their ranks were generally expected to gain expertise in at least one policy area, including running a government ministry or being a member of the Central Committee secretariat, which ran the policy arm of the party. While policy expertise is not identical to competence at elite politics, the two tend to go hand in hand: If one heads the Ministry of Foreign Affairs, one does not simply gain a detached understanding of foreign policy. One also gains skills at dealing with diplomats and international organizations. Roughly the same is true of upper level positions in most policy areas, though the elite (and in Hungary, semi-independent) groups vary.

Indeed, anyone who climbed to the level of a Central Committee member would have to deal at least to some degree with both of these party fields. No one would advance this far without some skills in dealing within a large, bureaucratic political organization. Moreover, while the Central Committee membership did not control policy—policy-making was highly centralized, with the politburo and the Central Committee secretaries making the key decisions—the Central Committee was the party's legislative body. These members had to deal at least nominally with policy issues.

Finally, Socialist politicians during the Kádár era in or near the party center had to gain experience in the mass politics field. In the decades after the revolution, the party became acutely aware of how its actions might influence its public legitimacy. It was extremely careful to maintain its image as a party of experts that promotes cultural openness and economic stability. Indeed, its subsequent demise is linked directly to its unwillingness to permit the economic decline that would hurt this impression. While this is not identical to building public support in a competitive party system, it is nonetheless theater before a mass audience. In fact, the Hungarian Socialist Workers' Party gave a performance that seemed convincing to not only most Hungarians but also the

West until the mid-1980s. By most accounts, until the late 1980's, it held the greatest amount of public support of any communist party in a Warsaw Pact country. So, while these Socialist politicians had no experience in marketing or electoral campaigning, at least some of them understood how to build and maintain public support.

Socialist politicians during the height of Kádár's reign were seasoned, professional party politicians. But, competence is not the only factor that determines whether a party succeeds. Besides the distribution of other party resources, changes in the political setting can cause damage that the party cannot control. For Kádár's party, the problem started becoming clear in the 1970s. It could not sustain the consumerism and economic stability that it depended on to legitimate itself before the public. As the crisis developed, an intra-party struggle for power developed, and a new generation of reform communists emerged victorious and with a new party name.

**The Rise of a New Party Elite:**

> *By the late 1970s, the [New Economic Mechanism] had become the principle, if not the sole, device for the regime's self-legitimization. It was only then that the leadership realized that it had been a strategic blunder to hand over to the population a yardstick, that is, take-home pay and consumer prices, with which to measure the gap between the regime's political rhetoric and its economic performance. As long as the state had the resources to underwrite the costs of stable living standards, no one outside the party elites and a small group of dissident intellectuals took notice of the postponement of the contemplated political reforms. In any case, it was not the lack of political democratization but the stagnation and, by the mid-1980s, general deterioration of the economic system that fatally undermined Kádár's position. (Rudolf Tôkés,* Hungary's Negotiated Revolution*)[15]*

Over the twenty-year period from 1968 to 1988, the Hungarian Socialist Workers' Party gradually shifted towards a political crisis driven by serious economic problems. While that crisis and the eventual regime change it caused were related to similar economic problems and political changes in the Soviet Union, the Hungarian crisis was not simply caused by a changed CPSU leadership (or for that matter an accelerated arms race.) Instead, the Hungarian Socialist Workers' Party was forever fearful of the Hungarian public, and it's justification for power was based on consumerism and economic security. By the late-1980s, its unwillingness to accept the consequences of changing economic circumstances, coupled with a loss of economic support from Russia, put the Hungarian Socialist Workers' Party into a situation in which it would govern over a sharp, painful decline in most Hungarians' standard of living. As a soft dictatorship losing Moscow support, the party had a good reason to fear a violent reaction by the Hungarian public. To save itself, the Socialist leadership gradually decided to try creating limited pluralism in which it would share power (and responsibility for the economic crisis) with a few, select partners.

But, there was an intra-party aspect to this revised strategy. The leadership did not simply change its mind. Instead, there was an internal shift in power that helped bring about this change. This shift occurred in two main steps. The first was a generation change. In 1988, a younger, middle-age generation of Socialist politicians ousted the aging Kádár and many of his closest allies, taking over the party. Once Kádár was out of the picture, the fight developed between the reform and hard-line wings. The reformers won in mid-1989 by winning supporters within the party, including a rank-and-file rebellion that formed Reform Circles throughout the country, by systematically replacing hard-liners with their own people, and by building loose alliances with political groups outside the party, notably the Hungarian Democratic Forum.

Most important for our purposes, the shift of power in the party was overall a shift from one group of professionals to another. As the conflict intensified and the party became less stable, mid-level politicians began advancing much faster. Nonetheless, the leaders of the new party, the Hungarian Socialist Party, had on average over twenty years experience working in the party. Those at the absolute center had all been active party members since at least the early 1950s. Some in the leadership had been Politburo members; more than half were Central Committee members; and virtually all had been career party members that had climbed up to some administrative or leadership position in the party. The Hungarian Socialist Party leadership therefore entered the new regime period with significant experience in the party politics of the Hungarian Socialist Workers' Party, a politics which, as I argued above, had much in common with multi-party politics.

*The Slide Towards Crisis:*

The leaders of the Hungarian Socialist Workers' Party were faced with two fundamental problems after 1968. First, despite their best efforts, the New Economic Mechanism did not solve their biggest political problem: It could not sustain a steadily increasing standard of living in a fundamentally communist (i.e., command) economy. The specifics of this problem will not be dealt with here.[16] The critical point is that while Kádár's policies, including the New Economic Mechanism, produced a better life for Hungarians, it still had significant inefficiencies, and it produced a mounting foreign debt.

Second, while Moscow had given Hungary and some of its neighbors greater autonomy after the 1956 revolution, that autonomy was limited. The Hungarian Socialist Workers' Party was still at the end of a Kremlin held leash. While Moscow was willing to give its Central European satellites more latitude for reform, that latitude was intended to reduce the cost of maintaining its domination. Once reform would begin to threaten Soviet interests, the Kremlin would clamp down.

From Kádár's perspective, the main problem was not the reform wing of his party but the one next door in Czechoslovakia. It is no accident that Kádár would try to play "honest broker" between Brezhnev and the young, Czechoslovakian reform leader, Alexander Dubcek. It was clearly in the Hungarian general secretary's interest to have a peaceful resolution to the conflict. The problem shows the complexity of the Hungarian Socialist Workers' Party elite politics field. The party needed to maintain loyalty to Moscow without hurting its developing relationship with the West, especially West Germany. Moreover, it needed those economic reforms in order to sustain the growth that would continue to placate the Hungarian public. In the end, Kádár had to take a side. Hungarian troops assisted in the invasion of Czechoslovakia and helped crush the Prague Spring.[17]

1968 was the year of mass movements and student protests across the globe. It was also the year that intra-party and extra-party political shifts began in Hungary. Within the party, the hard-liners rebounded because of the invasion and its aftermath. Outside the party, the invasion marked the beginning of the democracy movement that would eventually produce political parties, as will be discuss in the next chapter.

The first shift back towards the hard-liners reached its zenith in 1973 and 1974. A primary reason was pressure from Moscow. Because of the Czechoslovakia crisis, Brezhnev became concerned about reform. There was a shift in the Hungarian Socialist Workers' Party center, and several key Kádárites fell from power. Nyers was removed from the Central Committee secretariat, the administrative head of the party, and the Politburo. Aczél was also removed from the secretariat, though he remained in the Politburo. Besides pulling back on economic reform, the energized hard-liners began a crackdown on dissidents. A number of intellectuals were thrown out of the university and expelled from the party, and the writer Miklós Haraszti was put on trial. The shift was serious enough that Kádár requested retirement as first secretary, a request that the Politburo denied.[18]

In the mean time, the economic situation worsened. At the same time that wages were raised significantly for many workers, oil prices skyrocketed worldwide. Hungary, dependent on export to the West, was hurt by the economic problems there. By 1980, gross foreign debt was nine times greater than what is was in 1970, and Hungary faced numerous other economic problems, including the nearly impossible task of selling in two markets, one capitalist and the other command, with completely different product demands.[19]

Again, Moscow was not the only elite group the party had to please. Western trade partners and creditors were also important. The party center needed to deal with the economic problems without offending the mass public. It had to keep the standard of living up. As the 1970s progressed, Moscow became less concerned about the economic reforms, possibly because the 1968 crisis became more distant and certainly because its stranglehold over East-Central Europe was more secure than a decade before. This factor, combined with the need to deal with the economic problems, prompted a shift in power back to the reformers in the late 1970s. A number of economic reforms were made in Hungary, including a certain amount of decentralization. For our purposes, the most important step came in 1982. Hungary entered the International Monetary Fund, which gave the country emergency credits to meet its repayment obligations and avoid bankruptcy. By joining the IMF, Hungary and therefore the Socialist party became more dependent on the West.[20]

During the period from 1978 to 1984, gross foreign debt stabilized at around eight or nine billion United States dollars. But, Hungary's economic problems were not being resolved, and an economic crisis loomed closer. It was at this point that the aging Kádár made a critical mistake that would speed the end of his career. Unwilling to accept a significant drop in the standard of living, he instead borrowed even more money and invested it into large-scale projects that he thought would fuel the economy. The effect was disastrous. By 1986, Hungarian foreign debt nearly doubled to fifteen billion United States dollars.[21]

With an economic crash becoming an immediate possibility, Kádár decided to make dramatic personnel changes in the administrative parts of the party. Younger party members (in their late thirties to mid-fifties) were advanced to important policy positions. (Kádár and his closest allies were in their seventies.) These politicians who advanced in the first half of 1987 would then play key roles in overthrowing Kádár and his closest allies.

*The Last Days of Kádár:*

Now facing economic problems that could no longer be ignored, Kádár devised a new strategy for staying in power: He would maintain control of the party while shifting the blame for the crisis onto the government. During the months following the Central Committee meeting in November 1986, Kádár pushed through a number of party reforms. He shifted administrative control (and therefore responsibility) over economic decisions from the Central Committee to the government itself. The party's administrative role was reduced to oversight and setting strategic priorities. Kádár also promoted younger party members to positions of greater responsibility. For example, he made thirty-eight year old Miklós Németh the secretary of the Central Committee Department of Economic Policy. While these policy areas would be moved to younger and more energetic politicians, he and his closest allies would continue to control the Politburo, the party center.[22]

Instead of helping maintaining his position, the changes were interpreted as the first strong signs that Kádár was about to lose his grip. This impression prompted moves towards ousting him. During this period, the hard core opposition of János Kis and his fellow dissidents composed the "Social Contract" issue of their underground (samizdat) journal *Beszélő*. The title of the first article was "Kádár Must Go!" Internally, three ambitious politicians in their fifties— Imre Pozsgay, János Berecz, and Károly Grósz—began making serious plans to replace Kádár.

Pozsgay was the most prominent younger reform communist. He was secretary general of the Patriotic People's Front, which was formally a mass movement but in reality a vehicle for promoting party policies, since 1982. Pozsgay used this organization to build support among poorly organized extra-party groups (including the populists and cultural houses throughout the country) and disgruntled intra-party groups (like younger reform communists.) He also built mass support with the help of the Patriotic People's Front's newspaper, *Magyar Nemzet* (or *Hungarian Nation*.)[23] In order to win support among reform communists, he also studied economics and published articles about economic reform.[24]

In comparison, Berecz was a hard-line neo-Stalinist. Berecz anticipated a hard-line victory in Moscow, and his primary strategy was to show unwavering loyalty to Kádár. To the dismay of the populists and many others, Berecz replaced Aczél as the Central Committee secretary of ideology in 1985. He then decided to set the record straight on the 1956 "counterrevolution" through a series of documentaries meant to discredit the so-called rebellion and its victims.[25] Determined to stick to a strict communist ideology, he followed this performance with further blunders, offending many in the public and the reform wing of the party. But, Berecz did maintain Kádár's support, and he was well connected in Moscow.[26]

Grósz was somewhere between these two, ideologically orthodox (including supporting a pro-Moscow foreign policy) but wanting economic reform. Grósz's rise coincided with the fall of reformers in the early 1970s, when he became linked with the hard-line critics of Kádár. He survived the elimination of many of these critics, promoted himself as a loyal Communist and an expert on economic reform, and climbed his way to becoming the first secretary of the Budapest party organization in 1984 and a Politburo member in 1985.[27]

In June 1987, Kádár appointed Grósz as Prime Minister, possibly to place blame for the economic problems on this young upstart and thereby eliminate him as a political contender. The move triggered Kádár's loss of control over the party. Instead of becoming the scapegoat, Grósz instantly became Kádár's most serious opponent. Grósz called for party renewal, and he announced that the party needed to change its justification for power from economic security and growth. He quickly built a (temporary) coalition of intra-party support among technocrats, government bureaucrats, reform economists, and younger Communists. He developed public support as well, such as in his first televised address before parliament, in which he gave a clear, direct speech quite unlike those common among communist leaders. Kádár, in turn, gave a long-winded, unclear speech which seemed to reflect his age. As the seriousness of Grósz's challenge became clear to Kádár, each began to travel the country in an effort to build mass and rank-and-file support for his respective side: Grósz to replace Kádár, and Kádár to remain in power.[28]

As often happens when a party center splits, the decentralization of power moves beyond the interest of the challenger, in this case Grósz. In January 1988, in an attempt to counteract Grósz, Kádár called for local party units to "debate" a thesis on ideology written by Berecz. Unfortunately for Kádár and Berecz, this is exactly what many local units did, and the first sign of a rank-and-file rebellion emerged. Then, an intra-party reform movement, the New March Front, was formed in February with Rezsô Nyers, the main architect of the New Economic Mechanism, as its head.[29] In the mean time, Pozsgay used his position as the head of the Popular People's Front to help form the Hungarian Democratic Forum, a political organization outside the party run by the populists, and then publicize it in *Magyar Nemzet*.[30]

Kádár's demise came in May 1988 at a special party congress less than a year after Grósz became Prime Minister. During the period leading up to the congress, there was an intense fight between Kádár and Grósz to build support and to influence the selection of delegates. In the end, Grósz was able to build a wider coalition, partially by gaining the support of Nyers, Pozsgay, and their respective followers. When Kádár's fall appeared inescapable, even Berecz, his closest ally from the next generation, abandoned him. Even Kádár's old friend György Aczél stepped aside to let him fall. On May 17, Grósz got Kremlin approval of the leadership change. Two days later, Kádár finally drank the hemlock; he resigned and was given the insignificant position of "chairman," which was invented just for him. After some further maneuvering, his closest allies fell as well, including Aczél, and a new generation of Socialist politicians took control over the politburo and the party. Kádár died a year later, on July 6, 1989, a few weeks after the entire country re-buried and publicly mourned the execution of Imre Nagy, an execution for which many Hungarians blame Kádár personally.

*Reformers' Maneuvers and the Negotiated Transition:*

In the summer of 1988, First Secretary Károly Grósz had won the extended struggle to become Kádár's replacement, or so it had seemed. The problem was that with the fall of Kádár came a decentralization of intra-party power. There were still various groups vying for power, and a number of challengers were looking to grab the leadership position from Grósz's weak hold. An economic crisis appeared more imminent, and the Socialist party's legitimacy—and with it, the party's control over Hungary—was in serious jeopardy. The international political scene was changing as well. Moscow was becoming more reluctant to aid Hungary and seemed unlikely to bail Hungary out of its economic problems. As Moscow pulled back, Hungary was becoming more dependent on the West. Besides its overwhelming debt to western creditors, trade with the West would become even more important in the future, especially if Moscow significantly reduced its trade and financial assistance.

With these changes in the economic and international situation, both wings of the party were shifting ideologically as well. By the summer of 1988, the hard-liners supported economic remedies and some minimal political reform as a way to maintain some public legitimacy. But, they wanted that reform limited and especially to keep their one party control over Hungary. In comparison, the reformers saw a need for greater westernization. Economic westernization would produce a need for some minimum multi-party pluralism. Correcting the economic problems would cause public pain that would undermine the party's justification for power and quite possibly public unrest. A multi-party system based on elections would help spread the blame and create a new legitimacy for the party's position. (At this time, when there were no serious extra-party challengers, hard-liners and reformers alike seemed to believe that they could largely control the make-up of any new government.) Moreover, a representative system would help Hungary build an image of modernization and westernization, both of which would help Hungary shift trade relations and possibly negotiate aid from the West. The developing idea of reformers seemed to be to oust the hard-liners and instead share power with other groups, like those with whom Pozsgay was building a relationship. Possibly a Polish-type compromise could be reached; the reform communists would control the administration through a presidency while it would share legislative power in parliament.

As 1988 progressed, the hard-liners' position within the party steadily weakened. Mass, elite, and intra-party pressure was building to end the one-party hegemony, and even the hard-liners were losing confidence in staving off multi-party pluralism.  In late November, Grósz had to give up his position as Prime Minister—he remained general secretary—to the reform communist and foreign minister Miklós Németh.  A few days later, on November 29, Grósz made what appeared to be a desperate move to maintain intra-party support against the reformers.  In a speech at a mass rally of the Budapest party organization he argued that the threat of "white terror" was looming in the horizon.  On the same day, the first Reform Circle was formed in the city of Szeged.  The Reform Circles would become the main forums for the developing rank-and-file, intra-party rebellion.

Pozsgay's next big move came on January 28, 1989.  While Grósz was out of the country, Pozsgay dropped a bombshell on the radio program *168–Hours*.  Pozsgay told the interviewers that according to a Central Committee-appointed subcommittee that he was heading, the events of 1956 were not a counterrevolution, as the party had long claimed, but a popular uprising.  Pozsgay went further.  To the question: "Will [the Hungarian Socialist Workers' Party] try to learn how to live with another party?"  Pozsgay responded: "We must learn which parties—not one but two or more—will be a factor in Hungarian life.  This [Hungarian Socialist Workers' Party] cannot say nor does it want to say.  Instead, a partnership will emerge, or an opposition role for those that cannot take the responsibility of this partnership or coalition."[31]  It became clear later that the Hungarian Democratic Forum and some other emerging organizations were supposed to be part of Pozsgay's partnership and the Alliance of Free Democrats and Federation of Young Democrats were the key examples of organizations not prepared for that responsibility.

Pozsgay is candid about having pulled this maneuver at a moment when Grósz could not respond.  He subsequently wrote:

> *I calculated for the timing of this declaration that it should happen while they cannot strangle the message before the idea would come before the public.  For this reason, I asked that the meeting of the [Central Committee-appointed] subcommittee, originally scheduled for January 19, be postponed to January 27.  I heard that Károly Grósz, the first secretary of [the Hungarian Socialist Workers' Party], accepted the invitation to a world economic forum in Davos, [Switzerland,] and was to spend the days towards the end of January out of the country.  Thus, Davos and Grósz had solved one of my problems.  At that time only Grósz could censor my message... Grósz, as I had hoped, learned belatedly about the interview, since he was surrounded by our representatives to Switzerland, and he had no time to pay attention to events at home...*[32]

He is also clear about his intentions to undermine the party's public legitimacy:

> *... one had to expect at least two consequences of basic significance.  One, with this action, one would blow the party out of the ground by its roots...  The other, whoever declared that a popular uprising rather than a counterrevolution happened in*

56

*1956, breaks down not only the identity and legitimacy of the Hungarian [Socialist] party; he also declares that the interference of the Soviet Union was unjust and base.[33]*

But, there is one problem in Pozsgay's account. Less then a year after this radio interview, Pozsgay helped lead a renamed version of the very party he claimed to be blowing up. Strictly speaking, Pozsgay was not destroying the party itself but undermining two key elements of the hard-liners' basis of power: The legitimate rule of Kádár's party, and the legitimacy of its relationship with the Soviet Union.

As Grósz raced home from Switzerland, he had two main options: He could discredit and reprimand Pozsgay, or he could treat Pozsgay's statements with some level of seriousness. The first approach was clearly more desirable, since accepting these criticisms would further undermine the party's legitimacy and force it to make unwanted changes. However, it quickly became clear to the First Secretary that a reprimand would provoke a severe backlash. There was widespread public and intra-party support for Pozsgay's statements. Furthermore, Moscow seemed unwilling to support any action against Pozsgay. During this brief period, the United States Ambassador to Hungary apparently assured Grósz that regardless of the political outcome, he would not be jailed or persecuted, an assurance clearly meant to quell fears that even the softest of dictators might have.[34]

So, instead, the Politburo decided to endorse limited party competition. Of course, the Hungarian Socialist Workers' Party would set these limits. It would shape the process and control the party divisions. Non-communist parties could participate if they accept socialism as the dominant paradigm as well as Hungary's military alliances. (With both points, the Alliance of Free Democrats and the Federation of Young Democrats, the two radical, liberal opposition organizations, would be excluded.) Part of this philosophy seemed to be based on a confidence by even the hard-liners in Socialist party that they could control the process and stay in power. After all, they still dominated Hungarian politics.[35]

As 1989 progressed, Pozsgay's position steadily improved. Power within the Socialist party continued to decentralize. Partially because of the Pozsgay interview, Reform Circles emerged through the party network, and these circles became the main vehicles for the emerging rank-and-file rebellion. The Reform Circles supported Pozsgay. At the same time, extra-party political groups put aside their differences to form the Opposition Roundtable. While the Opposition Roundtable included the Alliance of Free Democrats and the Federation of Young Democrats, irritants to both wings of the Socialist party, the strongest organization of this group was the Hungarian Democratic Forum, which Pozsgay helped form and was headed by Zoltán Bíró, a close associate of his.

The Opposition Roundtable demanded negotiations with the Hungarian Socialist Workers' Party on the transition to a multi-party system. Such negotiations were partially in the interest of the Socialist party. Besides creating legitimacy for the transition, the party might be able to shift part of the blame for the economic crisis on other groups. However, Grósz was hesitant to forfeit any real policy control. The party leadership tried to begin serious negotiation with only some groups. In particular, the party wanted to leave out the Federation of

Young Democrats. While there was no love lost for the Alliance of Free Democrats, the young, outspoken radicals in the Federation of Young Democrats disturbed the communist leadership to no end. Besides, the Young Democrats were sure to vote with the radical anti-Communists against the moderates, like the Hungarian Democratic Forum.

But the Opposition Roundtable held firm. As the two groups maneuvered, the pressure on the Socialist party to negotiate mounted: Poland had finished its own negotiations; President Bush was coming to Hungary in July; and worst of all, the re-burial of Imre Nagy and other martyrs of the 1956 revolution was planned for June 16. It was developing into a day of national mourning, a public relations disaster for the Hungarian Socialist Workers' Party. A declaration of intent to begin the Trilateral Negotiations for a regime transition was announced on June 13.[36] (It was called "trilateral" because there were three sides: the party, the Opposition Roundtable, and social organizations; the primary purpose of the third side was to diminish the adversarial image, a victory for the Socialists.)

In late June, Pozsgay's position advanced further. Over the previous months, Németh eliminated hard-liners from his cabinet and replaced them with reformers, and he had been continuing the earlier trend of shifting policy administration away from the Central Committee and to the government. Meanwhile, the opposition, led by the Hungarian Democratic Forum, was using reforms in the electoral law to recall hard-line members of parliament and replace them with "independents" (i.e., Democratic Forum members.) Besides forcing some of the most ardent hard-liners out of parliament, the opposition also succeeded in scaring (and to some degree pacifying) the remaining Grósz supporters in parliament. The Reform Circles held their national conference in May, and the delegates resolved that a party congress would be held in the fall to renew the leadership. Cornered, Grósz reluctantly agreed. Finally, Grósz's party position, First Secretary, was eliminated. It was replaced by a four-member presidium held by three reformers, Nyers, Németh, and Pozsgay, and one hard-liner, Grósz.[37]

With this internal shift in power, Pozsgay replaced Grósz as the head negotiator at the Trilateral Negotiations. He was also selected as the party's candidate for President of the Republic—in June, long before there was any agreement with the Opposition Roundtable or a decision by parliament to have a separate election for president![38] Pozsgay was aided further by another development. The chief negotiator for the Opposition Roundtable became József Antall of the Hungarian Democratic Forum. As it would become clear later, instead of negotiating strictly as opposite sides, Pozsgay and Antall met secretly during this period. (This relationship between Pozsgay and Antall will be discussed in the next chapter.)

There were a number of issues at stake at the Trilateral Negotiations, dealt with in more detail by Bozóki,[39] but for our purposes the most important issue was whether the President of the Republic would be elected by the public or by parliament. The Socialist negotiators wanted a public election to be held soon after the negotiations were complete. The radical opposition, notable the Alliance of Free Democrats and the Federation of Young Democrats, believed that this publicly elected, strong president was a stealth method to maintain Socialist administrative control.  Since there was little public recognition of candidates from other parties and no time to build that recognition before the election, Pozsgay was virtually guaranteed victory, and he could be expected to simply maintain the Socialist party domination of the government administration.

The Opposition Roundtable had been united on this issue, but one by one moderate organizations switched their positions.  Finally, near the very end, the Hungarian Democratic Forum switched its position as well, voting for the early, public presidential election.[40]  Pozsgay now seemed virtually guaranteed to become the next president of Hungary, and the reform wing of the Socialist party would most likely maintain their administrative control over the Hungarian government.  Moreover, the Socialists and the Hungarian Democratic Forum each held just under 25% public support; the next highest levels of support were about 7% for the Independent Smallholders' Party and 5% for Alliance of Free Democrats.[41]  The Democratic Forum also seemed more than willing to create a coalition government with the reform communists.  As Antall said in a press conference in October, after the Hungarian Socialist Workers' Party changed its name, "without the Hungarian Socialist Party there cannot be a stable coalition that will work in the nation's interest."[42]  The reform communists were now in a good position to maintain much of their power over the Hungarian government by sharing that power with patriotic-minded moderates within a new, pluralistic system.

*The Creation of the Hungarian Socialist Party:*

But one step still had to be taken; the hard-liners had to be removed from the party.  This ousting effectively occurred at the party congress that was held on October 7, 1989.  At this meeting, the Hungarian Socialist Party was formed.  By this time, the reform wing had become a wide variety of groups, and the new party at its conception was a coalition of these groups.  At the beginning of the congress, there were seven platforms with committed supporters.  By far the largest was the Reform Alliance, or the federation of Reform Circles, which supported Pozsgay.  The second most supported, but far behind the Reform Alliance, was Nyers' People's Democratic platform.  According to Rudolf Tôkés, Pozsgay and Nyers had negotiated an agreement before the congress.  Pozsgay agreed that Nyers would become party president, and the Reform Alliance would not provoke a party split.  In return, Pozsgay would remain the presidential candidate, and the Reform Alliance would get a fair number of positions in the presidium, or the party's governing committee.  In the end, because the Reform Alliance had a significant majority of votes, its members won the vast majority of presidium positions.[43]

In 1989, the new center of power in the party became career, reform socialist politicians who had gained most of their party experience during the Kádár era.  The absolute center of power went to four people: Rezsô Nyers (the former Kádárite who had been the primary architect of New Economic Mechanism,) Imre Pozsgay, Miklós Németh (the Prime Minister,) and Gyula Horn (the foreign minister.)  Mátyás Szûrös, the former Central Committee foreign affairs secretary and the Speaker of Parliament at that time, was also very close to the center, though he had no formal party title.[44]  On average, each of these five Socialist leaders had nearly forty years of experience working in the Hungarian

Socialist Workers' Party, the Hungarian Workers' Party, and in the case of Nyers, the Hungarian Social Democratic Party. All but Horn and Szûrös had been Politburo members, and all five had been high-ranking members of the Central Committee.[45]

The larger center of power was the twenty-member presidium. On average, these presidium members had been Socialist party members for twenty-two years before joining the Hungarian Socialist Party's center.[46] Table 2.1 shows the membership and party experience of this presidium. 75%, or seventeen out of the twenty-four members, were career politicians in the Hungarian Socialist Workers' Party.[47] A large portion these career politicians had been high ranking party members: Just under half of the presidium (42%, or ten) had been Central Committee members; a quarter (or six) had been members of parliament; and a quarter (or six) had been either government ministers or undersecretaries in a ministry. However, even this understates the point slightly. The table leaves out two other important groups: heads of mass organizations, like the Young Communist League or the Patriotic People's Front, and first secretaries of county party organizations. If these two groups are included with those on the table, then one can conclude that fifteen members (or 63%) of this twenty-four person body had been high ranking members of the Hungarian Socialist Worker's Party before forming the Hungarian Socialist Party. See Table 2.1.

With this final move, a new generation of career socialist politicians seemed to have weathered the worst of political storms without losing governmental power. Even with a regime transformation, the end of the Cold War, the death of Kádár, a decline in the standard of living, and the undermining of the party's legitimacy, the new version of the Hungarian communist party seemed a few months away from maintaining its dominant position in Hungarian politics. It appeared ready to win the presidency and then share control of parliament with a new set of allies. Pozsgay in particular was now in an especially good position. Having just presided over the negotiations with the opposition for a regime change and having led his party's move to reform, he was virtually guaranteed to become the next president of Hungary.

But, there was a problem. In the process of defeating the hard-liners and changing the political regime, party power had decentralized in Hungary. New parties had pushed their way onto the political stage. Some, like the Alliance of Free Democrats and Federation of Young Democrats, were more than willing—indeed, quite inclined—to undermine this cozy situation the Hungarian Socialist Party had built for itself and even try to steal power from the reform socialists. Just as Pozsgay had reached the pinnacle of his career, that career was about to end. He would not be elected president. His party would lose the parliamentary elections. His friends in the Hungarian Democratic Forum would abandon him, even going so far as to erase his figure from Lakitelek pictures.[48] And he would be pushed out of power in the Hungarian Socialist Party, the party he helped form. Broken, even ridiculed, he would spend the next years trying unsuccessfully to regain his foothold in Hungarian politics.

The career politicians of the Hungarian Socialist Party came extremely close to staying in power in 1989 and 1990. In the end, their defeat would stem from losing a referendum by less than 1% of the vote. The problem was that the party field had changed. Using the very stage that the Socialists had accidentally given them, new parties subverted the reform communists' strategy and pushed them out of government. In the late 1980s, secondary and mostly unknown figures built party organizations at breakneck speed. In 1990, they found themselves in parliament. Odd circumstances, coupled with intense political battle, led not only to the defeat of a party of career politicians but also the political ascent of party amateurs. This rapid rise of party novices is discussed in the next chapter.

From Dissident to Party Politics

**Table 2.1**
**Party Experience:**
**Hungarian Socialist Party Presidium of 1989**

|  | Party Career | Politburo | Central Committee | Member of Parliament | Ministry* |
|---|---|---|---|---|---|
| László Boros | Yes |  | Yes | Yes |  |
| Béla Fábry |  |  |  |  |  |
| József Géczi |  |  |  |  |  |
| Csaba Hámori | Yes | Yes | Yes | Yes |  |
| Gyula Horn | Yes |  | Yes |  | Yes |
| Béla Katona | Yes |  | Yes |  |  |
| László Körösfôi |  |  |  |  |  |
| Ferenc Kósa |  |  |  |  |  |
| Jenô Kovács | Yes |  | Yes |  | Yes |
| László Lakos | Yes |  |  | Yes |  |
| Ilona Maár | Yes |  |  |  |  |
| Lajos Menyhárt | Yes |  |  |  |  |
| Imre Nagy | Yes |  | Yes |  |  |
| Miklós Németh | Yes | Yes | Yes | Yes | Yes |
| Rezsô Nyers | Yes | Yes | Yes | Yes | Yes |
| Mária Ormos | Yes |  | Yes |  |  |
| László Pál | Yes |  |  |  | Yes |
| Imre Pozsgay | Yes | Yes | Yes | Yes | Yes |
| Lídia Rácz |  |  |  |  |  |
| György Szabó | Yes |  |  |  |  |
| Sándor Szili |  |  |  |  |  |
| Csaba Vass | Yes |  |  |  |  |
| Pál Vastagh | Yes |  |  |  |  |
| Iván Vitányi |  |  |  |  |  |
| n = 24 | 17 | 4 | 10 | 6 | 6 |
|  | 71% | 17% | 42% | 25% | 25% |

"Ministry" means either a minister (államminiszter) or undersecretary
(minisztériumi államtitkár.)

Sources: Documents provided by Hungarian Socialist Party Headquarters;
*Parliamentary Almanac.*

# Notes:

1. Interview with György Heltai, "Reform to Revolution", *The Hungarian Quarterly* Vol. 37, No, 142, Summer 1996, pp. 42–56.

2. Tibor Hajdú and Zsuzsa L. Nagy (1990) "Revolution, Counterrevolution, Consolidation", in *A History of Hungary*, edited by Peter F. Sugar. (Bloomington: Indiana University Press). pp. 295-318.

3. *Parliamentary Almanac.*

4. Éva Gál, et. al, eds. (1993) *A "Jelcin-dosszié": Szovjet Dokumentumok 1956-ról [The Yeltsin File: Soviet Documents on 1956]* (Budapest: Századvég Kiadó), p. 74; Vyacheslav Sereda and János M. Rainer, eds. (1996) *Döntés a Kremlben, 1956; A Szovjet Pártelnökség Vitái Magyarországról [Decision in the Kremlin, 1956: Debate by the Soviet Presidium about Hungary]* (Budapest: 1956 Institute] p. 80.

5. János M. Rainer (1996) "The Road to Budapest, 1956; New Documentation on the Kremlin's Decision to Intervene (Part Two)" *Hungarian Quarterly*, vol 37, no. 143, pp. 16-31.

6. For an extensive discussion on on Aczél's life and his role in the Kádár leadership, see Sándor Révész (1997) *Aczél és Korunk [Aczél and Our Times]* (Budapest: Sík Kiadó).

7. Gyula Illyés "Egy Mondat a Zsarnokságról" *Irodalmi Újság [Literary Gazette]*, November 2, 1956. For a discussion on its importance, see Mátyás Domokos (1995) "A Few Words About a Single Sentence" *Hungarian Quarterly*, vol. 36, no. 139, pp. 10–4. Also see the English translation by George Szirtes in the same volume, pp. 15–20.

8. See, for example, Bourgin's discussion on Nagy's birthday party in 1956, just before the revolution broke out. Bourgin wrote that "almost every writer of eminence in the country was there. One of them, in the presence of others, paid a tribute to Nagy. The writers also told him that collectively they felt a very great debt to him because it was he who, by standing up to Rákosi in 1952 and 1953, particularly after he was dismissed, had given them an inspiration for the Writers' Revolt." p. 20.

9. Tôkés, *Hungary's Negotiated Revolution*, pp. 178-9.

10. Központi Statisztikai Hivatal [Central Statistical Office], 1995, *Magyar Statisztikai Évkönyv 1995 [Statistical Yearbook of Hungary, 1995]*, edited by Csák Liget, (Regiszter Kiadó és Nyomda Kft: Budapest).

11. The convertible currency forint debt increased from 1.6 to 4.1 billion "devisa forints." Nagel Swain (1992), *Hungary: The Rise and Fall of Feasible Socialism*, (London: Versa) pp. 93-4.

12. Ibid, pp. 85–113.

13. Ibid.

14. *Parliamentary Almanac.*

15. Tôkés, *Hungary's Negotiated Revolution*, p. 254.

16. For extended discussions on these economic issues, see János Kornai (1980), *Economics of Shortage* (Amsterdam: North Holland); Nagel Swain, *Hungary: The Rise and Fall...*; and Tôkés, pp. 82-116.

17. Tôkés, pp. 47–55. Tôkés gives a detailed discussion on how Kádár tried to avoid this invasion.

18. Ibid, pp. 102–6.

19. J. F. Brown (1988) *Eastern Europe and Communist Rule* (Durham: Duke) pp. 208-14; Nagel, pp. 115-23, 147.

20. Brown, pp. 214–8.

21. Nagel, p. 147.

22. Tôkés, pp. 274-6.

[23] George Schöpflin, et. al. (1988) "Leadership Change and Crisis in Hungary." *Problems of Communism*, vol 37, September-October, pp. 28-31.

[24] For an English language example, see Imre Pozsgay (1979) "The Interaction of Economics and Politics" *The New Hungarian Quarterly*, vol 20, no. 76, winter, pp. 17-26.

[25] See Berecz, János (1969) *Ellenforradalom Tollal és Fegyverrel, 1956* [*Counterrevolution with Pens and Weapons, 1956*] (Budapest: Kossuth), which Berecz republished in 1986, causing another public relations disaster.

[26] Tôkés, pp. 240-3.

[27] Ibid, pp. 233-4, 243-5.

[28] Schöpflin, et. al, "Leadership Change...", pp. 31-6.

[29] Ibid.

[30] See Pozsgay's own account in Imre Pozsgay (1988) *Koronatú és Tettstárs* [*Star Witness and Accomplice*], (Budapest: Korona), pp. 158–63. Pozsgay used an interview with himself to publicize the Hungarian Democratic Forum. It appeared in the November 14, 1987 issue of *Magyar Nemzet*.

[31] For a transcript of this interview, see Imre Pozsgay (1993) *1989; Politikús–pálya a pártállamban és a rendszerváltásban.* [*1989; Political Career in a Party State and during a Regime Change*] (Budapest: Püszki) pp. 222-7. The quote is from page 226.

[32] Pozsgay, *Star Witness and Accomplice*, p. 169.

[33] Ibid, p. 170.

[34] István Bodzabán and Antal Szalay, eds. (1994) *A Puha Diktaturától a Kemény Demokráciáig.* [*From Soft Dictatorship to Hard Democracy*] Interview with Mark Palmer. (Budapest: Pelikán Kiadó), p. 130

[35] Tôkés, pp. 298–303.

[36] András Bozóki (1993) "Hungary's Road to Systemic Change: The Opposition Roundtable," translated by József Böröcz, *East European Politics and Society*, vol. 7, no. 2, spring, pp. 276–308.

[37] Tôkés, pp. 324-32.

[38] Ibid, p. 331.

[39] Bozóki, "Hungary's Road to Systemic Change".

[40] Ibid.

[41] Tamás Moldován, ed. (1990) *Szabadon Választott; Parliamenti Almanach 1990* [*Freely Elected; Parliamentary Almanac of 1990.*] (Budapest: Idegenforgalmi Propaganda és Kiadó), p. 14.

[42] Sándor Révész (1995) *Antall József Távolról [Joseph Antall from a Distance]* (Budapest: Sík Kiadó) p. 48. Révész took the quote from the October 24, 1989 issue of *Népszabadság*.

[43] Tôkés, pp. 348–55.

[44] Mihály Bihari (1996) "Az Állampárt Végórái; Egy Pártkongresszus Szociológiája" ["The Government Party's Last Hours; The Sociology of a Party Congress"] in Mihály Bihari, *Magyar Politika, 1945–1995: A Magyar Politikai Rendszer Történetének Főbb Szakaszai a Második Világháború Után. [Hungarian Politics, 1945-1995: The Most Important Stages of the Hungarian Political System's History after the Second World War].* (Budapest: Korona), pp. 85-95, especially 90.

[45] *Parliamentary Almanac.*

[46] This statistic is based on the year the presidium member joined the Hungarian Socialist Workers' Party, as it was reported in their biographies in *Parliamentary Almanac.* If a member quit and then rejoined the party, the latter date was used. Eight, or one-third, of the cases are missing. However, since these cases range from high level party members

to non-professionals, there is no reason to believe that there is a serious bias in this statistic.

[47] Of the other 25%, several advanced because of their role in the Reform Circles, the organization of rank-and-file dissent. Another in this group, Ferenc Kósa, was a populist filmmaker and a key figure in the creation of the Hungarian Democratic Forum; he became prominent in the Hungarian Socialist Party through his close relationship with Pozsgay.

[48] Pozsgay, *Star Witness and Accomplice*, p. 288, a newspaper interview with Pozsgay in *Népszabadság*, January 16, 1998.

Chapter 3:

# Ascent of Party Amateurs I: The Evolution of Pre-Party Organizations

In April 1987, József Antall, János Kis, and Viktor Orbán were virtually unknown in Hungary. Antall was a historian who worked as the general director of the Semmelweiss Museum of Medicine. Kis was a philosopher kicked out of the Hungarian Academy of Science in 1973 for his dissident actions. (More had heard of Kis than the other two because his name was regularly cited on Radio Free Europe.) Orbán was finishing his law degree and was part of what later became called the Bibó Collegium. All three were highly educated, well read, and widely admired for their intellect. All three were politically involved. Kis was the primary editor of Hungary's main underground (or "samizdat") magazine and the unofficial leader of a small band of intellectuals who called themselves the "democratic opposition." Antall headed a "political salon," a regular discussion group on Hungarian democracy. And Orbán was a student activist who had done research on the Polish democracy movement. But, even though Kis was a party member before 1973, none had any real experience in running a party or anything like it.

Three years later, Antall, Kis, and Orbán headed political parties competing in the first free elections in Hungary for nearly half a century. Antall was the president of the Hungarian Democratic Forum, which won the majority of parliamentary seats; he became Prime Minister. Kis was the president of the party that came in second, the Alliance of Free Democrats. It became the primary opposition party. Orbán led and later became the president of the Federation of Young Democrats, or FIDESZ, a party that had an age maximum of thirty-five. FIDESZ won 9% of the vote and became the smallest party in parliament. It also became the most publicly supported party by 1991.

All three found their ways into these important positions because of some combination of competence and personal charisma. They were, in some way, the best of the groups that they subsequently led. And this was exactly the problem. Any new party in Hungary during the 1980s had to be run by either novices at party politics or members of the Socialist party. As a historian of constitutional law and the Austro-Hungarian Compromise of 1867, Antall understood politics. While this was an excellent background compared to that of the writers and literary historians in the Hungarian Democratic Forum, it was hardly a preparation for party politics. Much the same was true for Kis. He was the primary mastermind behind the subversive politics of the Hungarian opposition, and he had run an underground, samizdat operation. However, this dissident politics was quite unlike the politics of leading a large, bureaucratized network in multi-party combat. Finally, while Orbán was an activist, his primary background was as a student. He had not reached his twenty-seventh birthday when, in a period of a few months, he was catapulted from a student on a fellowship at Oxford to the head of a parliamentary faction and major political party.

There was no way for the leaders of the Hungarian Democratic Forum, Alliance of Free Democrats, and FIDESZ to have directly gained experience at party politics before being flung into multi-party competition. The collapse of Socialist rule came too fast, and the parties were built too quickly. But, the analysis does not end there. These parties did not simply appear. Instead, they evolved from other groups, each of which was involved in some form of politics. The primary question is the degree to which the pre-party experiences of these dissidents provided backgrounds useful to party politics. In brief, to what degree did the Hungarian dissident movement promote people with higher party competence or give them experience that built party competence?

This chapter will explore this questions. It will discuss the first stage of the rise of the Hungarian dissident movement as a set of pre-party organizations. The focus will be on the networks that built three main parties, the Alliance of Free Democrats, the Democratic Forum, and the Federation of Young Democrats, through the Trilateral Negotiations, or just before the organizations began running campaigns and therefore began acting as political parties. The chapter will show that dissident politics in Hungary was significantly different from and therefore poor preparation for party politics. It will also show that these loose networks often promoted individuals based on implicit criteria unrelated to political competence, much less party competence.

### A Network of Radical Dissidents:
*The Socialist Roots of Liberal Opposition:*

During the 1990 parliamentary campaign, both the Alliance of Free Democrats and the Hungarian Democratic Forum accused each other of being closet supporters of the socialist regime. The Free Democrats claimed that the Democratic Forum was involved in a secret pact with reform socialist Imre Pozsgay. The Democratic Forum distributed a leaflet titled "Apák és Fiúk" (or "Fathers and Sons") which claimed that the Alliance of Free Democrats was run by disgruntled communists thrown out of the Socialist party.[1] Oddly, the first presidents of both organizations, Zoltán Bíró for the Democratic Forum and János Kis for the Free Democrats, were former party members, though neither of them were career party politicians. Nonetheless, the claims of each group against the other were exaggerations. While the Democratic Forum had a cozy relationship with the reform socialists in 1989, it was not a puppet organization but a group trying to advance politically. Similarly, while some of the Free Democrat leaders had been party members, many had not been, and the group had abandoned its Socialist ideology nearly twenty years before the regime change.

The Democratic Forum claim that the Alliance of Free Democrats was run by disgruntled ex-Communists was clearly a political tactic; it was meant to counter the Free Democrats' claims that it was the true opposition to communism.

Yet, in a different way, the organizations' roots are from within the Hungarian Socialist Workers' Party. The starting point of this dissident group was the philosophy and sociology departments at Eötvös Lóránd University in 1961 and 1962, when the beginnings of cultural reform opened the university doors to students who were willing to consider critical thought on the regime. A number of these students associated themselves with the Lukács School and became known as the Young Lukácsians, or the "Lukács Nursery." While there were a number of professors who influenced these young students, the main point of connection seemed to be the Lukácsian philosopher György Márkus[2]. János Kis was one of the Young Lukácsians that worked closely with Márkus.

The unifying characteristic of the Lukácsians was their belief in a purest reading of Marx—which is to say that, at a philosophical level, they rejected the Stalinist model as well as Russian control over Hungary. Politically, the Lukácsians were sympathetic to the reform socialists who began gaining power in the party during the 1960s. But, following the invasion of Czechoslovakia in 1968, the Lukácsians lost faith that Socialism could be reformed. Possibly more important, this loss of faith produced a generation split within the group. The older group became central to the earliest wave of anti-government dissident work, but they were slow to reject Marxism. The younger Lukácsians began pulling away from their teachers and then broke ties entirely in the early 1970s. Unlike their teachers, this disenchantment with communism led the Young Lukácsians to shift ideologically from Marxism to British liberalism by the mid-1970s.[3]

A critical moment came in 1973 for the Lukács School. All its members and associates who taught at Budapest universities were dismissed from their jobs. The older members subsequently accepted visas and left the country. The two main Young Lukácsians, Kis and his close friend at the time György Bence, remained in Hungary. No longer having jobs to lose and now having significantly more free time, the two began working towards more serious opposition thinking.

This crackdown on the dissident community in 1973 included another pre-founding event for the radical opposition: the arrest and trial of Miklós Haraszti. In the 1960s, Haraszti was a Maoist, a group of young, radical, purist Marxists. Like the Lukácsians, the Maoists were opposed to Soviet-style communism and had connections to the New Left in Western Europe. They were forced underground by the late-1960s, and they subsequently split. Following the invasion, those Maoists who later found their way into the democratic opposition also concluded that communism could not be reformed and began shifting ideologically towards liberalism. The best known (former) Maoist by 1970 was Haraszti. After being thrown out of the university system twice (first in 1967, and then after being readmitted, in 1970) Haraszti was forced to take a job at the Red Star Tractor Factory. He used the experiences there to write the book *Darabbér* about dictatorship and the working class.

Haraszti was arrested and put on trial, and many of the Hungarian dissidents had their apartments searched for copies of Haraszti's manuscript. The point was clearly to intimidate the Budapest intellectual circles and stop their writing of illegal (samizdat) publications: Prominent dissidents were called as witnesses against Haraszti specifically to show them that they too could be arrested. The problem was that the prosecution could not accuse Haraszti of having written anti-government literature. Having now developed an economic policy that requires both loans from and trade with the West, they could not take repressive actions that might upset the relationship with western governments. So, instead, Haraszti was accused of mechanically reproducing his writing. (In translation, it is legal to *write* whatever one wants about politics, but it is strictly illegal to *reproduce* that writing through any copying machine.) This made it rather easy for the dissidents to band together. The witnesses admitted to reading the book and liking it, but nothing else. Haraszti also admitted to writing it. However, he flatly denied having mechanically reproduced it. Instead, he had repeatedly retyped the book by hand. The government was caught without a way of punishing him without potentially hurting its relationship with the West. Haraszti was given a suspended prison sentence. From the party's perspective, the dissident community got the wrong message: The trial showed them that if they banded together and exploited the reform socialists' relationship with the West, they could be protected from government repression.[4]

*A Politics of Moderate Subversion:*

The next critical year for the opposition was 1976, but not because of anything happening in Hungary.[5] The first wave of mass strikes in Poland began. Possibly more important than the strikes (though partially a product of Polish unrest) was a talk given in Paris by the Polish dissident Adam Michnik on the twentieth anniversary of the 1956 revolution. Michnik proposed a new strategy for subverting communist parties, which he called "New Evolutionism," a strategy that would influence the thinking of Kis and his colleagues and would be its guiding force in the struggle that would soon emerge.

Michnik's argument, in sum, was that the dissidents of Poland and the region needed to create a new, evolutionary strategy for subverting communist parties. He argued that the Nineteenth Century debate among leftists between pursuing revolution or reform made no sense in the Poland of the 1970s. A revolution would not succeed when Soviet tanks back the state; it would only lead to a shift in power to militants. Reform would also not work because, while it might be in the interest of party leaders to give concessions, those concessions are only made to solidify their own positions. They would not reform the party out of existence or willingly create a democracy that would create their fall from power. The evolutionary theories of Polish dissidents did not work, he argued, because they depended on the communist party simply giving up its own bases of power, either its own position in the country or its dependent relationship on the Soviet Union.[6]

But this did not mean that evolutionary change towards the end of communist party control was not possible. Instead, Michnik wrote: "[The invasion of] Czechoslovakia is an example of the fragility of totalitarian stability, and also of the desperation and ruthlessness of an empire under threat. The lesson of Czechoslovakia is that evolution has its limits and that it is possible."[7] The democratic opposition, the Polish political leadership, and the Soviet Union have a critical interest in common. For all three, military intervention would be disastrous. An uprising would end effective opposition. The Soviets would lose international prestige by attacking Poland. And a critical faction among the

Warsaw communists—the "pragmatists" who support reform not as a means to democracy but as a way to promote their own interests—would also lose much power. So, both the Soviets and the reform communists are willing to give concessions in order to avoid violence.

The trick, argued Michnik, is for the opposition to form organizations independent of the party and to push for concessions that lead to more organizing. The simple act of independently organizing undermines the communist party's fragile control over Polish society at the very moment that it produces the foundations of organizations (like parties) that could subsequently run the country.[8]

Implicit in the argument is a division within the communist party—an implication not lost on the Hungarian dissident community. The reformists have a different interest than the hard-liners. The strategy, at least as the Hungarian dissidents reformulated it, was to push the intra-party conflict between the two wings, especially on issues related independent organizations. The opposition would create new organizations bordering on illegality. They would challenge the government to imprison them, knowing full well that arrest and other forms of repression would damage Hungary's relationship with the West and undermine the interests of the reform communists. They would gamble repeatedly that the reform communists would concede to them. Once the public became aware that the communists' threats were only bluffs, other organizations would emerge. The more organizations that would emerge, they guessed further, the more power would slip from the hands of both wings of the Hungarian Socialist Workers' Party.[9]

Kis and his colleagues now began to develop a politics of moderate subversion. Their goal was nothing less than the collapse of communism in Hungary, and their method was to provoke conflict between the reform and hard-line communists. But they had a critical problem: Hungary was not Poland. There was no mass worker or democracy movement in Hungary, nor could anyone expect that one would emerge. The 1956 revolution and the repression that followed were a vivid memory for many Hungarians. While the reform communists' fear of violence was a chip that could be used against them, the same fear by the public and intelligentsia insured that no one would take steps that echoed the events of October 1956.

To make matters more difficult, the Hungarian dissident community was ideologically split between the "ruralites" and the "urbanites." The ruralites are more commonly referred to as the populists, or "népiek" in Hungarian. They are generally associated with the rural intelligentsia and with ideas of preserving the Hungarian culture and nation. In a tradition dating back to the Sixteenth Century, most are writers or poets. The urbanites, on the other hand, were mostly Budapest intellectuals who supported westernization and modernization and were much less concerned about traditional Hungarian culture. The Hungarian Democratic Forum founders were ruralites. The Kis group, which eventually built the Alliance of Free Democrats, were a specific group of urbanites who called themselves the "opposition", or "ellenzék" in Hungarian. Solidarity between these groups was unlikely.

The self-defined founding step of the Hungarian democratic opposition came in January 1977. Kis and Bence organized a petition that expressed solidarity with the Charter 77 movement in Czechoslovakia.[10] (Indeed, the characterization "organize" is an overstatement. Kis and Bence went from apartment to apartment asking people associated with the Budapest intelligentsia to sign.)[11] The critical effect of the petition was psychological, not organizational. The party reacted with mostly indifference; it even awarded one signer, the pianist Zoltán Kocsis, a prestigious award that year. The petition also did not lead directly to any form of organizing by the signers. But, it did give the petitioners and the Budapest intelligentsia the impression that political opposition is possible in Hungary, that they could take action and get away with it. The signers subsequently heard their statement and names read repeatedly over Radio Free Europe, which added to that sense of accomplishment.[12] The vast majority of signers—all but three—would become involved to a greater or lesser extent in the political actions that defined the Hungarian democratic opposition.[13]

The petition was the first, tiny step towards forming the Alliance of Free Democrats. It provided a symbolic resource that would later be essential for building a successful party: It defined a group with a political goal—at this time, opposition to Warsaw Pact human rights violations—and it created public exposure over Radio Free Europe. However, it also barely defined the membership of that group. This was partially because networks within the intelligentsia overlapped significantly at this time and partially because a group transition was underway. Fifteen of the thirty-four signers were from the Lukács School or Young Lukácsians. By the next petition, two years later, the older Lukácsians were gone, to play lesser roles in the developing struggle.[14] Furthermore, other members of the Budapest intelligentsia were soon to join the opposition. Indeed, of those involved in this petition, only two (Haraszti and the historian Miklós Szabó) would become members of parliament and three (Kis, Haraszti, and Szabó) would become part of the Alliance of Free Democrats' Administrative Board.

It took this new opposition movement two more years for another important step. On October 25 and 27, 1979, this group sent petitions in protest against the arrest of Charter 77 leaders, including Václav Havel.[15] These petitions contain far more signatures, respectively 127 and 186 names. Most of the people who would become key players in the democratic opposition in the 1980s and the subsequent building of the Alliance of Free Democrats had signed this petition. Unlike the 1977 petition, those of October 1979 contained the names all the 1990 members of the Free Democrats' Administrative Board except Haraszti and latecomer Péter Tölgyessy. In contrast—and not unimportantly—the older members of the Lukács School, who were central to dissident work in the early 1970s, were all absent. The membership of the opposition was more or less defined at this point.

*The Evolution Towards Pre-Party Organizing:*

A political network was gradually forming, but that network was involved in a politics dramatically different from party politics. The method of communication, while reaching a mass audience over Radio Free Europe, was intellectual and argumentative—quite different from the sound-bite simplicity of parties' mass politics communication; the elite politics strategies were, strictly speaking, subversive; and real organizing was virtually non-existent. The last point is especially important. The intelligentsia was nervous about anything that smacked of party formation. On a strictly political level, they considered it an overt and dangerous provocation against the Socialist party. On a philosophical level, they saw it as Bolshevik and extremely undesirable. And as intellectuals, they were simply not interested in being lower rungs on a hierarchical structure. The leaders of the opposition were beginning to develop political competencies, but these were competencies at dissident politics, not party building.

The creation of organizations and the starting of samizdat publications marked the period following the 1979 petitions. An early samizdat operation that reflected the oppositions' early political strategy was the Rajk Samizdat Boutique. The younger László Rajk was born in 1949, the year that his father and namesake was executed. Following the revolution and the subsequent amnesty, Rajk met through his mother the surviving group that had formed the Imre Nagy government in 1956 (who would become known as the "1956-ers" within the democratic opposition.) This group influenced the young Rajk's political thinking, and they were an impetus of his subsequent decision to join the opposition.

In 1981, Rajk founded the Rajk Boutique. Avoiding the felony of reproduction, Rajk paid typists four forints per page to retype samizdat writing—they typed on multiple layers of carbon paper—and then sold it to whoever came to the door. There was more to this subversive strategy than the distribution of underground writing. Rajk knew that his arrest, simply because of his name, would produce international embarrassment for the party. A second Rajk trial would be the best thing that ever happened to the opposition, and everyone knew it. Moreover, the opposition strongly suspected that Kádár had been emotionally scarred by the Rajk trial and execution, and they were not above exploiting a potential psychological advantage. The Rajk Boutique was established partially to taunt Kádár and to maybe even push the aging party secretary just a bit closer to cracking.[16]

However, by far the most important organization in the evolution from opposition to party was the underground operation *Beszélő*. *Beszélő* was the first mechanically printed samizdat publication in Hungary, and it is unique among the opposition's organizations. It is also the organization formed before 1987 that most resembles a political party as well as the foremost organization onto which the Alliance of Free Democrats was built in 1988.

Kis, Haraszti, and three other dissidents (Ferenc Kôszeg, Bálint Nagy, and György Petri) formed *Beszélő* in 1981. Their long-term strategy was to instigate conflict between the two wings of the Socialist party and spur the reformers into concessions that would gradually lead to a multi-party system. Effectively, they would goad the reform communists on issues related to freedom and civil society, forcing the latter to chose between concession and repression. The reformers, they gambled, would concede in order to placate the Hungarian intelligentsia and western governments, especially West Germany. But, they calculated further, those very concessions would produce the autonomous and eventually anti-Communist action that would undermine the government. This strategy could be implemented only gradually; calling for the end of communism in 1981 would have led simply to the isolation of *Beszélő*. The first step was therefore instead to encourage and publish information about autonomous social action.

The *Beszélő* operation, while certainly not a political party, was significantly more like a party than the other anti-Communist organizations before the late 1980s. It was the first organization geared entirely towards fulfilling an expressly defined goal (building civil society and undermining the regime) through a thoroughly developed political strategy, even though neither the goal nor the strategy was presented publicly until much later. *Beszélő* was also the first to develop a national network of constituencies. Indeed, the first year of work (before the first issue was published in October 1981) was spent constructing a sociological map of Hungary to determine where people were interested in information on autonomous action. Third, it regularly communicated to a mass audience over Radio Free Europe—which produced national recognition for the *Beszélő* group and others in the opposition, a critical resource for the Free Democrats in 1989 and 1990. Finally, and probably most important, it was the first (and for the longest time, only) hierarchically structured opposition organization.

*Beszélő* was constructed to function like a Mafia operation. The critical issue was that parts of the operation (printing and the large-scale end of distribution) were illegal and extremely dangerous. The dangers involved made it imperative that *Beszélő* be run in the most systematic, efficient manner possible. Beyond being the primary strategist, Kis also became the main organizer. There were three branches to the operation: the editorial staff (i.e., the five who formed *Beszélő*), printing, and distribution. The editorial staff met at the same time weekly in Kôszeg's tiny dentist office room, since all their apartments were bugged by the secret police. They used varying techniques to throw off the police that were regularly spying on them. This group edited the volumes and wrote much of the material. Following the technique of Russian samizdat, they always listed their names and telephone numbers. The printing was done entirely in secret. The printing, including the movement of supplies needed for printing and the communication between Kis and the printers, was organized through a clandestine system with multiple steps in order to bypass police efforts to stop the operation. Finally, distribution was done in layered system: Passing large amounts of printing material at once was illegal, so it had to be done in the middle of the night in deserted parking lots. But, once the lower levels of distribution were reached (when the distributor was no longer handling many issues) the issues could be passed along in relative safety. Moreover, by this stage, stopping distribution was virtually impossible.

The point to recognize is that this was an expressly political, hierarchically structured organization. Compared to the loose, small, and fluid organizations the other Budapest dissidents established, this was by far the most like a party. It therefore should have provided the best experience for party politics available to the opposition. Yet, according to Kis, the experience did little to prepare him (and one can assume, his group) for party politics:

> *Running Beszélő and [the Alliance of Free Democrats] were*
> *completely different, and the experiences I had with Beszélő were*

> *more harmful than helpful. The analogies were completely*
> *wrong... Even though Beszélô was an organization, nevertheless*
> *it was an organization built on personal networks and personal*
> *confidence. The Alliance [of Free Democrats] had to be a formal*
> *organization. It had to have a bureaucratic-type procedural code,*
> *and we had to learn how to separate personal attachments from*
> *official relationships. That was not very easy.[17]*

The point is critical. Even though *Beszélô* was the pre-party opposition organization most like a party, the very fact that it was an underground, dissident operation made it a bad analogy for party building. Moreover, the politics were different. *Beszélô* and the related opposition organizations were built on a strategy to subvert the regime. Jumping forward to 1989, there is little doubt that this group became quite proficient at undermining the existing system and pushing for changes that would create civil society and a liberal state. But, ingenious tactics in late-1989 and early 1990 were followed by gaffes once real multi-party politics began. The struggle would change, but the radical liberal dissidents would prove slow to adapt to party politicians.

**The Populist "Founding Fathers" of the Democratic Forum:**

If leaders of the democratic opposition had little experience related to the party politics that they would be thrust into, their political backgrounds were nonetheless significantly greater than that of the founders of the Hungarian Democratic Forum. The problem for the hard-core opposition was that they were experienced in a form of subversive politics. The problem for the Democratic Forum founders was that they had no background in practical politics whatever. There were two reasons for this difference. The first was profession. While the hard-core opposition was led by philosophers and sociologists, the Democratic Forum founders were primarily writers and literary historians. The hard-core was able to pull together a great deal of political information from the academic training of its members. The populists had no such resources. The second difference was their goals: The opposition was attempting to undermine the regime; the populists were not. The enemies of the populists were the Stalinists, who would potentially turn back Kádárist reforms and certainly not defend the rights of the Hungarian minority in neighboring countries. Moreover, the populists believed that the road to democracy included a reawakening of Hungarian culture squashed by forty years of Russian hegemony. While the opposition wanted to undermine the entire Socialist system, the populists were content with getting the hard-liners out of power and getting reform communists like Imre Pozsgay into power.

Because their backgrounds and goals were different, the methods of the opposition and the populists were also different. The radicals of the opposition studied politics, and their strategies were strictly political. They followed government policies, Hungary's international relations, and the internal conflicts within the party. The cultural goals of the organizations that *Beszélô* supported were far less important to the opposition than that these organizations were independent from the Socialist party. The moderates of the populist movement, on the other hand, followed a more covert approach. They wrote about the decay of

Hungarian society. They took symbolic moves towards democracy. They formed groups that promoted the redevelopment of Hungary's traditional culture. They lobbied party members for changes in cultural policy. They also joined the opposition on certain petitions, publications, and meetings. The populists had a critique of the Kádár regime, but they had no clear political strategy, and so they gained no experience constructing and implementing such a strategy.

*The Populists' Path to Organizing:*
By the mid-1980s, there were four main groups in the developing political struggle: the reform communists, the hard-line communists, the opposition, and the populists.[18] The reform communists disliked the hard-line communists but disliked the opposition more. They wanted to get rid of the pro-Moscow hard-liners without losing power themselves. The opposition wanted to undermine the entire Socialist system and was therefore an enemy of both the hard-liners and the reformers. The populists were therefore in the best position; both the reform communists and the opposition needed them. The reform communists needed an external ally that could help legitimate them before the public and the Western countries. The opposition needed the populists to help them create a somewhat united challenge against the Socialist government. The populists took advantage of this situation, shifting between the opposition and the reformers through the 1980s.

The first step towards unified work between the populists and the opposition was the *Bibó Memorial Book* in 1981.[19] István Bibó was one of Hungary's premier political thinkers, possibly second only to Lukács. He is virtually unknown out of Hungary, partially because he wrote specifically about Central European politics and partially because there are few translations of his work.[20] Bibó was important for two main reasons. First, he proposed a political strategy that promoted a compromise position with the Russians without giving up individual rights and multi-party democracy. It was an absolute failure in the 1940s, but some (including Kis) believed that it was a theoretical starting point in the changing politics of the 1980s. Second, he was respected among all the groups that might unify in opposition against the regime. He was a ranking member of the National Peasant Party, the populist party of the 1940s, so he was revered by the populist writers. Bibó was also a surviving member of the Nagy government during the revolution and was therefore respected by the "1956-ers"—those who were also in the government, weren't executed, and were still alive in the 1980s. The opposition also respected Bibó because he promoted individual rights and multi-party democracy.[21] Even the reform communists found Bibó an acceptable thinker, since the political thinker was also a Socialist.[22] He was therefore a symbolic starting point from which different factions of the infant Hungarian democracy movement could unify.

The *Bibó Memorial Book* became a thousand-page manuscript with authors from a wide range of intellectual groups. Authors included the most prominent populist from the previous generation, Gyula Illyés, the two rising stars of the new populist generation, Sándor Csoóri and István Csurka, several members of the opposition, including Kis and Haraszti, and the 1956-er Ferenc Donáth.[23] The party hesitated in publishing the book; the official publishing house requested that the articles by opposition writers be removed. The editors refused. The debate apparently reached the Politburo, which requested further research by a Central Committee department. In the end, the party gave in, it seems, because the book wasn't inherently subversive and because they knew that the book would be published either through official channels or in samizdat.[24]

The next step in the interaction between the opposition and the populists came in 1985 with the Monor meeting. By this time, the opposition had developed a clearly articulated plan, a number of organizations and samizdat publications, connections throughout the East and Central European dissident community, and a working relationship with Radio Free Europe. Yet, they continued to be an isolated group in Hungary. The populists, on the other hand, had no such development but held higher prestige within Hungary. They could both gain from such a meeting. The opposition would gain in stature and be able to partially unite opposition against the regime. (As Kis put it: "Monor brought the democratic opposition out of the ghetto. It was after Monor that we were treated as part of national politics and not simply as marginals who you can consider perhaps brave but certainly isolated.")[25] The populists would gain a forum at which that could present their critiques of the regime. Some members of the opposition claimed that the real aim of the populists was to demonstrate to the party that if they did not get their much awaited journal, *Hitel,* (which could be translated to *Credit)* they would work with the opposition. But, Csizmadia and others have argued that what the populists really gained at Monor was knowledge; it was by helping to plan and run the Monor meeting that they began learning how to organize.[26]

The Monor conference was held in June 1985. Its primary organizer was the 1956-er Ferenc Donáth. The main speakers were the opposition leader János Kis, the populists István Csoóri and Sándor Csurka, and the reform economist Tamás Bauer. The speeches reflected the differences between the populists and the opposition. Csurka spoke about moral decline and the cultural crisis in a period of soft dictatorship. Csoóri's speech was about maintaining the Hungarian cultural heritage and increasing awareness of the plight of ethnic Hungarians in Rumania and other neighboring countries. Kis' presentation was on the differences between the populists and opposition and how these groups and other critics of the regime could unify into a political movement. Monor was a critical step towards party development: It was both the height and the end of any real united effort by the populists and the opposition.[27]

*The Foundation of a Forum:*

The next critical moment came two years later in June 1987. During the months before June, power was shifting within the Socialist party. A new generation of party members was rising in position and stature. The head of the Patriotic People's Front, Imre Pozsgay, had spearheaded a national debate on the future of economic reform in December, 1986, and now he was seen as a rising contender for Kádár's position. Another young star, Miklós Németh, was made the Central Committee head of Economic Policy during this period. The most dramatic step, however, was Kádár's decision in June to make Károly Grósz Prime Minister. Possibly, Kádár was trying to dump the economic crisis onto Grósz's shoulders, but almost everyone else got a completely different message: Kádár was on his way out and a new generation of Socialists were on their way into power.

The *Beszélő* group reacted to these changes by publishing their most famous and controversial issue: "The Social Contract."[28] The issue laid out a set of demands for a changing relationship between the party and the population. It did not demand a multi-party system, but it did proposed a "compromise" which included constitutional checks on the party, freedom of the press, legal protection for employees, social welfare policy, and freedom of association. To make matters worse, in the eyes' of *Beszélő* critics, the title of the first article was "Kádár Must Go!" and included a pointed attack on the First Secretary as "personally responsible for the paralysis of leadership."[29]

The populists responded to this issue with anger, claiming that the *Beszélő* group had violated their "gentlemen's agreement." They complained that Kis and his colleagues had been secretive about their intentions and should have informed them that the issue would appear. At the time, the two groups were negotiating plans for a second Monor meeting. The populists canceled the meeting and cut ties with the democratic opposition, claiming that the *Beszélő* group had been using them and that Kis and his circle was trying to gain a hegemony over the entire democracy movement. Kis and his colleagues rejected the argument that any tacit agreement existed. Announcing the publication of a subversive issue of an underground journal was dangerous; it increased the risk of police intervention as well as arrests. They argued that the populists were simply shifting blame for their own strategic decision: With Pozsgay rising in stature, they were better off working with him than with the much weaker hard-core opposition.[30] Regardless of the reasons, a permanent cleavage emerged among the Hungarian dissidents.

The populists decided to hold their own meeting at the home of populist writer Sándor Lezsák in the village of Lakitelek. At this meeting, they would officially form the Hungarian Democratic Forum. In order to promote this organization, they decided to invite the first secretary of the Patriotic People's Front, Imre Pozsgay. Pozsgay described these events as follows:

> With the publication of the "Social Contract," the democratic opposition also expressed in essence that it was taking steps towards organizing itself as an independent, liberal party. With this, it took the first steps towards political stratification from mutually agreed upon opposition cooperation. The hard core of the democratic opposition left the populist opposition out of its initiative. This gave the signal that they were striving for a hegemonic role within the opposition movement. At least the populist-nationalist intellectual opposition interpreted it this way...

> *As they prepared to answer this provocation, the leaders of the*
> *populist intellectuals involved me as well in the preparation of*
> *their own initiative. Following some preceding discussions and*
> *complaints on their part, they invited me during the summer of*
> *1987 to the apartment of Zoltán Bíró. Outside of me and the host,*
> *Sándor Csoóri, István Csurka, Gyula Fekete, and Lajos Für were*
> *present. They asked me to provide the introductory speech of the*
> *meeting. I was to prepare a report on the situation of the country*
> *and to suggest a program for short-term development... My goals*
> *was not to become a member of a developing organization, but to*
> *assist at the birth of one, to assist their appearance under the*
> *protective umbrella of the Patriotic People's Front.*[31]

The founding meeting of the Hungarian Democratic Forum in September
1987 was organized much like Monor: four main speakers, two minor speakers,
and then open discussion. The meeting was attended by invited guests only. These
guests included populist writers, sympathetic intellectuals and economists, a few
members of the opposition not directly connected to *Beszélő*, and even a few
young sociologists who would later be important figures in the Federation of
Young Democrats.

At this meeting, they formed a national, political organization, which later
became a political party. There are signs in the meeting transcript that the
founders were intending to create a political organization like a party. But, true to
its name, the meeting reflected not the creation of a party or a "coalition," the term
repeatedly used by Gyula Fekete, the emcee. It was instead a forum of open
debate and discussion. István Csurka outlined the threats facing the Hungarian
"nation"—to be understood as Hungarian language and culture—and introduced
his "Hungarianism anti-catastrophe program." Pozsgay's colleague Mihály Bihari
presented an argument of how to unify socialism, democracy, and the cause of
Hungarianism. The reform economist László Lengyel gave a blistering attack at
some aspects of the meeting, arguing that ideas of cultural renewal were for
naught without serious economic and political reform. And most presented some
variation on the cultural theme, often disagreeing with each other on the specifics.
There was no articulation of political goals. There was no discussion of strategy.
And beyond the issue of meeting regularly and the creation a journal, there was no
discussion on how to organize this new political entity. (See Table 3)[32]

The colorful discussions seemed to reflect the background of the group.
As Table 3.1 shows, nearly half of the participants described their profession in
literature or art; common descriptions included "writer," "poet," "literary
historian," "filmmaker," folk singer," and "sculptor." Some of the participants,
like the sociologists, had a background that might have helped the construction of
an organization with political goals, but they were in the background. At this
stage, until at least the middle of 1989, the Democratic Forum was run mostly by
writers, artists, and literary historians. The meeting organizers were all
professionally involved with literature or art, except the historian Lajos Für. The
host was the young writer Sándor Lezsák, and the meeting emcee was the writer
Gyula Fekete. None had a professional background remotely related to practical
politics.[33]

From the foundation, one can see signs of the two directions that the Democratic Forum would take; it defined itself at once as a "party" and as a "movement." In truth, while some participants used the term "party," there were no signs at this stage that the group was trying to form a hierarchical organization geared towards winning governmental power. Indeed, any such plans in 1987 would have been very premature. But, there were clearly discussions of forming some organization to influence Hungarian politics and open dialogue with Prime Minister Grósz. On the other hand, they also had the intention to create forums throughout the country for political discussions by culturally minded, patriotic Hungarians. This intention was spelled out in the meeting's declaration, approved by a majority vote of the participants:

> *For this reason we recommend the establishment of the Hungarian Democratic Forum which can become the forum of open, public dialogue. This forum would be suitable for the discussion of our weighty problems, for the analysis of some thematic areas, for the preparation of recommendations for alternative solutions. The participants perceive this forum as open, at once imbued by democracy and national spirit. They expect the participation of people who have different world views and party orientations.[34]*

**The Race to Organize:**
*The Expansion of the Democratic Forum Network:*

In 1988, with the economic crisis looming closer and the Kádár group's stumbling from power, the struggle for power began swelling beyond the Hungarian Socialist Workers' Party. New organizations were emerging to challenge the old structure and to grab some part of the expanding political pie. These organizations defined themselves various ways. Some defined themselves as movements. Others, like the Independent Smallholders' Party, explicitly called themselves political parties. Yet others, like Bajcsy–Zsilinszky Association, defined themselves as intellectual circles. Unable to decide it if was a party or a movement, the Hungarian Democratic Forum fell into both of these categories. Regardless of how they defined themselves, all were preparing to compete in the changing structure of the Hungarian political fields.

The Hungarian Democratic Forum had months to organize and develop before any other major organization appeared on the scene. Partially because of Pozsgay's backing, the organization had a first year of exciting successes. On November 14, 1987, the Democratic Forum gained national, positive press when Pozsgay described the Lakitelek meeting in an interview in *Magyar Nemzet*, one of Hungary's most widely read newspapers. On January 30, it held a large public meeting at the Jurta Theater in Budapest. In the coming months, it would hold a number of forums in the countryside and another meeting at the Jurta Theater, all of which were condoned by the regime. In June, with the government's approval, the Democratic Forum held a giant demonstration to protest the human rights violations of Rumania against its Hungarian minority. Then, in September 1988, the organization held its second Lakitelek meeting, in which it decided to transform itself into a large-scale, political organization. At this stage it was the dominant group in the democracy movement. The Budapest radicals were relegated to the sidelines with little choice but to watch the rising prestige of the populists.

During this period, the Democratic Forum quickly expanded into a large network, bringing in members across the country. The writer István Csurka is credited with much of the work of building the grass roots part of the organization, and most observers believed that the rank-and-file membership were loyal followers of Csurka. (It is impossible to determine whether this is true, but that perception would have a dramatic impact on the organization's internal politics by 1992.) Moreover, the Democratic Forum built this network largely by expanding into three groups. The first group, those already closest to the populists, was the network of writers and literary historian directly or indirectly connected to the Hungarian Writers Organization. The second group, the vast majority of new recruits after the Democratic Forum organized, were people associated to local cultural houses or other cultural organizations. For these groups especially, competence in politics or a related area seemed to be incidental. Accidental or not, their primary criteria for membership development was some connection to the literary or cultural groups of that period.

The third group was the Budapest intellectuals connected to the political salons of the late-1980s. The political salons were seminars or discussion groups on democratization held in Budapest apartments.[35] While the liberals had their discussion groups as well, the groups important to the Democratic Forum were organized by historians and conservatives. Sociologically, the conservatives emerged from the groups that had supported the Horthy regime between the two world wars. They tended to come from the ennobled middle class, which was sometimes called the "gentry", which maintained its status following feudalism by working in the rapidly expanding government bureaucracy. Ideologically, they have been referred to as "royalists", though in the 1980s they would be better compared to Christian Democrats in Western Europe. Ironically, the conservatives and populists were opposing groups in the Horthy era, when the regime regularly harassed the populists. But, the two groups were unified in their concerns about maintaining the Hungarian national identity and protecting the Hungarian minorities in neighboring countries. With the exception of Democratic Forum founder Lajos Für, a historian with close ties to both the populists and conservatives, no conservative played a central role at this time. Géza Jeszenszky, the future foreign minister, attended and spoke at the first Lakitelek but was not one of the core members. József Antall, the future prime minister and Democratic Forum president, was not even known by most of the Founding Fathers before 1989.

During the second Lakitelek meeting, in September 1988, the Democratic Forum formally established itself as an independent social organization and as a democratic intellectual and political movement. It also created its internal structure at this meeting. The organization had three levels: a nine-member presidium, a much larger national committee, and local organizations. The first nine member presidium—also referred to as the "Founding Fathers"—were all populists: Zoltán Bíró (literary historian and close associate of Pozsgay), Dénes Csengey (young writer, secretary of Attila József Young Writers Circle), Sándor Csoóri (writer), István Csurka (writer, elected into presidium of the Hungarian Writers' Organization in 1981 against the party's wishes), Gyula Fekete (writer), Lajos Für (historian with close ties to the writers), Rudolf Joó (a less known figure who did research on nationality issues), Csaba Gy. Kiss (literary historian), and Sándor Lezsák (a writer, also in the Attila József Young Writers Circle, at whose country house the Lakitelek meetings took place.) Of the Founding Fathers, the key players would be Bíró, Csoóri, Csurka, Für, and Lezsák.

At this stage, then, the primary drive behind the development of the Democratic Forum leadership was not the desire to maximize competence at politics, much less party politics. It was instead to bring together intellectuals with cultural political outlooks under a single organizational roof. The populist network was expanded by connecting it to informal groups (like culturally minded Budapest intellectual circles) and other organizations, like rural cultural houses. There is no evidence that the populists worked to bring in people with any political expertise at this stage. There is also no evidence at this point that one's position in the network related to one's expertise. Status seemed more related to one's position within Hungarian cultural life (books one wrote, literary awards one has won, cultural organizations one has led, etc.) and one's personal relation to the Founding Fathers. While the populists had the head start in building a national organization and gaining wide public recognition, the Budapest radicals would gain the head start in attracting experts in politically related fields who were not already in the Socialist party.

*The Radicals Rebound:*

In late 1987 and early 1988, Kis and the radical opposition had to watch from the sidelines as the Democratic Forum quickly rose in stature. The central figures in the Hungarian dissident movement until this point, they were now relegated to a minor role in the developing political changes. To make matters worse, the Kis group strongly suspected that the populists had secretly developed a pact with the reform communists, which they referred to as the "Csurka-Pozsgay Pact." The point of this secret pact, they believed, was for a parliamentary system to be monopolized by two parties: the Hungarian Democratic Forum and a new socialist party dominated by the reform communists. The hard-line communists would be eliminated, and the Kis group would also be kept out of power. The populists, they believed, would be given control over the cultural arm of the government, including the media, cultural institutions, and schools. Instead of completely democratizing Hungary, they believed that this system would be a Finland-like compromise in which the Socialists would continue to play the dominant role in Hungarian politics.[36]

To some degree, the problem for the radical liberals was that they were stunned by the turn of events. They had been working for years to build a semi-unified opposition, and their primary strategy was based on Michnik's New Evolutionism: They were promoting the development of organizations independent from the Socialists party. Now, the democracy movement was divided, and one side had an open relationship with the most prominent reform communist. The Democratic Forum's president, Zoltán Bíró, was even a former assistant to Imre Pozsgay. The Kis group needed to build an organization to counter the Democratic Forum, but they were still not confident that the Budapest, liberal intelligentsia would be open to the idea of joining a hierarchically structured political organization.

The opposition's first step was to create an umbrella organization, called the Network of Free Initiatives (in Hungarian, *A Szabad Kezdeményezések Hálozata)*, which would link various intellectual groups. It would include not only the democratic opposition but members of newly emerging groups, like the Greens—who were protesting the joint development of a damn on the Danube River by the Hungarian and Czechoslovakian governments—and the Bajcsy–Zsilinszky Association. It would also bring in previously unattached dissidents and intellectuals. In its original *Appeal*, the founders declared that "the Network of Free Initiatives will help the exchange of information between different groups. It will follow attentively the fate of Hungarians both within and outside our borders, the development of living conditions, the situation of minorities within Hungary, the development of social initiatives, and the activities of public institutions." At this stage, the opposition was still applying the strategic framework that it used with *Beszélő*.

official formation, it had over 700 members (i.e., The loosely structured Network was an odd step towards party building. But, it did help promote this process in a critical way: The organization expanded the network with which the opposition was in direct contact. There was significant overlap in Democratic Forum and Network membership in 1988, but the focus was different: The Democratic Forum was connected closer to intellectuals with a cultural outlook while the Network was closer to intellectuals at Budapest universities and the Hungarian Academy of Sciences. In this way, the Kis group expanded its network farther among experts in sociology, law, economics, and social policy. The two groups therefore began with opposite strengths. With Pozsgay's help, the populists were able to build mass support but had few people who understood politics and policy. The radicals, on the other hand, had surrounded themselves with people who understood policy (though not party politics), but the Network had virtually no support outside the Budapest intellectual circles.

Like the Democratic Forum, the Network expanded rapidly. Forty-six people, mostly dissidents involved with the democratic opposition, signed the original document. By May, when the Network announced its signers of the *Appeal*). By July, it had over 1500 signatures.[37] Throughout this expansion, Kis and his circle held the dominant position in the organization. When the Network officially formed itself in May 1988, it created a fifty member Provisional Coordination Council. From those fifty, nine were elected spokespeople, to be the key people running the Network. Six were core members of the democratic opposition.[38]

Ironically, the critical moment came while several core members of the opposition—Kis, Haraszti, Gábor Demszky, the future Mayor of Budapest, and the writer Miklós Gáspár Tamás—were in the United States teaching at universities. On November 13, 1988, the Network held its first general meeting, at the Jurta Theater, with over 1000 participants. The vast majority of participants supported a proposal to eliminate the loose, decentralized Network of Free Initiatives and replace it with a more centralized, party-like Alliance of Free Democrats. The Free Democrats tended to be more liberal while the Democratic Forum tended to be culturally oriented and patriotic, and the Alliance tended to be the organization of Budapest intellectuals while Democratic Forum members tended to be rural intellectuals. But the critical difference was that the Alliance of Free Democrats wanted a complete elimination of Socialist rule while the Democratic Forum supported a compromise with the reform communists within a parliamentary setting. The defining characteristic for the Alliance of Free Democrats at this point was not liberalism but radical opposition.

*A Party of Dissidents and Intellectuals:*

Reflecting its roots in dissident opposition and a Central European intelligentsia, the Alliance of Free Democrats was loosely organized despite the leaderships' intention to build a bureaucratically structured party. This was partially an issue of experience. They understood conceptually how a bureaucratic organization is supported to run, but they had no experience in such a venture. Partially, the formal structure conflicted with the real power dynamics within the network. The members of the first administrative board were all connected to the democratic opposition;[39] but, it did not include the central figure of the opposition, János Kis, because he had been abroad during the founding meeting.

The first Free Democrat administrative board was quite disorganized: There were no formal agendas; the meetings barely followed any rules; and there was no enforcement of quorums or even the most basic rules of voting. Board meetings were regularly attended by at least two non-board members: Kis and Iván Petô, a peripheral member of the opposition who was now rising in importance in the group. Kis became the de facto leader of the party, even though he had no formal position. On the one hand, Kis attempted to build a bureaucratic party organization with clear rules and authority based on well-defined positions. On the other hand, his inclination was to run the party the way that he ran the underground *Beszélô* organization, where informality and interpersonal trust were far more important than rules.[40] In this way, the Kis circle became the dominant figures in the party with only a few of them holding positions in the governing body.

In the very beginning, one's position in the Alliance of Free Democrats was determined primary by one's status in the former democratic opposition, especially how close one was to the *Beszélô* group. This network could be seen as a set of circles with Kis at the center. The dominant players, those nearest the center, were the people closest to Kis in the opposition, including the *Beszélô* group and also people like Rajk and Demszky who were close to the *Beszélô* group. This "hard core" of the opposition would dominate the party until 1992. After the key players of the opposition, the next group was peripheral members of the opposition who brought the party some valuable competencies. The two best examples of this are Bálint Magyar and Iván Petô. Both were sociologists; Magyar was also a filmmaker. In the opposition, Magyar was secretly a runner for *Beszélô,* helping move copies from the printer to distributors, and Petô wrote in

*Beszélő* under the pseudonym "Pál Ada" to avoid being fired from the university. Like the Democratic Forum, this would begin to change in 1989: the Free Democrats would bring in complete outsiders to help with the negotiated transformation, and some of those outsiders—notably the lawyer Péter Tölgyessy—would become prominent members in the organization.

## Spring of the Young Democrats:

And then, seemingly out of nowhere, the Federation of Young Democrats, or FIDESZ (pronounced "FEE-des") was formed on March 30, 1988.

From the start, FIDESZ was the most radical of all the major players in the developing Hungarian dissident movement. But, radical had a particular meaning in this setting. FIDESZ was considered radical because of its opposition to the Socialist regime as well as because of the direct language its leaders used to express that opposition. It was certainly not "radical" in terms of leftist thought. Ideologically, FIDESZ was actually the most "moderate" of the main dissident organizations: They were closest to the center on the urbanite-ruralite split, largely because they did not take the debate between these groups seriously. This might be one reason why FIDESZ had a good relationship with the other groups of the democracy movement even as tensions grew between the hard-core and the Democratic Forum. Nonetheless, in the period before the transition, FIDESZ was somewhat closer to the group that would form the Alliance of Free Democrats. They were both hard-core opponents of the regime that wanted the Socialist party stripped of its power. They were both more closely tied to the Budapest universities and intellectual networks than the Democratic Forum or the other parties being formed. And both groups of leaders had studied British liberalism as well as samizdat of other Central European opposition movements. It was their uncompromising opposition to the Socialist regime that made FIDESZ radical.

FIDESZ was also considered radical because of how it expressed this opposition. The founders of the Alliance of Free Democrats were known for being thoughtful and deliberate in their actions. It was not uncommon for them to decide to create an organization months before actually forming it. The founders of FIDESZ, on the other hand, met and organized in a day. They openly challenged and ridiculed the regime. The FIDESZ icon, for example, later became the orange, partially a reference to the ill-fated attempt in the 1950s by the Stalinists to grow oranges in Hungary, a country with long and often cold winters. They spoke in a bold and direct manner, in contrast to the unclear double-talk of the Kádár regime. The FIDESZ founders also made a point of wearing blue jeans, not shaving, and not wearing socks. It was a style that irritated many Hungarians and seemed to especially unnerve the regime. But much of the Hungarian youth—and later, many older Hungarians—found this approach to be a refreshing change from the status quo.

The most common description of the FIDESZ organizers is that they were students from the Bibó and Rajk Collegiums. While technically true, FIDESZ was dominated from the start by a handful of law students from the Bibó Collegium. The collegium system was a regime method, within the communist tradition, of bringing the best young people from the country and educating them in Budapest. The Rajk Collegium, for economic students, was formed a number of years before, and the Bibó Collegium, for law students, was formed in 1988. Each collegium was a semi-democratically run dormitory in which the students were given a significant amount of freedom. A number of the Bibó students used that freedom to study the dissident movements of Eastern Europe. The regime had accidentally produced a breeding ground for opposition intellectual thought.

Ironically, a Socialist had organized the founding meeting, on March 30, 1988. He wanted to create an independent but nonetheless Socialist youth organization. The participants, who came from a number of universities and technical institutes, quickly rejected the idea of creating a Socialist organization and instead chose the name Federation of Young Democrats. This name was accepted partially because the Hungarian pronunciation of the name, "Fiatal Demokraták Szövetsége," could be shortened to FIDESZ ("FEE-des"), meant to sound similar to fidelity in Latin.[41] The unofficial leader from the beginning was the young, charismatic lawyer and former Bibó student Viktór Orbán. Four other Bibó students at the meeting would play central roles in the FIDESZ story: Orbán's roommate Gábor Fodor, Orbán's close friend László Kövér, József Szájer (the assistant university teacher who advised how FIDESZ could become a legal organization according to the new Association Act,) and the future "rock star" and heart throb of Hungarian politics, Tamás Deutsch. In all, of the thirty-seven signers from the meeting, eight became among FIDESZ's twenty-two members of parliament two years later: six Bibó students, one Rajk student, and one with a teacher's diploma.[42]

Within days, FIDESZ began an explosive expansion of membership. It's rapid increase in support and recognition, not to mention its jump into the center of Hungarian politics, was created by a number of factors. In the first place, FIDESZ positioned itself well symbolically. It defined itself as the alternative to the Communist Youth League *[Kommunista Ifjúsági Szövetség],* one of the primary organizations of the regime. Second, the regime-controlled media gave FIDESZ a surprising amount of free media attention. Especially helpful were the repeated radio announcements that it was an illegal organization, which seemed to peak interest among Hungarian university students. Finally, the leadership was aggressive in its promotion of the new organization and seemingly fearless in challenging the regime. This was especially true of Orbán and Kövér.[43] Despite repeated and often serious threats by authorities, including threats of imprisonment, the early FIDESZ members spared few opportunities to promote the organization.

There are no reliable figures on exactly how fast FIDESZ's membership grew. However, the chronology of events demonstrates quite clearly that the organization grew exponentially over the next few months. On March 30th, FIDESZ held its founding meeting; there were thirty-seven charter members.[44] It then held a press conference before the Hungarian and international press on April 1st. Two weeks later, 200 FIDESZ members held a meeting to create some basic structure: They elected spokespeople, a self-defense Committee, and legal representatives. On April 30th, 400 members met at a cinema, and then on May 14th, 500 members met at the famous Jurta Theater. Meanwhile, groups within FIDESZ were popping up across the country. Some of these groups were regional, connected to a city, village, or university. Others were identified by some issue or group, such as the Liberal Circle, the radical FIDESZ Workers' Group, and the Alice Madzsar women's group. There was even a film documentary made about FIDESZ, which was presented in August, a mere five months after its inception.[45]

Within the first few months, virtually all the critical players of FIDESZ had joined the rapidly expanding organization. Most of these individuals emerged from three groups. The first group was the Bibó law and Rajk economic students. Six Bibó and one Rajk student formed an informal leadership that dominated the organization during this period.[46] Most became prominent members of FIDESZ.

The second group was young sociologists and other researchers from Budapest research institutes and libraries. These researchers were younger than the intellectuals that formed the Hungarian Democratic Forum and Alliance of Free Democrats, and they were at the periphery of the Hungarian democracy movement until this point. (Some of their names can be found in earlier documentation on the movement, but none played central roles.) FIDESZ became a way for them to play a more significant role in the developing movement than if they joined either the Free Democrats or Democratic Forum.[47] They rose quickly in the organization because they brought a particular competence to FIDESZ: To the core's legal and economic knowledge they added an understanding of sociology, which would prove helpful in developing the organization, constructing policy, and producing a campaign before the mass public.[48]

The third group was those who gained prominence because of their positions in the many FIDESZ groups formed during its rapid growth. Unlike the sociologists, the rise of these individuals seemed to have more to do with intra-organization politics than any competence that they brought to the leadership. Some gained prominence by voicing opposition to the informal leadership of Orbán and his colleagues. This group, while having influence in this period, never positioned themselves well enough to win control over the organization. While they succeeded in winning seats in the "governing" Committee, real internal power followed Orbán and his group. The most successful of this third group were those who found themselves on the FIDESZ national list for the 1990 parliamentary elections because of a compromise between the Budapest and non-Budapest branches. Those high enough on the list became MP's and close to the center of power.

A great strength of FIDESZ would prove to be that young, bright, and well-educated lawyers, economists, and sociologists ran it. The individuals at the center of this network, especially the lawyers, had backgrounds that could be more easily translated into party politics than the backgrounds of the other dissident organizations. Furthermore, because they were mostly in their mid- to late-twenties during the transition, the FIDESZ leadership could adapt to changing circumstances faster. They had less to unlearn than, for example, the populist writers or the hard-core Budapest dissidents.

A second factor, with a mixed impact, was the incredible speed that the FIDESZ organization expanded in 1988 and 1989. This expansion certainly helped establish the credibility that FIDESZ needed to become a central player. But, the organization expanded so fast that it became nearly impossible to structure. Serious internal opposition to the leadership developed already by October 1988, during the first FIDESZ congress. Possibly more damaging,

FIDESZ would have great trouble mobilizing this loose organization once it began serious campaigning. Ironically, the loose, decentralized structure made effective opposition to the Bibó group virtually impossible—since winning positions on the Committee or other formal governing bodies did not necessarily increase one's internal power—thereby helping maintain the domination of Orbán and his colleagues.

**The Opposition Roundtable:**

It was in this context and with these backgrounds that these three organizations were thrust into the center of a negotiated democratic transition. As discussed in the previous chapter, in early 1989 the ruling Hungarian Socialist Workers' Party decided to begin negotiations for a multi-party democracy. The Socialist party scrambled to find a way to stay in power, that is, to transform Hungary into a multi-party democracy without giving up its central role in the Hungarian political system. The hard-liners, led by Károly Grósz, General Secretary of the party, positioned themselves to create "socialist pluralism," in which the Hungarian Socialist Workers' Party would control the division of power and Hungary would not leave the Warsaw Pact.[49] The reform communists, led by Imre Pozsgay, worked to build a coalition with a select group of opposition organizations and rid themselves of the hard-lines.

At this point, the party—that is, both wings of the Socialist party, including the hard-liners—needed the independent organizations in the rapidly growing democracy movement. In the first place, multi-party pluralism requires other players, even if they were only supporting cast. In the second place, the party needed external actors to legitimize the transition. For the hard-liners especially, the idea was to involve other organizations in the transition symbolically while giving them as little real influence as possible. The Grósz group clearly hoped that token organizations would sign a "negotiated" transition with only minor concessions by the regime.

The Socialist representatives had proposed to negotiate with each organization separately. It therefore became in the interest of these organizations to unify into a single group. The Free Democrat leadership proposed an opposition roundtable, but the Democratic Forum was very hesitant to accept any proposal from its rival. A new figure in the democracy movement, Imre Kónya, became the person who pulled the various factions together into the Opposition Roundtable. Kónya had formed the Independent Lawyer's Forum in November 1988; on March 19, 1989, he invited other independent organizations and parties to begin their own discussions on the transition. Three days later, the first meeting of the Opposition Roundtable was held at the law university. It gradually developed into a union of nine voting organizations: FIDESZ*, the Hungarian Democratic Forum*, the Alliance of Free Democrats*, the Bajcsy-Zsilinszky Association, the Christian Democratic People's Party*, the Hungarian People's Party, the Independent Smallholders' Party*, the Social Democratic Party, and the Trade Union League. (An asterisk indicates that the organization became a party with a recognized faction in parliament in 1990.) The Independent Lawyers' Forum did not have a vote.[50]

*Intra-Party Shifts, and the Rise of József Antall:*

The Opposition Roundtable produced another shift in the Democratic Forum and Free Democrat networks, this time entirely related to political competence. People with related professional backgrounds were needed to negotiate with the Socialist party. In this case, the shift was small (in terms of the number of people) but important: A few new people were brought into the organization and quickly given prominent roles; in other cases, less important people in the network suddenly became central figures. The key example of an outsider being brought in was Péter Tölgyessy in the Alliance of Free Democrats. A lawyer, Tölgyessy joined the Free Democrats in 1989 and quickly became its chief negotiator. Another example, in a slightly different way, were husband Imre Kónya and wife Katalin Kutrucz of the Independent Lawyer's Forum; both became prominent Democratic Forum members after the Trilateral Negotiations, and Kónya subsequently became the Democratic Forum's faction leader in parliament. The most important example of a less important person in a network rising to power because of political competencies, though, was József Antall. Joining the Democratic Forum at the second Lakitelek meeting, and declining invitations to be party president by both the Independent Smallholders' Party and the Christian Democratic People's Party, he catapulted from obscurity to the chief negotiator for the Democratic Forum (and then the entire Opposition Roundtable) virtually overnight.

The specifics of when and how Antall gained prominence are not clear. Reports by those involved are conflicted. However, a number of issues are certain. First, contrary to the claims of his closest allies, Antall rose in importance in the Hungarian Democratic Forum only in 1989. The most common claim among Antall apologists is the he could not attend the first Lakitelek meeting because he had an appointment outside Hungary that weekend. While this may be true, it is also true that Antall's name is absent in any documentation on the dissident movement before 1988. The first clear piece of information is that he attended the second Lakitelek meeting in late 1988. Second, his primary proponent within the Democratic Forum leadership was Sándor Csoóri, and potentially his greatest opponent was Sándor Lezsák. Conflict with Lezsák would become steadily more important in 1993 and 1994.

Third—and the most important piece of information here—Antall was advanced because of his understanding of constitutional law. The historian had studied the negotiations behind the Austro-Hungarian Compromise of 1867, which had created the Dual Monarchy and dramatically increased Hungary's status in Europe. He had also come from a political family. His father, József Antall, Sr., was a high ranking civil servant during the war and both a member of parliament and a minister after the war. He resigned from his position after the communist takeover. From this background, the junior Antall brought a competence needed for the Trilateral Negotiations that was far greater than that of the populist leadership of the Democratic Forum.[51]

The relationship between Antall's background in constitutional law and his late but quick rise in the Hungarian Democratic Forum, or MDF, is illustrated in the following statement by Sándor Csoóri:

*"I knew [József Antall] well, and he had no relationship with MDF at this time. And the roundtable negotiations began sometime in May. My book was published in Finnish, and they invited me to Finland. While I was out there, they sent two people to the roundtable negotiations. When I got home, I asked Zoltán Bíró (he was the MDF president): 'Zoli. Who did you send?' He said: 'Don't worry, these roundtable negotiations aren't all that important.' I said: 'What do you mean that these aren't important. They are the most important.' He replied: 'It's no big deal. We sent György Szabad and Lajos Für.' I said: 'You sent the two orators to the roundtable negotiations?' He said: 'So, who should I send?' I said: 'József Antall and Iván Timkó.' He replied: 'Who is Antall?' He never heard of him. But I still had a voice in MDF at that time, and then we sent Antall in place of these two people. Antall had very serious constitutional law education, and so did Iván Timkó."[52]*

*An Alternate Political Field:*

The Socialist party eventually conceded to negotiating with the Opposition Roundtable, and these talks became known as the Trilateral Negotiations. The Opposition Roundtable and the Trilateral Negotiation quickly became primary political field in the rapidly changing Hungarian political system. Being a member organization of the Opposition Roundtable was an important resource in a particular context (a regime transformation) that these organizations used to win more resources and influence that context.

All five of the new parties that entered parliament in 1990 had been members of the Opposition Roundtable. In other words, involvement in the Trilateral Negotiations became the first dividing line between the parties that survived politically in 1990 and the parties that would play insignificant roles in Hungarian politics. These parties gained prominence, and they also used the Opposition Roundtable and Trilateral Negotiations to build public support. For example, during the re-burial of Imre Nagy in June—seen by a quarter million Hungarians packed into Heroes' Square in Budapest and viewed on televisions by most of the nation—these organizations were able to present themselves and some of their politicians to the entire country. FIDESZ was especially successful at this event. Its leader, Viktor Orbán, gave an impassioned, anti-Communist speech that became famous in Hungary. During the months of the negotiations, the Democratic Forum gained the most public support, probably because of Antall's role as the chief negotiator. From June to September, 1989—that is, from the first month to the last month of the negotiations—the percentage of Hungarians who would vote for the Democratic Forum rose from around 12% to just under 25%.[53] Antall also gained public exposure and support, which became another resource in his quest to take charge of the Democratic Forum.

These organizations were also able to influence the structure of the new political system to their own perceived advantages. A good example was the negotiations over the electoral system, with each party attempting to design the system in a way that most improved their chances of winning seats in parliament.[54] But, the most important example of trying to influence the context was with the question of whether the President of the Republic should be elected by the public before or appointed by parliament after the parliamentary elections. The Socialists wanted a separately elected president soon after the negotiations were over because, it seems, they believed that their candidate, Imre Pozsgay, would win easily. Pozsgay was much better known and more widely supported than the other parties' potential candidates, and the other parties would have little time to build an effective campaign.

The Free Democrats and FIDESZ were the most adamantly opposed to the early presidential election. They believe that this was a hidden trick to create a "Polish style" compromise in which the Socialists retained control over the administration and gave up or shared power in the parliament. Moreover, the Free Democrats believed that Pozsgay had reached a secret agreement with Antall in which the former would become President of the Republic and the latter would become Prime Minister. They called this suspected agreement the "Pozsgay-Antall Pact." The Free Democrat leadership also believed that Antall and Pozsgay were meeting secretly during the Trilateral Negotiations to share information about their respective sides and construct strategies.[55]

The first clear evidence of these surreptitious meetings came from Pozsgay himself. In 1990, during a television interview with him and FIDESZ leader Viktor Orbán, Pozsgay admitted to the meetings. According to an article in *Magyar Hírlap*, which reported about this interview:

> *He had such a good relationship with Mr. József Antall then that they met almost regularly. In the course of these meetings, he received significantly precise information about the events of the unified roundtable. What's more, at times—as he said—Mr. Antall would even provide him with pieces of advice.[56]*

Pozsgay would subsequently claim that, while he had been friends with Antall for many years, even meeting in each other's apartments during the 1980s, they had no secret dealings during the Trilateral Negotiations, nor did they reach a secret pact. He said in one interview: "I told Antall that I could imagine him Prime Minister in a regime in which I am the President of the Republic. But there was not one word about a pact..."[57] He also denies having had secret meetings. Antall did meet him at his office as an opposition leader, Pozsgay said, but so did other opposition leaders at this time. Moreover, while he admits that during this period he met several Democratic Forum leaders, including Antall, in his summer home near Lake Balaton, he insists that the discussion was about who should replace Zoltán Bíró as president of the Democratic Forum.[58]

Yet, according to a Democratic Forum leader at the time, Sándor Csoóri, there were indeed secret meetings between Antall and Pozsgay during this period. In an interview with the author, Csoóri said:

> *...and during the Trilateral Negotiations, I constantly brought Antall together with my old friend Imre Pozsgay, for whom I had*

*great respect. But I had to bring them together secretly, because Pozsgay was a [Socialist] party member—but [the Socialist party] had more than one wing. One wing was led by Grósz, Károly Grósz, and he sent György Fejti to the Trilateral Negotiations, the other was Imre Pozsgay. Well, Pozsgay was close to us, and Fejti was far from us. And I brought Pozsgay and Antall together so that they would create such a situation at the Trilateral Negotiations, that indeed there would be no civil war during the transformation. Instead, we tried to accomplish this quietly.[59]*

To the question of where they met, Csoóri responded: "Once in Imre Pozsgay's ministerial office, the second time in my apartment, and the third time in Pozsgay's kitchen. Pozsgay cooked."[60]

At the beginning of the Trilateral Negotiations, the Opposition Roundtable was united in its conviction that the president should be chosen by parliament. But, one by one, organizations in the Opposition Roundtable began to change their votes. The first organization to change its position was the Christian Democratic People's Party. It was followed by the Hungarian People's Party. Then, the Independent Smallholders' Party and the Bajcsy-Zsilinszky Association changed their stands as well. Finally, the Democratic Forum changed its position, producing five votes for a separately elected president. The other four organizations—FIDESZ, the Alliance of Free Democrats, the Social Democratic Party, and the Trade Union League—argued that the Opposition Roundtable should stick to its original position, but without success. In the final agreement, the public would elect the President long before a new parliament was elected.[61]

Pozsgay now seemed virtually guaranteed to become the next president of Hungary, and the reform wing of the Socialist party would most likely maintain its administration control over the Hungarian government. Moreover, the Socialists and the Democratic Forum each held just under 25% public support; the next highest levels of support were about 7% for the Independent Smallholders' Party and 5% for the Free Democrats.[62] The Democratic Forum also seemed more than willing to create a coalition government with the reform communists; as Antall said in a press conference in October, after the Hungarian Socialist Workers' Party changed its name, "without the Hungarian Socialist Party there cannot be stable coalition that will work in the nation's interest."[63] The reform communists were now in a good position to maintain much of their power over the Hungarian government by sharing that power with patriotic-minded moderates within a new, pluralistic system.

The loss on the presidency issue was a devastating blow to the FIDESZ and Free Democrat leadership. If they signed the agreement, they would help legitimate the Socialists' stay in power and undermine any ability they might have to challenge that outcome. If they did not sign, they would appear like extremists and put themselves back into the periphery of Hungarian politics. Moreover, it appeared to the FIDESZ and Free Democrat politicians that they would almost certainly be beaten in the parliamentary elections and have to watch from the sidelines as an Democratic Forum-Socialist coalition designed the new Hungarian government.

But then, a countermove was proposed: Since Antall was arguing that a publicly elected President would be more democratic, why not make it really democratic and have the public decide the presidency issue through a referendum?[64] The critical day came on September 18, 1989, when Pozsgay was to preside over the negotiated end of one party rule. As the cameras rolled, organizations signed the agreement between party and opposition one by one. Then, the cameras reached Péter Tölgyessy, the chief negotiator for the Free Democrats. Tölgyessy put his pen down and announced that the Free Democrats would not sign the agreement because it was a veiled method for the Socialists to stay in power. Moreover, the Alliance of Free Democrats was announcing that it would hold a public referendum on four issues, including on whether the president should be elected by the public or appointed by parliament. The FIDESZ representative followed by announcing that he would also not sign. Caught completely off guard, Pozsgay reacted with open anger and even threw his pen.

The reform communists' strategy for remaining in power had backfired. The hard-core dissidents and their allies would win the referendum on the presidency by a vote of 50.07%. The Socialists would be soundly defeated in the 1990 parliamentary elections, and the political career of Imre Pozsgay, the key reform communist, would rapidly collapse. He would never be President, and he would lose virtually all his supporters, including the reform communists and Democratic Forum populists, within a year. Yet, despite the end of the Cold War, the stagnating economy, and its intra-party struggle for power, the Hungarian Socialist Party came within one-tenth of 1% of a referendum vote of staying in power.

But this defeat of the Socialists also speeded the democratic transition, increasing the pace at which dissident networks would become the key political parties in Hungary. That gradual evolution of dissident networks over decades and then breakneck transformation into political parties helped created party competence problems a number of ways. First, generally speaking, a politicians' position in the new party became based much more on that's person's position in relevant pre-party networks than on the skills or other resources he or she brought to the party. The Alliance of Free Democrats would be run by the hard-core Budapest dissidents until the party nearly collapsed internally, and FIDESZ would be dominated primarily by a small group of friends that met at the Bibó Collegium. For the Democratic Forum, it would become a tug-of-war between the small network of writers and those close to Antall. Second, the former dissidents had little time to develop competencies at this new politics. Within a few months, they would be in parliament, and in the case of the Democratic Forum, running a government.

This rapid transition from dissident networks to party organizations produced party competence problems another way, already hinted at above. The rapid expansion of the networks into massive, national organizations meant that these new parties, especially the Democratic Forum and Free Democrats, had to promote people with little connection to the dissident politics and no political background whatever. People with no political experience became party candidates and were propelled into parliament in a matter of months. This problem will be explored further in the next chapter.

**Table 3.1**
**Participation in Hungarian Democratic Forum Founding by Occupation**

| Occupation | Participants | |
|---|---|---|
| Literature, Literary History, Art | 70 | 40% |
| Sociology, Political Science | 19 | 11% |
| Teachers | 15 | 9% |
| Economists | 10 | 6% |
| Reporters, Editors, Television | 9 | 5% |
| Skilled Labor | 9 | 5% |
| Historians | 7 | 4% |
| Party Politics, Members of Parliament | 5 | 3% |
| Students | 5 | 3% |
| Other (categories of three or less) | 26 | 15% |
| Total | 175 | 100% |

(There are six missing cases, four because of insufficient information, two because they were from the United States.)

Source: *Lakitelek, 1997* (Budapest: Püski), pp. 215-8.

# Notes:

1. "Apák és Fiúk", *Magyar Forum*, March 31, 1990.
2. The key figures of the older Lukácsians were György Márkus, Ágnes Heller, Ferenc Fehér, and Mihály Vajda, all of whom studied with Lukács. Márkus is considered especially important, since he was the mentor of János Kis, Kis' collaborator György Bence, and most of the other younger Lukácsians that would become involved in the opposition.
3. See interview with György Márkus in Ervin Csizmadia (1995). *A Magyar Demokratikus Ellenzék (1968-1988): Interjúk [The Hungarian Democratic Opposition, 1968-1988: Interviews]* (Budapest: T-Twins Kiadó), p. 13-26.
4. Interview with Haraszti; Ervin Csizmadia (1995). *A Magyar Demokratikus Ellenzék (1968-1988): Monográfia [The Hungarian Democratic Opposition, 1968-1988: Monograph]* (Budapest: T-Twins Kiadó), pp. 45-8. The communist party's reaction is expressed in a speech by Kádár in 1973 before the Central Committee, in which he states: "The other thing is this Haraszti affair... There is a man whom I can hardly describe as a writer... they printed his writings in ten or more copies and, at the end, there was a trial. In addition to this hostile phenomenon and the fact that they have become quite impertinent, another characteristic of this case is that it helped unite all opponents of the regime..." Rudolf L. Tôkés (1996) *Hungary's Negotiated Revolution; Economic Reform, Social Change, and Political Succession,* (Cambridge: Cambridge University Press), pp. 172–3.
5. For the interrelationship of the dissident opposition in Eastern Europe, see Janusz Bugajski and Maxine Pollack (1989) *East European Fault Lines; Dissent, Opposition, and Social Activism*, Westview Special Studies on the Soviet Union and Eastern Europe, (Boulder: Westview Press). For the earlier period of dissident activity, see Rudolf Tôkés, ed. (1979) *Opposition in Eastern Europe*. (Baltimore: Johns Hopkins University Press) as well as Walter D. Connor (1997) "Social Change and Stability in Eastern Europe", *Problems of Communism*, vol. 26, no. 6 (November–December), pp. 16-32.
6. Adam Michnik, (1985) "A New Evolutionism", *Letters from Prison and other Essays*, (Berkeley: University of California Press) pp. 135–48.
7. Ibid, 139.
8. Ibid.
9. Interviews with Haraszti and Kis.
10. The actual petition can be found in Magyar Hirlap January 9, 1992 or Ervin Csizmadia (1995) *A Magyar Demokratikus Ellenzék (1968–1988): Dokumentumok [The Hungarian Democratic Opposition, 1968–1988: Documents],* (Budapest: T-Twins Kiadó), p. 75.
11. All the signers were associated with Budapest intellectual life, even though not all were directly related to the Academy of Science. For example, the pianist Zoltán Kocsis signed as did a number of writers and poets. Of the thirty-four signers, fifteen were associated with the Lukács School—they were preparing to emigrate later that year—or Young Lukácsians. It is worth noting that one signer was the populist writer Sándor Csoóri, who would later become a central figure in the Hungarian Democratic Forum.
12. Interview with Kis, and interviews with Márkus and György Dalos in Csizmadia, *Interviews*, pp. 23–25 and 171-3.
13. This was determined by examining petitions that followed this one, based on the collection gathered by Csizmadia in *Documents*. While petition signing was neither the only nor the central work of the opposition, it was considered important. Effectively, anyone involved with the democratic opposition would sign at least some of these petitions, even those who used pseudonyms when writing in Hungarian samizdat.

[14] It is essential to note that group membership is always a slippery issue at this time. For example, the sociologist and former prime minister András Hegedüs was associated with the Lukácsians, though based on the description of Márkus I would not count him as a member of the school. The point is that any conclusion about groups and group changes at this stage of the democracy movement should be treated as very general.

[15] See Csizmadia, *Documents*, pp. 82–88 for the petitions.

[16] Interview with Haraszti, and interview with László Rajk in Csizmadia, *Interviews*, pp. 254–67.

[17] Interview with János Kis.

[18] Two other groups were also important: the reform economists and the 1956-ers. The reform economists were growing steadily more concerned about the state of the Hungarian economy and, as the country moved toward crisis as the 1980s progressed, they developed steadily more open relations with the opposition and the populists. Neither the reform economists nor the 1956-ers were central to the development of political parties, so their otherwise important roles will not be highlighted here.

[19] Ferenc Donáth et al., eds. (1980) *Bibó Emlékkönyv [Bibó Memorial Book]* (Budapest: Samizdat)

[20] One exception is István Bibó (1991) *Democracy, Revolution, Self-Determination; Selected Writings*, edited by Károly Nagy, translated by András Boros–Kazai. (Boulder: East European Monographs). Distributed by Columbia University Press.

[21] Interview with János Kis.

[22] Anonymous interview with diplomat and former Hungarian Socialist Workers' Party Central Committee member.

[23] Donáth *Bibó Memorial Book;* Csizmadia, *Documents*, pp. 133-5.

[24] Tôkés, *Hungary's Negotiated Revolution*, pp. 184-6. See especially the quote on page 186 from the internal Hungarian Socialist Workers' Party report on why the book should be accepted for publication.

[25] Interview with János Kis.

[26] Csizmadia, *Monograph,* pp. 310-17.

[27] Ibid.

[28] János Kis, et al., eds. (1987) "Társadalmi Szerzôdés, a Politikai Kibontakozás Feltételei" ["Social Contract: Conditions of Overcoming the Political Deadlock"] *Beszélő*, no. 20.

[29] János Kis, et al. (1989) "Kádár Must Go!" in János Kis, *Politics in Hungary: For a Democratic Alternative*, (Boulder: East European Monographs), Distributed by Columbia University Press, pp. 143-52.

[30] This issue is so widely discussed it barely deserves citation. Along with the discussion on this debate in almost any text on this period, it was also discussed during the author's interviews with Sándor Csoóri, Miklós Haraszti, Géza Jeszenszky, and János Kis, all of whom held firmly to the position of their respective groups.

[31] Imre Pozsgay (1988) *Koronatú és Tettstárs [Star Witness and Accomplice]* (Budapest: Korona) pp. 158-9.

[32] Sándor Agócs, ed. (1991) *Lakitelek 1987, A Magyarság Esélyei; A Tanácskozás Hiteles Jegyzôkönyve. [Lakitelek 1987, The Chances for Hungarianism; The Authentic Minutes of the Conference]* (Budapest: Püski).

[33] Ibid, pp. 215-18.

[34] Ibid, p. 177-8.

[35] Interview with Géza Jeszenszky. Jeszenszky pointed out to me that a critical dividing line among the conservative political salons was when someone finished at the Academy of Sciences. The group he headed had finished a few years after the group that József Antall headed, for example.

[36] Interview with Miklós Haraszti.

---

[37] Csizmadia, *Monograph*, pp. 430-6.

[38] These six people were Kis, Haraszti, János Dénes, Iványi Gábor, Imre Mécs, and István Vass. The other three were Iván Bába, Ferenc Miszlivetz, and Levente Ruttkay.

[39] The first Alliance of Free Democrats administrative board was: Árpád Göncz (a dissident writer who later became the president of Hungary), Gábor Iványi (who was involved with the opposition since 1979), Ferenc Kôszeg (a member of the *Beszélô* editorial board), Bálint Magyar (a sociologist who was a peripheral member of the opposition), Imre Mécs (an opposition member since 1979), Ottila Solt (a founder of opposition organization SZETA, the Organization to Support the Poor), Miklós Szabó (a core opposition member who signed the original petition in support of Charter 77 in 1977), István Szent–Iványi (a minor figure in the opposition), and István Vass (whose name does not appear in any documents on the opposition before the Network).

[40] Interview with János Kis.

[41] Interview with Iván Csaba.

[42] The full list of signers are as follows, with an asterisk after each person who subsequently became an MP: Miklós Andrási, Zsolt Bayer, István Bajka, György Balassa, István Bartók, Gábor Bartus, Éva Bánszky, Mária Bekk, Zoltán Benedek, Attila Bégány, Vilmos Both, Iván Csaba, Balázs Csongor, Tamás Deutsch*, Gábor Fodor*, Péter Gyöngyössy, István Hamecz, Péter Kaderják, József Kardos, Péter Kata, Attila Kliment, László Kövér*, László Langauer, Péter Molnár*, Zsolt Németh*, Viktor Orbán*, András Rácz, Szilárd Sasvári*, Gábor Szabó, Lóránt Szajkó, József Szájer*, Péter Szemerei, Szávó Sztilkovics, Sándor Petô, Miklós Tár, and Tibor Vajda. Bozoki, András, ed. 1992. *Tiszta lappal: a FIDESZ a magyar politikában, 1988–1991 [With a clean slate: FIDESZ in Hungarian politics, 1988–1991]*, (Budapest: FIDESZ Press), pp. 23-5.

[43] The following is one of many stories that illustrated this point: During one of their "invitations" to police headquarters, the Public High Prosecutor apparently asked the group to hand over their passports—which meant that they would be barred from travel. According to one of the FIDESZ members there, Orbán responded: "Sure we'll hand you our passports, if you hand us yours." The group kept their passports. Interview with Iván Csaba.

[44] *With a Clean Slate*, pp. 23-5.

[45] Zsolt Enyedi, "The organizational structure of FIDESZ" (Unpublished article); *FIDESZ; Az elsô száz nap* [FIDESZ: The First One Hundred Days], (Budapest: FIDESZ document); *Federation of Young Democrats; Hungary, 1991*, (Budapest: FIDESZ Documents), pp. 23–7.

[46] This informal leadership was Orbán, Fodor, Kövér, Deutsch, Szájer, Péter Molnár, and Zsolt Németh, the Rajk (economic) student. All seven were at the first meeting and subsequently became MP's.

[47] Interview with András Bozóki.

[48] This group included János Áder, István Hegedûs, Zoltán Rockenbauer, and András Bozóki.

[49] Tôkés, *Hungary's negotiated revolution.* pp. 299-303.

[50] András Bozóki (1993) "Hungary's Road to Systemic Change: The Opposition Roundtable" *East European Politics and Society*, translated by József Böröcz, vol. 7, no. 2, spring, pp. 276–308.

[51] For Antall's biography, see Zsolt Horváth, ed. (1992). *Az 1990-ben megválasztott országgyûlés almanachja. [The almanac of the parliament elected in 1990].* (Budapest: Magyar Országgyûlés). pp. 10–2. In English, see Tôkés, *Hungary's negotiated revolution.* pp. 365–8. For an extended discussion, see Sándor Révész (1995) *Antall József Távolról [Joseph Antall from a Distance]* (Budapest: Sík Kiadó).

[52] Interview with Sándor Csoóri.

[53] Tamás Moldován, ed. (1990) *Szabadon Választott; Parliamenti Almanach 1990* [*Freely Elected; Parliamentary Almanac of 1990.*] (Budapest: Idegenforgalmi Propaganda és Kiadó), p. 14.

[54] Bozóki, "Hungary's Road to Systemic Change".

[55] Interview with Miklós Haraszti. It is important to note that the Free Democrat leadership did not accuse the Democratic Forum of simply being a strategic arm of the Socialist Party. Instead, they argued that Antall was trying to improve the position of his party and advance his own political career by shifting between the opposition and the reform communists.

[56] "Antall Instruálta volna as MSZMP-t?" ["Did Antall Instruct MSZMP?"] *Magyar Hírlap*, September 27, 1990.

[57] Bodzabán and Szalay, p. 144.

[58] Pozsgay, *Star Witness and Accomplice*, interview with Ferenc Szekely, p. 300–11.

[59] Interview with Sándor Csoóri.

[60] Ibid.

[61] Bozóki, "Hungary's Road to Systemic Change".

[62] Tamás Moldován, ed. (1990) *Szabadon Választott; Parliamenti Almanach 1990* [*Freely Elected; Parliamentary Almanac of 1990.*] (Budapest: Idegenforgalmi Propaganda és Kiadó), p. 14.

[63] Sándor Révész (1995) *Antall József Távolról [Joseph Antall from a Distance]* (Budapest: Sík Kiadó) p. 48. Révész took the quote from the October 24, 1989 issue of *Népszabadság*.

[64] Interview with Miklós Haraszti.

## Chapter 4:

# Ascent of the Party Amateurs II:
## Referendum, Campaign, and the
## Construction of Parties

The call for a referendum by the Alliance of Free Democrats, the Federation of Young Democrats, or FIDESZ, and their allies was the first serious mass politics move of the new political system. This referendum on whether the President of the Republic should be elected before the parliamentary elections or selected by the new parliament after its election changed the dynamics among the developing Hungarian parties. The referendum catapulted the Alliance of Free Democrats into the center of Hungarian politics; once openly ridiculed by Kádár as insignificant, the former hard-core opposition was now in the limelight. The referendum also damaged the Socialists' public image. Having long presented itself as different from the other ruling parties in the Warsaw Pact, it was now accused of attempting to maintain its position of power with an underhanded trick. The Hungarian Democratic Forum was also implicated in this alleged scheme, which would force it to redefine itself as the most anti-Communist of the new parties.

The referendum and then the parliamentary election forced the dissident networks to finish transforming themselves into political parties. During the Opposition Roundtable and the Trilateral Negotiations, the groups performed mostly as elite organizations competing in an elite forum. At that stage, the new parties were really more of organized factions. With the call for a referendum, mass opinion suddenly became a primary stake in the struggle among these groups, and the upcoming election would force them to run a national campaign with candidates in districts throughout the nation. The loose connection of local Democratic Forum and FIDESZ organizations would no longer be enough. These networks would have to expand throughout the country and reorganize themselves into structures that could campaign effectively at both the national level and in individual districts. But, as the organization with the most to gain from winning the referendum, the Alliance of Free Democrats was the quickest to make this transformation. Known as an "elite" organization through most of 1989, the Free Democrats began rapidly building a national organization that could get the necessary signatures for the referendum, build mass support for a president selected by parliament, and get voters out to the polls.

But, this rapid transformation would exacerbate the party competence problems of these dissident networks. The original, small networks had to expand dramatically, pulling in people to fill the many jobs of running a party. The high demand for new people, combined with the Socialists' virtual monopoly over experienced party politicians, meant that the new parties brought in people with absolutely no political experience and gave them important positions, including as candidates for parliament. With the dramatic political changes in late 1989 and early 1990, the new parties would win a flood of party resources, including widespread public exposure, significant amounts of free labor from people energized by the transformation, and then parliamentary seats and public money. This would catapult these political neophytes into the center of national-level politics.

This chapter will explore the last stage of party development before the new government was formed. It will demonstrate through both qualitative analysis and quantitative data how the rapid expansion of the new parties in late 1989 and early 1990 deepened their party competence problems, and it will show further how oddities in the Hungarian electoral laws made that problem even more acute for the Hungarian Democratic Forum. The chapter will also set the stage for the analysis of the rest of the book.

## Mass Politics Field I: Referendum and Danube-Gate

The referendum on presidential elections and three other issues was critical to the rise of the Alliance of Free Democrats as a major political party in Hungary. The campaign to win the referendum was run by a coalition of four organizations—the Free Democrats, FIDESZ, the Independent Smallholders' Party, and the Hungarian Social Democratic Party—but it was really the Free Democrats who led the charge. The coalition had to accomplish three goals. First, it had to get at least 100,000 signatures for a referendum; they decided to make 200,000 signatures the goal to avoid problems with rejected signatures. Once the referendum was accepted by the government and put on a ballot, the coalition had to convince people to vote. This would not be an easy task, partially because the issue was not immediately obvious to the public and partially because there had not been a real national election in over forty years. Finally, they needed to convince those who voted that the President of the Republic should be chosen by parliament, not by popular election. This too was a difficult goal since effectively they were asking the public to give up its direct vote for the President.

The fight to win the referendum forced the new parties, especially the Free Democrat leadership, to learn how to perform political struggle before a mass public. The first issue was how to construct the referendum in such a way that the public would support it. The group decided to present not just the primary issue, the presidential election, but all four major issues that the radical side of the Opposition Roundtable had lost. In truth, Imre Pozsgay, the chief Socialist negotiator, had promised to resolve the second and fourth issues with parliament. They were non-issues by the time the actual voting occurred. The real purpose of putting them onto the ballot was to increase turnout as well as to indirectly increase support for the first issues. The leadership, apparently at the suggestion of Péter Tölgyessy, also decided to word the referendum items in positive language. They guessed that people would be more likely to vote for than against an item. The referendum therefore became called the "Four Yeses" by the organizers. These four items were: [1]

## Ascent of Party Amateurs II: Referendum, Campaign, and Construction of Parties

1. Should the President of the Republic be chosen only after the parliamentary elections?[2]

2. Should the party cells withdraw from workplaces?

3. Should the Hungarian Socialist Workers' Party account for all assets in its possession or under its control?

4. Should the workers' militia be disbanded?

The Free Democrat leadership, made up of former dissidents and the lawyer Tölgyessy, also had to learn for the first time how to simplify their messages in order to attract support. During the first stage of the referendum battle, when the coalition was getting signatures, their key slogan became: "Let the people decide!" which in Hungarian *["Döntsön a nép!"]* had an effective double-meaning: It could also mean: "The people should topple!" The slogan was also meant as a way to counteract the inevitable argument by the other side that the people should choose their own president. The slogan was also a joke. The line was taken from a poem by the leftist Hungarian poet Attila József, who used the same imagery for the toppling of capitalism.[3]

The Free Democrat leadership struggled to keep its message simple. The weight was on the Free Democrats to simplify the issue and convince the public. A counter-strategy by the Socialists was to confuse the issue, since confusion would keep the public thinking that voting directly for a president would be the most democratic. The coalition put together four simple, positive referendum items. Parliament, controlled by the Socialists, added "explanations" that made the issues more difficult to understand. The Free Democrats, in turn, created a poster with the referendum ballot—with both the items and the explanations—with each "Yes" box checked with a red magic marker.[4]

The Free Democrats had fallen behind the Democratic Forum in developing a national organization, but in late 1989 the Free Democrats quickly caught up. The excitement of political change drew swarms of people into becoming active members of the Alliance of Free Democrats. Local offices were established at a breakneck speed. By most accounts, the referendum brought in people who were hard-core anti-Communists, most of whom had listened to the Free Democrat dissidents on Radio Free Europe.[5] But the pace of organizing and organizational inexperience of the Free Democrat leadership, not to mention their distaste for bureaucratic authority, led to the local offices gaining much independence.

The plebiscite was held on November 26, 1989. The coalition won the presidential election issue by an infinitesimal 50.07%—a mere six thousand votes. Each of the other issues was won with 95% of the vote. The Free Democrats had now jumped from almost complete obscurity to a primary position in the developing party field. Moreover, it put other parties into more difficult situations. The Hungarian Socialist Party, still widely supported in late 1989, would slip in public support. It was caught appearing to hold onto power through a backdoor deal. The Hungarian Democratic Forum now had to deal with the potentially serious public relations problem of seeming to have been in bed with the former regime, the very group it claimed to oppose. FIDESZ, much less organized than the Alliance of Free Democrats, was in danger of developing the reputation of simply being the Free Democrat youth organization.

The Free Democrats had gained the most during the referendum. The party was in a good position to win the upcoming parliamentary elections and lead a governing coalition. But the party was run by former, radical dissidents who spent over a decade working to undermine the Socialist state. Even after the Socialists lost their foothold, the Free Democrats set their sights on completely eliminating the Socialists from any power in Hungarian politics. The former radicals, by their own admission, did not distinguish between two very different strategic goals: Eliminating the Socialists from Hungarian politics, and winning control over the government.

*The Danube-Gate Scandal:*

The Hungarian mass politics field was changing rapidly as the election approached. The most dramatic changes were with the popular support of the Hungarian Socialist Party and the Alliance of Free Democrats. Socialist support was at 25% in October 1989—and its predecessor, the Hungarian Socialist Workers' Party, was supported by over 35% of the population in July 1989—but that support dropped to around 10% by January 1990. The Free Democrats, on the other hand, had less than 5% support in July and less than 10% in October. By January, it was a few points under 20%. The Alliance of Free Democrats was also catching up to the Hungarian Democratic Forum, which had been hovering between 20% and 25% since November. The contest was no longer the once popular post-Kádár Socialists against the new parties, but the party of the populist moderates against the party of the radical opposition.

If the loss of the referendum was a serious setback to Socialists' hopes of staying in power, the Danube-Gate Scandal was the final blow. A member of the secret police approached an independent MP by the name of Gábor Roszik with information that the Ministry of Interior was continuing to spy on members of the former opposition and that they were also quickly shredding old documents. Roszik, who had joined the Democratic Forum, suggested that the secret policeman take the information to Black Box [*"Fekete Doboz"*], a film company which had been documenting the transformation. (Black Box had created the FIDESZ Movie and had filmed much of the debate within the Opposition Roundtable.) Black Box, in turn, informed the Free Democrat and FIDESZ leadership. Television cameras were sneaked into the Ministry of Interior, and documents—both shredded and complete—were smuggled out of the building. [6]

The Danube-Gate Scandal story broke in the Hungarian press and electronic news media on January 5. Here was another example of changing dynamics in the elite politics field leading to changes in the mass politics field. Before this point, the Socialist party controlled the media; the only real fight was when one faction in the party was using a media outlet to gain an advantage over another faction, such as when Pozsgay would use the media against Grósz. Now, the Socialists' were abandoned by the once loyal Hungarian news organizations. These new outlets published extensively about the scandal, which was extremely damaging to the public image of the Hungarian Socialist Party. The Minister of Interior denied the accusations, as did Prime Minister Németh, Pozsgay, and other ranking members of the party. Then, the secret police agent stepped forward, and evidence emerged that these ranking officials were receiving those reports. All this was presented to the public. The Minister of Interior resigned. This in turn seemed to end any credibility the Socialists had with most of the public.[7]

## Mass Politics Field II: The Campaign for Parliament:

*Alliance of Free Democrats: From Mouse to Kangaroo:*

The rapid decline in Socialist support in the period leading up to the 1990 parliamentary election made it an open field for the new and re-formed Hungarian parties. The Antall led Hungarian Democratic Forum had been the most widely recognized and supported of these parties. Now, the Alliance of Free Democrats was quickly catching up. But, after several months of dramatic victories, the Free Democrats made a strategic mistake that potentially cost them the role as head of the new government. Having spent a decade attempting to undermine the Hungarian Socialist government, they did not recognize that after Danube Gate their chief rival was not the Socialists but the Democratic Forum.

During the parliamentary campaign, the Free Democrats tried to present a front of westernization and anti-Communism. In Hungarian political discourse, "westernization" is closely associated with liberalism as well as "modernization" and "Europeanization." The roots of this ideology might date back to the sixteenth century and certainly can be connected to the reform period in the nineteenth century. In the sixteenth century, the Ottoman Empire conquered a large portion of Hungary. The country was divided into three parts: An independent Transylvania (now northern Rumania), a Habsburg controlled region (now roughly Slovakia, eastern Austria, and western Hungary), and a region controlled by the Ottoman Empire. The country experienced almost constant warfare for 150 years, during which the population and economic conditions dropped significantly. Following the liberation of Hungary from the Ottoman Empire, a significant portion of the Hungarian nobility and intelligentsia began calling for Hungary to "catch up" with Western Europe, or as it is more often put, to "join Europe" [in Hungarian, *"Európához csatlakozni"*]. This theme has been repeated through a number of historical moments, including in the 1990s, when many groups argued that the Russian period had caused Hungary to again fall farther behind "Europe." Hungarian liberals—mostly proponents of limited government in both the social and economic spheres—were especially strong proponents of "Europeanization." Unlike the populists or conservatives, they were less concerned that westernization might threaten Hungary's national identity.[8]

The Free Democrats presented this westernization, Europeanization theme in a number of ways. Its party icon showed three westward flying birds in the colors of the Hungarian flag. It emphasized the word "freedom", like in its name (the Alliance of Free Democrats) and in slogans like "Some Like it Free," a play on the Marilyn Monroe movie of a similar name. The term has connotations of both anti-communism and pro-westernization. The Free Democrats also claimed repeatedly that they had the most "experts" of all the parties.

For our purposes, the more important aspect of the Free Democrat mass politics strategy was its ardent anti-Communism. The party's best-known slogan in this campaign was "We know! We dare! We do!" The intended message was that the Free Democrats know how to challenge the communist regime; they dare to make that challenge; and they did indeed topple the regime. It was meant to be a strong message of the party's courage and capability.[9] The anti-Communist flavor of this slogan was made particular clear in the party's best-known television commercial, which starred cartoon characters Tom and Jerry. Tom, the cat, was beating Jerry, the mouse, with a frying pan. Jerry then took a magic pill that made him much larger than Tom. The now enormous mouse grabbed the frying pan and began beating the cat over the head. With each hit, the cat got smaller, until it finally ran into the mouse hole. The commercial ended: "We know! We dare! We do!"

One can always speculate in retrospect how much a particular set of advertisements had on a voting public. Rarely is there enough empirical evidence to reach any definitive conclusions. What is clear, however, is that the Free Democrat leadership maintained a strategy throughout the campaign of aggressively attacking the former regime. Their primary goal, besides winning, was to stop the Socialists from simply maintaining power under a new governmental system. They even coined a word for what they were trying to stop: *"hatalomátmentés"*, which meant the saving of power from one regime to another. They spent most of the campaign beating an already dead communist cat. These attacks may have had virtually no impact on support for the Socialists after the Danube-Gate Scandal, which did not move significantly after January. By focusing its attacks on a party that seemed to fall as far as it would fall, the Free Democrats effectively allowed the Democratic Forum not only to set the agenda but also to redefine the mass politics field to its own benefit.

*Hungarian Democratic Forum: The Moderate Spring Cleaning:*
With the Hungarian Socialist Party now eliminated as either a partner or a serious contender, the Hungarian Democratic Forum was also potentially in serious trouble. The Democratic Forum seemed to be the party most caught off guard by the call for a referendum. Having presented itself as the moderates who also led the democracy movement and the Opposition Roundtable, it was suddenly accused of having been in bed with the reform Communists. Throughout the referendum campaign, the Democratic Forum was unable to take a clear stand on the issue. Instead of encouraging Hungarians to vote either for or against the presidential election issue, it called on its supporters to boycott the election. The Democratic Forum also announced its candidate for president: Founding Father Lajos Für. Ironically, the call for a boycott may well have kept just enough pro-presidential election voters away from the polls to create the slim victory for the other side.

The Democratic Forum stood on the sidelines as the Free Democrats and other parties ran a successful campaign against the old system. Then, in January, it stood on the sidelines again as FIDESZ and the Free Democrats led a successful media campaign that undermined the Socialists' spying operations. The Democratic Forum was not only associated with the sinking, Socialist ship; it's old rivals, the radical, liberal Free Democrats, were now quickly catching up to them in popular support.

## Ascent of Party Amateurs II: Referendum, Campaign, and Construction of Parties

The rise of the Free Democrats and decline of the Hungarian Socialist Party were clearly among the factors that prompted the now Antall led Democratic Forum to shift ideologically from populism—which in Hungary had a leftist, anti-capitalist flavor—to a "center-right" ideology. Antall would repeatedly claimed that this center-right ideology had three roots in the development of the Democratic Forum: National liberalism (which has a long history in Hungarian politics and is arguably the ideology of the social group from which Antall emerged), Christian democracy (a clear reference to the right of center in Western Europe), and the populist movement (from which the Democratic Forum founders emerged.)[10]

Certainly, this move is not a complete break from the Democratic Forum's past. There is evidence that this shift away from strict populism to a more general nationalist ideology had begun as early as the second Lakitelek meeting in 1988. But, Antall had clear reasons to make a more explicit redefinition in early 1990. In the first place, he had to redefine the party's ideology in a way that would justify his central role; as long as the Democratic Forum was defined as a populist organization, Antall would have to play the role of talented outsider. Second, if the Democratic Forum won the election and became the government, it would have to deal with the capitalist West, which Hungary owed a great deal of money and needed as a trade partner. Finally, by defining itself as politically right, the Democratic Forum could distinguish itself from its former, now falling partners: the reformers who built the Hungarian Socialist Party.

But there was another trick behind this move. If the Democratic Forum and other parties, including the Christian Democrats and the Independent Smallholders, were defined as the right, and if the Free Democrats and FIDESZ were defined as the left, then the Democratic Forum's main competitor, the Free Democrats, could be pushed into one camp with the Socialists. With this move, the Democratic Forum could try to take credit for being the real anti-Communists, undermining the Free Democrats' claim to being the hard-core opposition against the former regime.

This Democratic Forum maneuver is best shown by a document that the party wrote and distributed into mailboxes: "Fathers and Sons", or "Apák és Fiúk" in Hungarian. The gist of this short essay—apparently written mostly by Sándor Lezsák, not Antall—is that the Free Democrat leadership is made up of disgruntled ex-Communists. They were Communist zealots who came from Communist families, but the Communist party had rejected them. So, Free Democrat leaders, especially Kis and Haraszti, were trying to regain power by pretending to be anti-Communists. "Fathers and Sons" includes the following excerpt:

> More and more people are becoming aware that under the Alliance of Free Democrats' anti-bolshevism garb beats a different type of heart. "Among the Free Democrat leadership are numerous former zealot Communists, and you can still hear it in their bleats from under the radical anti-communism sheep's cloth." (Nyugati Magyarság [Western Hungarians], Montreal, 1989, November–December.) Among those in the administrative

*board are quite a few who not long ago were brave fighters for the governing party—yes, the Hungarian Socialist Workers' Party. They were not common soldiers but strategists working to advance Marxism and related doctrines. Miklós Haraszti's parents were founders of the Israeli communist party, and around 1970 he was brought before a judge and accused of a Maoist conspiracy... János Kis was the party secretary of the MTA Philosophy Institute; in 1973 he was expelled from the party for his "too leftist" views... Miklós Gáspár Tamás' mother was a founder of the Rumanian communist party; after they moved from Kolozsvár [in Rumania] to Budapest, she received one of the biggest party pensions. Tamás Bauer's father was known as "Clawed Bauer" for his specialization at 60 Stalin Street [where there was a political police prison.] His son, Mihály Laki, and Attila Károly Soós, currently Free Democrat experts, together brought to life the Economic University's local organization. Iván Petô's party and Péter Tölgyessy's government management careers were performed "independently." Both were Hungarian Socialist Workers' Party members.[11]*

The essay continues by claiming that the Free Democrats are both anti-democratic and dangerous. It includes the statement: "Add up the expulsions, the placing of everyone 'else' under one hat, and the aggressive style, and from this political arithmetic we reach the final, painful result for Hungary: dictatorship. Expulsion + aggression = dictatorship. We have already had enough of this, once and for all!"[12]

Here we see an early example of Hungarian politicians applying their former competencies to the new political setting. Just as the Free Democrat dissidents would repeatedly take political steps more in line with opposition politics than party politics, the Democratic Forum populists would repeatedly revert to tactics they knew instead of tactics that were best suited for party politics. Writers write, and more than once the populists would take political moves through written tracts, which were often long essays. In this case, a 700-word discussion that accuses the other side of being closet Communists and potential dictators is a risky tactic that can easily backfire. However, the tract did not seem to hurt the Democratic Forum—though the Free Democrat leadership reacted to it with outrage—and may well have helped define the Democratic Forum's line of attack against their rivals.

After successfully redefining the mass politics field into a socialist–liberal left and a populist–conservative right, the Democratic Forum's mass politics maneuver was to present itself as both more anti-Communist and more moderate than the Free Democrats. The Democratic Forum had two main campaign slogans in 1990. The first was "calm strength," an effective method of distinguishing itself from a party that represented itself through cartoon animals beating each other with a frying pan. Indeed, it played effectively on the Free Democrat's inability to distinguish itself from its radical past. The second slogan was "the great spring cleaning." For example, this slogan was presented on a poster that pictured a broom next to a giant garbage can with communist artifacts. In the same vein, another Democratic Forum poster showed the back of a Russian soldier from head to upper shoulders, with the caption, in Russian: "Comrades! The End!"

*FIDESZ: The Radical, but Liberal Alternative:*

Like the Democratic Forum, the Federation of Young Democrats entered the 1990 parliamentary campaign with possibilities and problems. FIDESZ had gained positive public recognition over the previous two years and was widely recognized even when the Alliance of Free Democrats was largely unknown. FIDESZ gained wide recognition already in 1988 through its aggressive tactics against the government as well as because the government controlled media repeatedly denounced it. In 1989, Viktór Orbán gave a stirring speech over national television during the reburial ceremony for Imre Nagy,[13] which made him a national figure. That same year, FIDESZ played a role in the Opposition Roundtable and the referendum campaign. Now, the FIDESZ core decided to run for parliament with the hope of passing the 4% minimum vote. They had no illusions that they would win a plurality of votes. Their goal was simply to enter parliament as a political party.

However, FIDESZ began the campaign with a number of problems. One problem was that the FIDESZ core had trouble re-organizing its network from a loose web of groups into a hierarchical organization geared towards campaigning. Part of the problem seemed to be their choice of organizer during the referendum: Tamás Tirts. While the Free Democrats quickly built a national campaign organization, the FIDESZ organization under Tirts progressed at a turtle's pace.[14] Most likely this was not simply the choice of organizer: Running this type of campaign would force the loose, decentralized organization to become more hierarchical and bureaucratic. Regardless of the reasons, this difficulty in organizing helped make FIDESZ a secondary player to the Alliance of Free Democrats during the referendum, and it did not give FIDESZ much lead-time in organizing for the parliamentary elections.

Another problem developed in FIDESZ at this time. Viktor Orbán, the head of FIDESZ from the beginning, had been accepted to study at Oxford with a scholarship. He left for England after the Trilateral Negotiations had ended, and his former roommate Gábor Fodor became the de facto head of FIDESZ. This was the first moment in FIDESZ history that Orbán was not the dominant figure. It is not clear whether it started before, during, or after the referendum, but Fodor would develop a following within the party independent of Orbán. Moreover, Fodor was openly building closer ties with the Free Democrat leadership. At the time of the referendum campaign, he was even living in János Kis' apartment; apparently the leader of the Federation of Young Democrats was walking the president of the Alliance of Free Democrats' dog.[15] FIDESZ was now in danger of losing its independent identity and appearing to be little more than the Alliance of Free Democrats youth organization, a problem made worse by Antall's maneuver to invent an Socialist-Free Democrat-FIDESZ left.

As the parliamentary campaign began, the internal structure of the network shifted again. One important change was the rising importance of the young sociologists, most of whom were older than the core from the Bibó

Collegium but younger than the Free Democrat radicals. The most important case was the sociologist and lawyer János Áder. Tamás Tirts, the person who others felt had poorly run the FIDESZ organization during the referendum campaign, was called up for military duty. His role of organizer was handed over to Áder. This shift of power in the FIDESZ center would prove important in the subsequent internal struggles for power. Áder, a secondary figure in 1989, would build the organizational structure that would help secure Orbán's internal power, and Áder in turn would become one of the four or five central people in FIDESZ.

Another shift was with the creation of the Image Group, formally run by Áder but effectively run by sociologist András Bozóki. Bozóki was a key figure in the Eper Street 56 group, a FIDESZ group that met at this address. This group had been formulating campaign ideas for FIDESZ since 1989. It had, for example, proposed that orange become the organization's color, and it developed the key ideas that FIDESZ would adapt as its campaign image. The Eper Street 56 group, especially Bozóki, was therefore fundamental in constructing the FIDESZ party image in 1990. As the election approached, Bozóki's informal role as image builder was translated into his primary role in the image group as well as FIDESZ spokesperson.

Bozóki's idea was that FIDESZ's image could be summarized in three words: Radical, liberal, and alternative.[16] These ideas were then represented through three people. Viktor Orbán, who returned from Oxford and reclaimed the role of the head of FIDESZ, was chosen to represent FIDESZ radicalism, partially because of his well known, fiery speech at the Nagy reburial. The quieter Gábor Fodor, who was more like the liberal Free Democrats, was chosen to represent liberalism. And the young and handsome Tamás Deutsch was used to represent alternative. Deutsch became well known after being arrested for participating in a demonstration in Prague, for which he received significant press coverage. In order to fit with his image as the FIDESZ alternative, he wore long hair and an earring. He became known as the rock star of Hungarian politics and grew quite popular among Hungarian teenage girls. These three became the best known members of FIDESZ at this time, and Fodor in particular gained further national recognition.

During this period, many rose within FIDESZ because they brought a particular resource, usually some competency, to the party. For example, a person by the name of Zoltán Lovas became press secretary because of his background as a journalist. Another example was Csaba Földvári. Földvári was a psychology student who, instead of listening to lectures, apparently spent class time inventing jingles. He was brought into the image group—a group very close to the FIDESZ center—in order to make up rhymes for the FIDESZ campaign. Földvári's best-known creation came to him as he was singing along to the Roxette song "Listen to Your Heart" in his car. Wanting to learn English, Földvári translated the line to Hungarian and then immediately came up with the rhyming slogan: "Listen to your heart. Vote for FIDESZ!" [In Hungarian: "Halgass a szivedre. Szavazz a FIDESZ-re."] The rest of the image group initially rejected the slogan on the grounds that it was synonymous with "ignore your brain." But, it was accepted after the "focus group" of teenage girls hanging around Deutsch said that it was fantastic.[17]

## Ascent of Party Amateurs II: Referendum, Campaign, and Construction of Parties

The FIDESZ organization developed in other ways during the campaign. During this campaign, it exploded in size partially because of better organizational moves but mostly because of youthful excitement. Distribution of posters was accomplished largely by handing out piles of posters to the swarms of young people who came to the office volunteering to put them up. People of useful training, especially those in public relations, simply provided their services. Its most famous poster, for example, was neither made by the FIDESZ image team nor paid for by the party. Someone simply brought the finished product to the main office. It was an organization run more through excitement than structure. Within the context of a collapsing Socialist state, FIDESZ's youthful image helped pull in a critical resource, unskilled labor, without which the Young Democrats would have been very unlikely to run a successful electoral campaign. In 1994, in a completely different context, FIDESZ would hold no such advantage.

The key to FIDESZ's popularity at this time seemed to be its youthful image. Its young leaders were well known for their unkempt look and their willingness to make statements in a blunt and uncompromising manner. Their advertisements tended to be direct and powerful. For example, the most famous FIDESZ poster had two pictures. In the top picture, Brezhnev was kissing the East German Prime Minister on the lips, a common practice among communist leaders. In the bottom picture a young couple held hands and kissed. Between the pictures sat the statement "PLEASE CHOOSE," or "TESSÉK VÁLASZTANI," which also has the double meaning "Please vote for."

For some, especially younger voters, this was a refreshing change from the careful, evasive discourse of the Kádár era. For others, it seemed to be inappropriate, adolescent aggressiveness. To become a major player, FIDESZ would need to branch out from the smaller group in the mass public that liked this radicalism to a larger group that was not likely to support FIDESZ with its direct speech and long hair. The FIDESZ leadership would have to go the farthest to prove that they were capable of governing. However—as the Orbán group would learn too late—they would have to prove this point without contradicting their self-produced image as the young, radical, liberal, alternative party.

*The Hungarian Socialist Party: The Secure Change:*

The months leading to the parliamentary elections were a disaster for the Hungarian Socialist Party. First, it lost the campaign to have the President of the Republic elected by the public instead of selected by the parliament. This loss destroyed the Socialists' chance of maintaining power by running the executive branch of government. Then, in January, party leaders were caught spying on other parties. The Socialists became the focus of all the other party's attacks. The former friends of the reform Socialists now abandoned the Hungarian Socialist Party and were instead competing to prove that they were the most anti-Communist.

The Socialists' solution to this situation was to present an image of security to the public. As the only party with real experience running a government, they would be the best suited to lead Hungary through the difficult transition ahead. Like the other parties, the Socialists showed this theme through generally but not explicitly consistent advertisements. One such ad was a poster showing nothing more than the party icon, the party name, and the line: "Choose the secure future!" [In Hungarian, *"Válaszd a biztos jövôt!"*] Another showed a mother holding a baby with the baby seeming to be saying: "Tell Papa that he too should vote for the Socialist Party!" [In Hungarian, *"Mondd a Papának, hogy Ô is a SZOCIALISTA PÁRT-ra szavazzon!"*] [18]

At the same time, some of the internal shifts within the party leadership were beginning. The four most important figures in early 1990 were Imre Pozsgay, party president Rezsô Nyers, Prime Minister Miklós Németh, and Foreign Minister Gyula Horn. Németh would soon be out of the picture; after the election, he would accept a job in Germany, leaving both the party leadership and Hungary. This would help open the door for his ally, Horn, to grab more power in the party. At the same time, Pozsgay was beginning his descent in power. He was still prominent and well respected among the Socialists, but the events of the previous few months had devastated his career possibly most of all the Socialist leaders. His position was built partially through his relationship with the moderate opposition. The destroyed relationship with the Democratic Forum and several other parties translated into a weakened internal position for Pozsgay.

Moreover, this devastation went beyond rational politics. The shattering of his dream to lead the Hungarian government seemed to have dealt a psychological blow as well. According to one of his assistants at the time, Pozsgay ran himself ragged trying to revive his fallen party. But all he accomplished was to exhaust himself physically and emotionally to the point that he would not have the energy to fight the intra-party battle that would come after the election.[19] Just as Pozsgay had worked with Grósz just long enough to eliminate him, Horn's good relationship with Pozsgay would end with the former pushing the latter out of power.

**The Selection of Candidates:**

The next critical step in the development of each party's network was the selection of candidates for parliament. The selection of candidates is one of the central tasks of a political party. Not only do they represent the party before the mass public, but if the party is successful, those candidates become the governmental arm of the party. Successful candidates also tend to gain internal party power: Their public exposure and positions in government become resources within the party's internal distribution of power.

Parties choosing candidates for office must face two primary considerations. The first consideration is what the individual adds to the party's attempt to win power. This is partially a question of what resources the candidate brings to the party. How well known is the candidate? Is she a nationally known figure, like a famous actor, athlete, or politician? Does the candidate have other resources like contacts and money that can be brought into the struggle? This is also partially a question of competence. Is the individual skilled at public relations and other thing needed for campaigning? Does the individual bring skills that can be valuable to a parliamentary group, like an understanding of law, negotiation, or some area of policy?

The second consideration is related to internal politics. How does the selection of candidates influence the power dynamics within the party? This is part of the fundamental dilemmas political parties face. On the one hand, those in power within the party (the party center) need to find and promote candidates who will help increase the party's support among the mass public and elite groups. On the other hand, in doing so, they might forfeit internal power to another set of individuals. The party might inadvertently create a new center of power (the party faction in parliament) that could compete for internal control against the old center of power (presumably, the main governing committee.) The easiest way to avoid this crisis is for the very same people to be in the governing body and the parliamentary faction. Effectively, if the same smaller network within the party controls both the governing body and the parliamentary faction, there is no possibility of one challenging the power of the other, since they are the same people.

The question is therefore whom each party chose as its candidates for parliament in 1990. In the rather complex Hungarian electoral system, a candidate can win a seat in parliament in one of three ways. First, the candidate can run for an individual mandate, which is equivalent to running for a winner-take-all seat that represents a single district. If no candidate wins a majority of the vote during the first round, the top two candidates and every other candidate with at least 15% of the vote can run in the second round. Whoever wins a plurality in the second round wins the seat. Second, the candidate can be placed on one of twenty county lists. If a party wins at least 4% of the list vote nationally, that party wins the same percentage of county seats as its percent of list votes in that county. Third, the candidate can be placed on the national list. After the election commission determines how many seats each party wins from county lists, there is a recalculation to offset the biases in that system. They then use that recalculation to determine how many seats each party above 4% receives from its national list. So, the best position for any candidate wanting to win a parliamentary seat is to be number one on the national list, number one on a list in a county that supports the party, and a local candidate in a district that supports the party. See Figure 4.1.

The Democratic Forum selection of candidates indicates how the populists were allowing control of the party they founded to slip from their hands. Central figures of the Democratic Forum populists, including founders Zoltán Bíró, Sándor Csoóri, and Sándor Lezsák, each of whom was still in the presidium, did not run for office. Similarly, of the Founding Fathers, only four were even on the national list, and only three were high enough to possibly win a parliamentary seat. (The historian Lajos Für was #3, the writer István Csurka was #5, and the writer Dénes Csengey was #6.) György Szabad, a historian well connected with the populists and a member of the presidium, was also high on the list; (he was #4). The other candidates in the top ten of the national list were not from the populist core. József Antall (#1), was the Democratic Forum president and it's candidate for Prime Minister, but as was discussed above, he entered the organization late. The two pre-1990 members of parliament, János Szentágothay (#2) and Zoltán Király (#10), were both nationally recognized figures, but while Király had some relationship with the populists, neither was from the founding group.[20] Similarly, Katalin Kutrucz (#7), a lawyer and wife of lawyer Imre Kónya, entered the organization after playing a role in the Independent Lawyers' Forum; she and her husband, who was number one on the Pest County list, had much closer ties to Antall than the populists. The other two in the Democratic Forum top ten—Ernô Raffay (#8) and József Debreczeni (#9)—were relative unknowns at this point with weak ties to the populists at best.

So, while the populists did not simply hand to Antall power over the parliamentary faction, they also did not secure that power for themselves. The decisions by many Democratic Forum founders to not run, and the populist's collective decision to let Antall lead the parliamentary arm of the party, opened the door for an intra-party struggle for power between the populist founders and the developing Antall group. Their candidate selection process would also open the door for other problems. For example, Debreczeni became a key figure in the near implosion of the Democratic Forum a few years and was thrown out of the party after he publicly called Csurka a Nazi.

There was another problem with the candidate decisions the Democratic Forum made. Of the candidates chosen for the national list, only 27% also ran as single district candidates. The decision making that led to choosing single district candidates was decentralized. From what can be determined by the biographies of those who ran as local candidates but not on the national list, a large percent won those candidacies because they were leaders and often founders of local Democratic Forum organizations. In other words, soon after the party formed, the organization began building a national network, often by connecting the party to local organizations, like cultural houses. Often individuals who were leaders in these local organizations—often teachers, doctors, and clergy—founded or led the local Democratic Forum branches. Because of their status within the local group, many of these individuals then became the Democratic Forum candidates in their local districts.

There were two strategic problems with this selection process. First, these local leaders were only loosely tied to the center of the party, whether the populist founders or the rising Antall group. Second, these candidates rarely had any skills needed to either govern or run a party. Ironically, a critical reason for the low party competence of the Democratic Forum parliamentary faction is only indirectly related to the lack of experience of the founders. Lacking political experience, they created a mechanism for internal promotion that advanced people with neither loyalty to the leadership nor backgrounds that would be useful to the party.

If the Democratic Forum selection of candidates is best described by the founding group giving up control over the party, the Free Democrat selection process is best described by its centralization. In the first place, the hard-core, radical dissidents, now securely in control of the governing body, also placed itself as the primary candidates for parliament. Though many of his colleagues wanted him to run for Prime Minister, János Kis decided that he did not want be a member of parliament, much less the head of government. Because Kis was such a central figure, the party did not want to choose another top candidate, and so the Free Democrats had no candidate for Prime Minister. The other ten members of the administrative board gave themselves the first ten positions on the national list. Péter Tölgyessy, the Free Democrat candidate for leader of its parliamentary faction, was the first name on the national list. The other nine members were placed in spots two through ten in alphabetical order: Gábor Demszky (#2),

## Ascent of Party Amateurs II: Referendum, Campaign, and Construction
of Parties

Miklós Haraszti (#3), Ferenc Kôszeg (#4), Bálint Magyar (#5), Imre Mécs (#6), Iván Petô (#7), László Rajk (#8), Miklós Szabó (#9), and Miklós Gáspár Tamás (#10). They also received choice spots on county lists. All but Miklós Szabó were first on a county list; he was number three on the Budapest list, where Free Democrat support was expected to be high.

The rest of the list was devised through a test, a system that the Free Democrats would perfect before the 1994 election. Perspective candidates were judged on a number of "criteria" and from that criteria they were given a quantitative score. (However, the criteria were never specified, and at times this system was employed in a rather unsystematic way.) The higher someone scored, the better spot she got on national or county lists.

By accident or not, the system seemed to promote two main categories of people. The first were members of the democratic opposition. Of the 116 people on the national list, 28% were somehow involved in the democratic opposition between 1977 and 1988, a large percent if one considers that the democratic opposition was a small network of dissidents. Moreover, these dissidents tended to get the best spots on the lists. Of the first fifteen people on the Free Democrat national list, for example, all but two were involved in the democratic opposition and all but four had signed the petitions in support of Charter 77 in 1977 or 1979.[21] The second group seemed to be people who the party leadership thought could bring some competence or other advantage to the party. They included lawyers and economists. However, the party was hesitant to allow any former Socialist politicians to join. So, the competence that these individuals brought, while it may have helped the faction construct policy, was not in party politics.[22]

If the Democratic Forum founders did little to maintain control over their faction, the Free Democrat hard-core did little to hide the fact that they dominated the party. To make matters worse, the party leadership allowed itself to become the Budapest section of the party. All ten members of the administrative board ran as local candidates in Budapest—which is to say that none ran as local candidates in the country. (There is a long-standing clash in Hungary between those who live in Budapest and those who live in other parts of the country.) The all too clear domination of the party by former democratic opposition members, all of whom resided in Budapest, would make an internal challenge easier later.

When the Young Democrats decided to run candidates in the 1990 election, their primary goal was to pass the 4% minimum threshold needed to enter parliament. Possibly because no one within the party expected FIDESZ to win much more than this minimum, the process of selecting candidates was rather lax. The construction of the national list was done in at an informal meeting chaired by András Bozóki. Bozóki described the selection process this way:

> In 1990, only the first 15 places were regarded as important. Some experts said that if FIDESZ is able to beat the 4 percent limit or go over the 4 percent limit, we could have between 14 and 18 members in parliament. And nobody believed that FIDESZ could reach 9 percent in the first election. They said that the best scenario is 6 percent and that is why it was that only the first 15 to 18 places were regarded as important. For

other spots, we just put people into them. But the campaign proved to be very successful. FIDESZ became popular, and we won 22 seats.

So some guys surprisingly entered the parliament that nobody thought would. There was this guy Szilárd Sasvári, who was the 21st. I remember because I was there. Maybe there was a little discussion about places between 15 and 20, but not over 20. And we asked, 'who else,' 'who is there,' 'who has an idea,' and 'who has a good friend,' because there were even problems filling the list, because we had to present 50 names. And not everybody wanted to be an MP. For example, I put my name in the 49th place to be sure that I cannot be there. Anyway, Szilárd was a kind of worker in a theater moving furniture. He had a low-level job to finance himself while he went to teacher training school. He found himself in parliament a month later.[23]

The group took a number of factors into consideration as it developed the FIDESZ national list. The first was the person's position within the organization. Viktór Orbán and Gábor Fodor, as the two symbolic heads of the party, were given spots one and two, respectively. Other central figures received key spots as well. Spots three and five were given to founding members József Szájer, the Bibó student who designed the FIDESZ legal strategy, and László Kövér, another Bibó student. According to Bozóki, another important consideration was whether the individual had some expertise that could be used in parliament. János Áder was given the fourth spot because of his knowledge of the law, and Klára Ungár was given the sixth spot because she was considered an excellent economist.

After spot six, according to Bozóki, another consideration became to appease the countryside parts of the organization. These groups complained that FIDESZ was creating a Budapest elite, and that leaders of other FIDESZ groups should also be represented on the list. This is how two virtual unknowns, Zoltán Trombitás and Mihály Varga, became numbers seven and nine on the list. Before his association with FIDESZ, Trombitás had a rather undistinguished career as a medical student, which included being thrown out of medical school in 1983. Varga was an economist who helped form the Szolnok County group, but in terms of bringing expertise, the group would have preferred long time FIDESZ members from the prestigious Rajk Collegium. The eight and tenth spots were given to economist and FIDESZ founder Zsolt Németh and the young sociologist Zoltán Rockenbauer, both of whom were important members of FIDESZ at this time.[24]

A number of key FIDESZ members were pushed lower on the list in order make room for Trombitás, Varga, and a few other lesser-known members. Tamás Deutsch, the young Bibó student who was used to present FIDESZ's "alternative" image, was given the twelfth spot. The same was true of Péter Molnár, a Bibó student and FIDESZ founder who had been a central figure from the beginning, and István Hegedüs, a young sociologist who has become a key member. They received spots fourteen and eighteen, respectively. In the end, this had little effect on the outcome, since FIDESZ received far more votes than anyone had expected.

Contrary to the situation of the other parties, the Socialists had a deep reserve of politicians that it could use when selecting candidates. The national list was constructed by the presidium, and it clearly reflected both internal and external politics considerations. At this time, the Hungarian Socialist Party was a fusion of factions that had roughly formed the reformed wing of the party. It included, for example, both the reform circles, which followed Pozsgay, and the New March Front, an organization formed by Rezsô Nyers. The lists were therefore formed with the same compromises in consideration that had guided the formation of the presidium during the founding party congress. Of that presidium, all twenty members were placed on the national list, though some were placed too low to win a seat.

On the other hand, the places on the lists were clearly influenced by what the candidates brought to the party. The first five people were nationally known figures: (#1) Imre Pozsgay, the head reformer and negotiator for the Socialist party; (#2) Nyers, who had been a prominent member of the Hungarian government since the Kádár takeover in the early 1960s; (#3) Gyula Horn, the foreign minister; (#4) Mátyás Szûrös, a former MP and a prominent Central Committee member for eleven years; (#5) and Miklós Németh, the prime minister.

After this point, the list varies from long-term members of the Socialist party apparatus to Hungarian Socialist Workers' Party members who did not work in the party bureaucracy or people who joined the Hungarian Socialist Party only in 1989. Overall, of the first twenty-eight names on the national list—all of whom entered parliament—just over half (16, or 57%) had long professional experience working in the Socialist party, mostly in very high positions. Others were party members who worked close to the party apparatus but not in it. Yet others were not party members but brought something else to the table, like the actor Attila Nagy (#18). Another example was Pál Demény (#14). Demény ran a nearly independent—and some claim the mostly widely supported—wing of the communist movement between World Wars I and II, sometimes called the "Demény movement". After the Soviet invasion, he was imprisoned multiple times, and the party gave him political rehabilitation only in 1989. Clearly, the candidates for the Hungarian Socialist Party brought a range of resources and experiences that the party could use, but the dominant positions were given to the most prominent politicians that had been in the party for many years.

**The 1990 Election and Party Competence:**

On March 25, Hungary held its first multi-party election in forty-three years. During this first round, voters selected among party lists and among individual mandate, or single-member district, candidates. Six parties received the minimum four percent of the list vote needed to enter parliament: the Hungarian Democratic Forum, the Alliance of Free Democrats, the Hungarian Socialist Party, the Federation of Young Democrats (or FIDESZ), the Independent Smallholders' Party, and the Christian Democratic People's Party. The Democratic Forum received the most list votes, about 25%, with the Free Democrats coming in a relatively close second with 21%. The first round also determined which single-member district candidates could run in the second round, on April 8. It was during the second round that the Democratic Forum established itself as the dominant party in the new parliament. It won 114 of the 176 single district seats, as compared to the Free Democrats, who won only thirty-five of those seats. The

Democratic Forum then formed its center-right coalition with the Smallholders' and the Christian Democrats with 229 members of parliament, or a 59% majority of seats. See Graph 4.1.

The complex Hungarian electoral laws produced a number of unexpected and unplanned consequences. First, even though the Democratic Forum received the most list votes, the Free Democrats received the most list seats.[25] However, the two-part electoral process produced a momentum for the Democratic Forum that led to a sweeping victory in the second round. While the Democratic Forum had won only 25% of the list votes in round one, it won 64% of the single-seat district elections. Because of this whopping second round success, the Democratic Forum could form a government without having to go into coalition with the Free Democrats, thought it could not avoid joining forces with the less predictable Independent Smallholders' Party.

But, there was a negative side to these unexpected factors for the Democratic Forum. 70% of Democratic Forum MP's won in single-member district elections. As had been discussed above, the selection of single-member district candidates was rather localized for the Democratic Forum in 1990. These candidates for "single mandate" seats tended to be people who had formed or led local Democratic Forum organizations. This opened the party to two problems. One, these people often had little relationship with the party center. If they had any loyalty, it was to István Csurka, who had traveled the country and built the Democratic Forum network in 1987 and 1988, not to József Antall, the latecomer who had taken over the party presidency and its governmental arm. Second, a large portion of these local candidates who became members of parliament had absolutely no background in politics or related fields. This lack of political experience was true of all the new parties and probably a far more serious problem for the Independent Smallholders' and the Christian Democrats. But, as the leader of a government coalition, the Democratic Forum was in a special situation. The weight of running a government in transition and a country entering an economic crisis weighed on this party and especially the shoulder's of the newly elected Prime Minister.

Indeed, the formation of parliamentary factions produced new centers of power within each of the major parties, even for the Socialists. The importance of this new center would vary from party to party. For FIDESZ, for example, the parliamentary wing would become the de facto governing body of the party until 1993, while for the Democratic Forum there would develop a power struggle between the presidium and the governmental arm. But, the immediate question is how much competence at party politics did these new members of parliament bring to their new, elite position in Hungarian politics?

*Party Competence and Years of Experience:*

Since competence is closely related to experience, one of the easiest ways to measure political competence is to examine the political backgrounds of individuals. One type of experience is time within a particular type of institution. Well developed bureaucratic institutions, including political parties, normally require most of their members to climb the hierarchy gradually. This promotes institutional stability, but it also gives individuals time to develop skills that the

116

institution needs. In this way, a person who has been a member of a party for thirty years before becoming a party leader will likely have higher competence at party politics than someone who won that position after only a year.

Of course, the new parties did not exist before 1989. This method can therefore be broken down to two questions. One, how much was the pre-1989 organization like a political party in a multi-party system? This question was explored in Chapters 2 and 3. Generally, the pre-party organizations were quite different from political parties, but to a greater or lesser extent they at least provided some level of political experience. Two, how many years were these MP's in the party or pre-party organization or network before becoming MP's? This question is explored here.

On average, the Socialist MP's had been party members for 25 years before entering the new parliament. Over 90% (30 of 33) had joined the Socialist party before 1980, a decade before the transition. Nearly three-quarters (24 of 33, or 73%) had joined before 1970. This provides further evidence to points made in Chapter 2 and above. The Socialist politicians of 1990 had significant party experience before entering the new parliament, even if that experience was in a party that did not have to compete against other parties to remain in power.[26]

In comparison, a minority of MP's from the other parties had political experience before 1988. 85% (238 of 280) of Alliance of Free Democrats, Hungarian Democratic Forum, FIDESZ MP's in 1990 joined their respective party or pre-party in 1988, 1989 or 1990.[27] Some of these 238 MP's could have be considered dissidents. For example, while there are indications that future FIDESZ leaders were involved at the periphery of the developing democracy movement a few years earlier, none had gotten involved in any serious organizing before FIDESZ was formed. The only FIDESZ MP whose name appears in documentation about the democratic opposition is István Hegedüs. He had attended the first Lakitelek meeting, though even he openly admits to have simply been a passive observer before joining FIDESZ.[28] However, most of these 238 MP's were not involved in any way before joining on of the major new organizations. They were jumping on board as the Socialist regime appeared ready to collapse.

In terms of time involved in political activity, the Free Democrat MP's were the most prepared of the three, or indeed, any of the new parties in parliament. But, only a fraction had been involved in the opposition movement over an extended period. (Fifteen, or 16%, are known to have been involved with the Hungarian democratic opposition for at least a decade.) Even here, the importance of this involvement can be overstated. In the first place, a number of these people were only involved at the periphery. In the second place, the democratic opposition was involved in a politics quite different from running a party in parliament.

While this measure of competence would indicate that among the new parties, the Free Democrat parliamentary faction was the most prepared for multi-party politics, two other factors should be considered. First of all, years of unrelated experience can be more damaging than no experience at all. Younger people can have a learning advantage over older people in moments of rapid change (for example, in their level of comfort with new technology.) In simple terms, younger people have less to unlearn. The more mature have more of a tendency to return to well-developed habits, and they will be more likely to resist changing behavior.

Second, even if a politician has no experience in party politics, a background in a related career can make the transition to party politics easier. Both Max Weber[29] and Pierre Bourdieu[30] have pointed out that law is an excellent preparation for party politics, for example. Similarly, as Ronald Reagan and others have demonstrated, a background in acting can be useful in multi-party competition. For these reasons, MP's pre-1990 career can be another indicator of the level of party competence for those factions that did not evolve directly from another political party.

*The Professional Backgrounds of MP's:*

Table 4.3 shows the non-party, professional experiences of the FIDESZ, Democratic Forum, Socialist, and Free Democrat party factions in the 1990 parliament. This table is based on biographies published in *The Almanac of the Parliament Elected in 1990 [Az 1990-ben Megválasztott Országgyûlés Almanachja].* Each member of parliament was put into a career category based on the biographical description. This is a rough measure of experience, for sure, but it does give a general indication of what professional experience each faction brought to the new political system. See Graph 4.2.

According to this table, the Young Democrats entered parliament with the best non-party, professional background for party politics. This was largely because the FIDESZ center was made up mostly of Bibó trained lawyers and Rajk trained economists, though this domination of lawyers and economists was also helped by the FIDESZ decision to put "experts" high on its national list. The Socialists also had high indirect experience, though the professional backgrounds of Socialist members of parliament were more varied. Instead of just lawyers and economists, the Socialist faction also included people who worked in the government bureaucracy (usually policy experts), leaders of the foreign affairs community, journalists, and business leaders.

There was another difference that did not appear on this table. Cases were coded by the main career of the MP. With this coding, there was no way to indicate how much experience the individual had in his or her career, nor was there any way to determine how much that experience related to party politics. For example, the FIDESZ economists were young professionals; they were mostly well trained but had only a few years experience at best. The Socialist economists included Rezsô Nyers (the former Minister of Finance who helped design the New Economic Mechanism), Lajos Bokros (the reform economists who worked for years in the Finance Ministry and was the managing director of the Hungarian National Bank), and László Békesi (who worked as the secretary of political economy in the Hungarian Socialist Workers' Party Budapest committee and as the Assistant Minister of Finance.)

In contrast, of these four factions, the Hungarian Democratic Forum entered parliament with the least professional experience related to party politics. Nearly two-thirds of Democratic Forum members of parliament began their new jobs with backgrounds completely unrelated to party politics. The Alliance of

## Ascent of Party Amateurs II: Referendum, Campaign, and Construction of Parties

Free Democrats began in somewhat better shape, with just over half of its members having had professional backgrounds related or partially related to party politics. To some degree, the political background of the Democratic Forum and Free Democrat factions is understated. The historians in the Democratic Forum did included Antall, who came from a political family and had studied political negotiation. The social thinkers among the Free Democrat MP's included people who had played serious roles in the opposition or who had significant knowledge in social policy. Both parties also had prominent and talented lawyers, like Kónya in the Hungarian Democratic Forum and Tölgyessy in the Alliance of Free Democrats. Nonetheless, these two parties entering parliament with two-thirds and one-half of their respective MP's having backgrounds completely unrelated to politics.

**Summary:**

Taken as a whole, the evidence of the past three chapters indicates that the Hungarian Socialist Party began the new political system with significantly higher party competence than its new opponents. Several key pieces of evidence were shown. First, Chapter 2 discussed how the Socialist party's reaction to the violent, anti-Communist public uprising of 1956 helped produce a generation of career politicians relatively well prepared for multi-party politics. It also showed how the reform wing of this generation took control over the party, which was reinforced by data presented above. Chapter 3 showed why the politics of the Hungarian dissidents was poor preparation for multi-party politics. Moreover, as this chapter demonstrated, because dissident networks tend to be small and parties are large, national organizations, these networks had to expand rapidly as the transformation neared and put people with no political experience whatever into important positions. In the end, the former dissidents tended to at least partially run each party apparatus, but for the Free Democrats and Democratic Forum, the vast majority of MP's were people with little connection to the dissident movement who had no political background. To the degree that FIDESZ was an exception to this last problem, it was because it had won only 22 seats in 1990.

**Figure 4.1**
**The Hungarian Electoral System in 1990**

| | Round 1 | Round 2 |
|---|---|---|
| **Local Mandate (176 seats)** | If a candidate receives a majority of votes, she becomes the MP. Otherwise, the top two or all those with at least 15% of the vote go to Round 2. | Whoever wins plurality of votes wins the seat. |
| **County Lists (120 seats)** | For those parties getting at least 4% of the list votes nationally, its number of seats is determined by the percent of the list votes it received in the county. | |
| **National Lists (90 seats)** | For those parties getting at least 4% of the list votes nationally, its number of seats is determined through an equation meant to offset the biases in the county list system. | |

Starting with the 1994 election, the minimum list vote needed to enter parliament was changed from 4% to 5%.

## Table 4.1
## 1990 Parliamentary Election Outcome

| | Percent of list votes | Seats won on county lists | Seats won on national list | Seats won in local elections | **Total seats won** |
|---|---|---|---|---|---|
| Democratic Forum | 24.73% | 40 | 10 | 114 | 164 |
| | | 33.3% | 11.1% | 64.8% | 42.5% |
| Independent Smallholders | 11.73% | 16 | 17 | 11 | 44 |
| | | 13.3% | 18.9% | 6.3% | 11.4% |
| Christian Democrats | 6.46% | 8 | 10 | 3 | 21 |
| | | 6.7% | 11.1% | 1.7% | 5.4% |
| Free Democrats | 21.39% | 34 | 23 | 35 | 92 |
| | | 28.3% | 25.6% | 19.9% | 23.8% |
| Socialists | 10.89% | 14 | 18 | 1 | 33 |
| | | 11.7% | 20.0% | 0.6% | 8.5% |
| FIDESZ | 8.95% | 8 | 12 | 1 | 21 |
| | | 6.7% | 13.3% | 0.6% | 5.4% |
| Agrarian | 3.13% | | | 2 | 2 |
| | | | | 1.1% | 0.5% |
| Independent | | | | 6 | 6 |
| | | | | 3.4% | 1.6% |
| Joint Candidates | | | | 3 | 3 |
| | | | | 1.7% | 0.8% |
| **Total** | 100.00% | 120 | 90 | 176 | 386 |
| | | 100.0% | 100.0% | 100.0% | 100.0% |

* Joint candidates ran in single seat elections under both the FIDESZ and Free
Democrat label, though Kristóf Kállay ran under the Christian Democratic label
as well. Kállay became an independent; Bertalan Komenczi joined the Free
Democrat faction; and László Kövér joined the FIDESZ faction.

Source: Gábor Tóka, "Parties and their Voters in 1990 and 1994" in *Lawful
Revolution in Hungary, 1989–1994*, edited by Béla K. Király, (Boulder:
East European Monographs), Distributed by Columbia University Press,
pp. 132–3.

**Table 4.2**
**Pre-Transition Profession or Training of 1990 MP's**

| | FIDESZ | | Democratic Forum | | Socialists | | Free Democrats | |
|---|---|---|---|---|---|---|---|---|
| **Related Fields:** | | | | | | | | |
| Gov't Bureaucracy | | | | | 4 | 13% | | |
| Economics | 5 | 23% | 14 | 9% | 5 | 16% | 6 | 6% |
| Foreign Affairs | | | | | 4 | 13% | | |
| Law–Political Science | 10 | 45% | 22 | 13% | 1 | 3% | 20 | 22% |
| Union Leadership | | | 1 | 1% | 1 | 3% | | |
| Subtotal | 15 | 68% | 37 | 23% | 15 | 45% | 26 | 28% |
| | | | | | | | | |
| **Partially related fields:** | | | | | | | | |
| Business–Trade | | | 5 | 3% | 1 | 3% | 2 | 2% |
| Film–Television | | | 1 | 1% | 1 | 3% | 5 | 5% |
| History | | | 9 | 5% | 1 | 3% | 4 | 4% |
| Journalism | | | 5 | 3% | 2 | 6% | 3 | 3% |
| Marketing | | | 1 | 1% | | | | |
| Social Thought | | | 1 | 1% | 1 | 3% | 11 | 12% |
| Subtotal | | | 22 | 13% | 6 | 18% | 25 | 27% |
| | | | | | | | | |
| **Unrelated fields:** | | | | | | | | |
| Agriculture | 2 | 9% | 11 | 7% | | | 2 | 2% |
| Architecture | 1 | 5% | 3 | 3% | 2 | 6% | 2 | 2% |
| Clergy | | | 3 | 3% | | | 4 | 4% |
| Engineering | | | 17 | 10% | 1 | 3% | 10 | 11% |
| Medicine | 2 | 9% | 29 | 18% | 3 | 9% | 7 | 8% |
| Teaching | 2 | 9% | 21 | 13% | | | 7 | 8% |
| Literature–Art | | | 9 | 5% | 2 | 6% | 5 | 5% |
| Other | | | 12 | 7% | 4 | 12% | 5 | 5% |
| Subtotal | 7 | 32% | 105 | 64% | 12 | 36% | 42 | 45% |
| **Total** | 22 | 100% | 164 | 100% | 33 | 100% | 93 | 100% |

Source: Compiled from data in *1990 Parliamentary Almanac.*

# Ascent of Party Amateurs II: Referendum, Campaign, and Construction of Parties

# Notes:

[1] In Hungarian:
1. Csak az országgyûlési választások után kerüljön-e sor a köztársasági elnök megválasztására?
2. Kivonuljanak-e a pártszervek a munkahelyekrôl?
3. Elszámoljon-e az MSZMP a tulajdonában vagy kezelésében lévô vagyonról?
4. Feloszlassák-e a munkásôrséget?

[2] This wording can cause confusion, especially since the word for "choose", "megválaszt," can also be translated as "elect." The issue was as follows. According to the agreement between the Hungarian Socialist Workers' Party and the Opposition Roundtable (which FIDESZ and the Alliance of Free Democrats did not sign,) the President would be elected by the public long before the parliamentary elections. If a majority of referendum voters voted for this item, then the parliament would choose the President after the parliamentary elections.

[3] Interview with Miklós Haraszti. Haraszti, a poet involved with the democratic opposition from the beginning, had written many of the Free Democrat slogans for the referendum and 1990 parliamentary election campaigns. According to Haraszti, the slogan came directly from József Antall, who had told him that the Alliance of Free Democrats should let the people decide who their president would be.

[4] Ibid.

[5] Haraszti and several other sources gave me this explanation, including someone who claimed to have joined the Free Democrats at this time for exactly these reasons.

[6] Tibor Kiss (1991), "A magyar titkosszolgálatok 1990-ben" ["The Hungarian secret services in 1990"] *Hungarian Political Yearbook, 1991*, pp. 262-7.

[7] Ibid.

[8] For discussions on this issue, see András Gerô (1995), *Modern Hungarian Society in the Making: The Unfinished Experience*, trans. by James Patterson and Enikô Koncz, (Budapest: Central European University Press); and especially Andrew C. Janos (1982), *The Politics of Backwardness in Hungary, 1825–1945*, (Princeton: Princeton University Press).

[9] Interviews with Miklós Haraszti and Béla Légar.

[10] Sándor Révész (1995) *Antall József Távolról. [József Antall from a Distance]* (Budapest: Sík). pp. 54–61.

[11] "Apák és Fiúk", *Magyar Forum*, March 31, 1990.

[12] Ibid.

[13] The speech can be found in *With a Clean Slate*, pp. 154–5 and *FIDESZ Press*, June 20.

[14] Interview with Bozóki.

[15] Interview with István Hegedüs. The story was also confirmed by another source. According to these sources, László Kövér called Orbán in England to tell him that the situation for FIDESZ was quite bad, that organizing was poor, and that FIDESZ was losing its independent image. Orbán quickly dropped out and returned to Hungary to take the reigns again. Fodor moved out of Kis' apartment soon afterwards in order to avoid the impression that FIDESZ and the Alliance of Free Democrats were not separate organizations.

[16] András Bozóki (1989), "Mi a Fidesz és mi nem" ["What is FIDESZ and what is it not."] *Magyar Narancs [Hungarian Orange]*. October 23, 1989.

[17] Interview with Bozóki. If Bozóki's account is accurate, Földvári's inclusion into the image group is an example of how informal networks and perceived competence can combine in odd ways during party building: Bozóki's wife was a fellow psychology student with Földvári.

123

[18] *Hungarian Political Yearbook*, 1991. pp. 62–7.

[19] Interview, László Vass.

[20] In 1985, the regime permitted independent candidates with no party affiliation to enter parliament. This was, of course, a process significantly regulated by the regime; there would be no chance that the hard-core opposition would enter parliament. A number of the independent MP's joined the Hungarian Democratic Forum and continued their work in the new parliament.

[21] Membership in the democratic opposition was determined by seeing if they had signed any of the petitions and other opposition documents, including the forming of opposition organizations, from 1977–1988. This information was gathered through Csizmadia, *Documents*.

[22] These conclusions are based on interviews with Haraszti and on biographies of the Alliance of Free Democrats members that entered parliament. József Kiss, editor. (1992) *Az 1990-ben Megválasztott Országgyûlés Almanachja [The Almanac of the Parliament Elected in 1990]* (Budapest: Jelenkutató Alapítvány).

[23] Interview with Bozóki. Bozóki had in fact not been on the national list, but he was number twenty on the Budapest list.

[24] Interview with Bozóki, plus the lists and biographies of members of parliament in *Parliamentary Almanac.*

[25] After the county list seats were determined, the numbers were recalculated to determine how many seats each party would win from their national lists. Because of this recalculation, the Free Democrats won fifty-seven list seats (thirty-four county and twenty-three national) as compared to fifty list seats for the Democratic Forum (forty county and ten national.)

[26] This data is based on MP's at the very beginning of the 1990 parliament, including what party they had belonged to at that time. It was compiled from biographical descriptions of MP's in *1990 Parliamentary Almanac* and *Freely Elected.*

[27] Among the 22 FIDESZ MP's in 1990, 20 joined in 1988 and 2 joined in 1989. Of the 94 Free Democrat MP's, 15 had been involved in the opposition before 1980 and 9 became involved from 1980 to 1987. 12 joined in 1988, 37 joined in 1989, and 21 joined in 1990. Thus, 70 of 94, or 74%, joined from 1988 to 1990. Of the 164 Democratic Forum MP's, 8 were involved before 1987, the year of the founding meeting at Lakitelek. 10 joined in 1987, 90 joined in 1988, 43 joined in 1989, and 13 joined in 1990. Thus, 95% of Democratic Forum MP's joined in 1987 or later and 90% had joined from 1988 to 1990. This data is based on MP's at the very beginning of the 1990 parliament, including what party they had belonged to at that time. It was compiled from biographical descriptions of MP's in *1990 Parliamentary Almanac* and *Freely Elected.*

[28] Interview with István Hegedüs.

[29] Max Weber (1946) "Politics as a Vocation", *From Max Weber: Essays in Sociology.* edited by H. H. Gerth and C. Wright Mills, (New York: Oxford) pp. 77-128.

[30] Pierre Bourdieu (1991) "Political Representation: Elements for a Theory of the Political Field," In *Language and Symbolic Power*, Edited by John B. Thompson, (Cambridge: Harvard University Press), pp. 171–202

## Chapter 5:

# The Implosion of the Hungarian Democratic Forum, 1990-1994

*Evidence from parties in other new democracies indicates that those who were most prominent in the formation of a party are not necessarily those who are best equipped to lead it subsequently. This is especially true of parties that regard themselves as movements. In other parts of the region most of the original leaders of movements soon vanished from political life. The Hungarian experience, particularly that of [the Democratic Forum], the Free Democrats, and the Young Democrats, seems to follow this pattern. Various examples can be noted. Among the Young Democrats the radicals who advocated direct democracy were forced to leave the party; some prominent figures within the Free Democrats (including some founding members) announced that they would not contest the 1994 elections; in [the Hungarian Democratic Forum] many of the 'movement-orientated' old guard have left the party or have been expelled. Optimistically this pattern can perhaps be interpreted as the replacement of 'amateur' by 'professional' politicians.*[1]

The 1990 election was a substantial victory for all five new and re-formed parties that passed the 4% minimum of list votes. By entering parliament, these parties won a fundamental resource in any multi-party, representative system: government seats. Parliament produces a clear platform on which parties can compete with each other for mass support. While advantages among the Hungarian parties would shift in the coming months and years, the critical difference at this point was between those in parliament and those not. The parliamentary parties would gain public exposure and a legitimacy that would give them a clear advantage in building or maintaining mass support. They were also in the position to create legislation to their own advantage, effectively to alter the political context to their own benefit, such as when they would raise the minimum list vote needed to enter parliament from 4% to 5%. Also, as the groups that most influenced legislation and had the greatest likelihood of winning parliamentary seats in the future, they were in a much better position to raise money from other elite groups. It is quite irrelevant that the Hungarian Social Democratic Party can claim the longest history of all the parties that competed in the 1990 election; its leaders now headed a secondary party in Hungarian politics. The critical division between haves and have-nots was made on election day in 1990, and the winners gained dramatic advantages in both the mass and elite politics fields.

125

But there is a price to victory. As a party gains political power, the difficulty of party politics increases. The party completely out of power, while usually damned with a lack of party resources, is also spared the burden of trying to maintain support among various groups. Its internal party network is usually a small group of ideologically driven activists. Mass support is usually isolated to a small, distinct fraction. And elite support rarely exists.

In contrast, a party in power has to maintain the support of groups that often have conflicting interests and views. In the first place, parties in parliament, especially governing parties, always have to deal with different elite groups, including other parties, interest groups, media outlets, and foreign governments. They also have to maintain a high level of support within the mass public. (Even to meet the 5% list vote minimum in Hungary, a party had to be supported by about half a million people.) Unlike appealing to a small fraction with a distinct agenda, these parties have to compete for the support of heterogeneous groups within the mass public. Finally, the competition for elite and mass support requires a large party organization. Unlike a party completely out of power, which can be run by a small group of faithful volunteers, the successful party is virtually always so large—and the stakes are always high enough—that internal factions develop. The party center must maintain support within all three groups at once (i.e., the mass public, elite organizations and active party members) while maintaining a consistent message, a task that can be extremely difficult when they have conflicting interests.

It is at this point that party competence becomes most important. While party competence certainly can help during the rise towards first winning seats, once the party is in parliament, competence becomes a critical factor. A new party usually finds its way into parliament with the help of an extraordinary amount of good fortune, such as the transformation of a political system. But good fortune runs out. As political winds shift, the party must be able adjust to those shifts without undermining the public image it used to build that support.

As will be shown in this and then next two chapters, this is exactly what the new Hungarian parties did not do. Instead of consistent and unified performances, the Hungarians were jubilant in 1989 and early 1990 watched the new parties slip into exaggerated rhetoric, about faces, and failed strategies. They read newspaper editorials by Hungarian Democratic Forum politicians that accused their fellow party members of being Bolsheviks and fascists. They watched the Independent Smallholders' Party divide uncontrollably into multiple parties, with each faction passing resolutions to expel other factions. They saw the Alliance of Free Democrats change overnight from a loyal opposition party to the "enemy" of the Democratic Forum government, which it called dictatorial. It even watched Free Democrats, the radical opponents to socialist dictatorship as late as 1990, join forces with the Socialists in 1991 to fight that Democratic Forum dictatorship.

The Federation of Young Democrats provided the only sense of relief from this unintended political slapstick. Then, FIDESZ abruptly changed the way that it presented itself, switching from a liberal to a conservative ideology and attempting to discard its overwhelmingly popular youth image. The only party to maintain a consistent presentation this period (except maybe the Christian

Democratic People's Party, which at this time acted mostly as a loyal follower of the Democratic Forum) was the Hungarian Socialist Party. Once FIDESZ support began to evaporate in 1993, support for the Socialist party began to rise steadily until it became the most widely supported party in Hungary.

**The Crumbling of the Hungarian Democratic Forum:**
Within three weeks after winning the first competitive elections in nearly a century, József Antall made the first strategic mistake that would lead to the Hungarian Democratic Forum's demise.

The new Prime Minister of Hungary, József Antall, was clearly the person who made the greatest gains during the political transformation. He shot from an obscure museum director to the head of state within a year. But, he took on this position facing problems. First, even as the clear head of the Democratic Forum, Antall was a relatively new figure in the party. He was a conservative historian in a party that emerged from the populist writers movement. It was István Csurka and the other Founding Fathers that had built the national party. Antall had assumed the leadership role because of his expertise in constitutional law. Now that a new government was formed, the populist writers, notably Csurka, wanted to be given a part of the spoils. Csurka was hoping to take charge of the mass media as his tool for rebuilding Hungary's ethical foundation. As the leader of a new government coalition, Antall had other problems as well; he would have to hold together what he referred to as his "natural" Christian-right coalition. The greater problem, besides the populists in the Democratic Forum leadership, was the Independent Smallholders' Party. The Smallholders' Party was calling for a radical re-privatization of farmland to pre-1945 owners, a plan that Antall was hard pressed to either promote or ignore.

The problems facing Antall were serious. The Hungarian populist tradition—or, the part of the tradition from which this generation of populists emerged—was leftist, anti-capitalist, and in this sense very suspicious of the West.[2] International communism had horribly damaged Hungarian national and religious values, populists argued, but international capitalism was capable of producing much the same effect. Populists therefore tended to promote a "third way" philosophy, a social and economic system that was neither entirely capitalist nor socialist but a Central European derivative of the two. The philosophy, while never spelled out in specific terms, did imply independence from both East and West.[3]

The politics of the Independent Smallholders' Party also posed problems for Antall. The Smallholders' won 11% of the parliamentary seats in the 1990 elections; the coalition could not stand without its votes. The primary issue for this party was land compensation. The Independent Smallholders' Party demanded a total reform of the land ownership, including a radical redistribution of rural land to their pre–Communist period owners. Taking this goal seriously was a price that the Antall government had to pay for building his coalition government, but it certainly produced political dangers.

Symbolically, land compensation would be a powerful move for a conservative, nationalist government. However, the radical reform promoted by the Smallholders' Party would produce a political disaster for the Antall government. The Smallholders' Party's goal was to produce an agricultural economy based on small, independently held plots. The chances of these minifarms producing the cheap food on which Hungarians could compete with the large, automated farms developing in Western Europe was, according to most economists, slim.[4] The politics of compensation was complicated further because it was extremely difficult to determine after forty years whom was the rightful owner of a plot of land or section of a state or collective farm. While some wanted to be compensated, others feared that they would be forced to leave the collective farms. The Independent Smallholders' Party was taking an ardent stand on a potentially explosive issue; radical reform would surely undermine the Democratic Forum's support in many circles.

The seriousness of Antall's intra-party and coalition problems becomes even clearer if one takes into consideration the changes in the elite politics field. An outcome of the Hungarian political transformations was that power shifted from Russia to western, capitalist countries: Hungary had to pay back enormous loans; it had to shift trade from eastern to western markets; and it could no longer depend on the Soviet Union for military protection and economic stability. Western pressures on the new government conflicted with many of the coalition's goals, especially those of the Independent Smallholders' Party and the populists in the Democratic Forum. Populists wanted Hungarian ownership of property, but the raising of hard currencies for loan repayment required the government to sell government property to foreign investors. The Smallholders' Party plan to return farm land to former owners would have led to an agricultural economy of minifarms, but to be competitive on western markets, Hungary would need large, automated farms. And Democratic Forum populists wanted to use the Hungarian media as a tool for a national revival, but to become part of the capitalist West, Hungary would have to liberalize its government, including the media. It became Antall's unfortunate job to try to hold together the factions in his party and coalition government and at the same time deal with intense pressures to westernize.

In a multi-party, pluralistic system, the heads of governing parties regularly have to hold together conflicting wings of their respective parties as well as coalition partners with varying interests. It is also not uncommon for the mass public or important factions within the party to place demands on this leadership that conflict with the demands of the elite politics field. To stay in power, these party leaders must be able to deal with these conflicting demands without seriously offending any group whose support they depends on. They must reward or at least placate differing interests while maintaining a consistent party image and keeping the organization unified.

Antall, however, handled his problems another way: the Democratic Forum-Free Democrat Pact. His goal seemed to be to surround himself with confidants—like his brother-in-law, the historian Géza Jeszenszky, and his old friend Árpád Göncz, the Free Democrat candidate for President—centralize power as much as possible, and in the process significantly limit the influence of the populists. Antall had *overtly* undermined the position of a powerful and widely supported group within the Democratic Forum, the populists who had founded the party. In doing this, he seemed unaware or little concerned that his intra-party support could diminish and that he might be provoking a challenge from groups he needed. Before even taking office, Antall had triggered an internal conflict that would resolve itself through the party splitting in half multiple times and virtually self-destructing.

**Sleeping with the Opposition: The Democratic Forum–Free Democrat Pact:**

On April 12, 1990—four days after the Democratic Forum's landslide victory during the second round of the parliamentary elections—the Democratic Forum held its third national meeting. According to Zoltán Bíró, the first party president, Antall used the occasion to dramatically increase his power over the party's governmental work and its relationship with coalition parties. Among other points, Antall emphasized that Hungary would be ungovernable if the parliament maintained the two-thirds requirements for passing certain laws.[5] The implication was clear enough. Some agreement had to be reached with the party's main opponent, the Alliance of Free Democrats, which held ninety-four parliamentary seats and therefore controlled a critical 24% of the votes.

Around the same time, Antall approached the Free Democrat party president, János Kis, to ask for private discussions about the new parliament. He proposed that the two parties secretly reach agreement on some critical issues before the term began. It would later become clear that the negotiations would be not between the Free Democrat and Democratic Forum party leaderships, strictly speaking, but between the Free Democrat leadership on the one side and Antall and his closest allies on the other. The preliminary meeting was between Antall and Péter Tölgyessy, who would become the parliamentary faction leader for the Free Democrats. The negotiations then took place on April 29 between two small groups. On the Free Democrat side sat Kis, Tölgyessy, and Iván Pető, all of whom were members of the Free Democrat administrative board. On the Democratic Forum side sat Antall, Imre Kónya, Katalin Kutrucz (Kónya's wife), László Salamon, and István Balsai. All five on the Democratic Forum side had been elected to parliament; only Antall was a member of the Democratic Forum presidium.[6]

The pact was approved by the Democratic Forum presidium the next day and then announced to the public on May 2, the first day of the new parliament. "In order to ensure the stability of the democratic institutions yet to be created," the pact shifted governmental power to the Prime Minister (and largely away from the Democratic Forum presidium) in several important ways. The Democratic Forum and Free Democrat sides agreed to eliminate a number of two-thirds requirements for legislation important to the Antall Government, making it possible to pass this legislation with a majority vote. The parties also agreed to create a constructive motion of no-confidence, meaning that there could not be a vote of no-confidence against members of the cabinet, only the Prime Minister, and in that case parliament had to propose a person to replace him or her. Third, the President of the Republic would become the Free Democrat candidate, Antall's long-time friend Árpád Göncz. Finally, and the most controversial, the presidents of the Hungarian television and radio companies would be appointed not by the governing coalition but by the President of the Republic, that is, Göncz.[7]

In terms of Hungarian Democratic Forum intra-party politics, the move was a critical blow to the positions of the populist wing. The constructive motion of no-confidence increased the prime minister's power at the expense of the government coalition parties, not the opposition. Antall had effectively given them two options: Either they support his government as a whole, or else they would have to replace the entire government. Moreover, many had expected the presidency to go to populist writer and Democratic Forum founder Sándor Csoóri or possibly a Smallholder MP. Antall instead handed the position to his old friend from the main opposition party. That friend, the liberal Göncz, was also given responsibility to select the presidents of the Hungarian television and radio stations, which took that power out of the hands of Csurka, the Democratic Forum founder who wanted to lead a media crusade against declining Hungarian ethics.

The final issue, choosing the heads of the electronic media, would turn out to be a driving force in the intra-party conflict within the Democratic Forum. If Miklós Haraszti's description is accurate, Antall probably did not even have to negotiate that control away. Haraszti, who focused on media issues in the Alliance of Free Democrats, claimed that the Free Democrats had brought it up in the negotiations with the assumption that Antall would not easily grant this request; it was too important to the Democratic Forum populist wing. However, Haraszti claimed further, Antall agreed with this proposal without much argument.[8]

With the pact, a split within the Democratic Forum leadership began. While Antall centralized governmental power in his own hands, the presidium would continue to be largely run by the populists. Conversely, many of the key populists, including Bíró, Csoóri, and Lezsák, continued primary roles in the presidium without even holding parliamentary seats. Effectively, one part of the leadership ran the government while another part ran the intra-party affairs. Antall had insulted a faction of the leadership that continued to have a considerable following in the party and the public.

As often occurs with these types of mistakes, the first reaction can appear moderate. However, that moderate reaction can hide a deeper conflict. If other factors also come into play, the impact of the initial problem can escalate. A prime minister who holds widespread support can stave off intra-party conflicts easier than one who presides over a dissatisfied public or elite. In the Hungary of 1990, however, Antall was in no position to insult the populist wing of his party. The pact, in and of itself, did not cause disaster for the Democratic Forum, but it would prove to be one of the key elements in a crisis that would soon develop.

## "The Government is Afraid of No One":

Many of the problems Antall faced were completely out of his control. The Antall government inherited an economy in crisis and already undergoing a massive transformation. A massive debt to international creditors and a host of other economic problems produced a situation in which the government had no good options.[9] Early hopes for an alleviation of the interest burden and financial support disappeared by the time the Democratic Forum and its coalition allies became responsible for the economic problems. The government's primary goal was to curb foreign indebtedness. To accomplish this, it needed to take a number of steps—including increasing the monetary base (or "printing money") and selling government securities—that caused inflation to continue rising. On the other hand, it also needed to decrease government spending, partially through privatization, which would reduce the government's financial burden at the same time that it would bring in capital through the sale of state property.

The circumstances at hand, however, made the task difficult and the burden heavy on the Hungarian population. The government had far more state property to sell than interested buyers. Those who did buy state run companies systematically fired large percentages of their workers. Full employment, a guaranteed inefficiency of state socialism, disappeared with the transformation. Unemployment skyrocketed at the same time that social support, like government subsidies to keep food prices low, were disappearing. Beyond even the state subsidies, the soaring inflation—no longer matched by equivalent wage increases, like in the late 1980s—caused the real incomes of even working Hungarians to drop. At the same time, the markets with former Warsaw Pact countries, previously subsidized by the Soviet Union, collapsed. Virtually all Hungarian industries were geared to this market and unprepared for the more competitive Western, capitalist markets. To further the crisis, Yugoslavia, one of Hungary's primary trading partners, soon fell into violent civil war. This market also collapsed partially by the destruction and partially by the subsequent United Nations economic sanctions against Serbia.[10]

Despite the worsening of Hungarians' standard of living, the Democratic Forum and its coalition partners continued to be supported by many Hungarians. In the list votes during the local elections in September, the Hungarian Democratic Forum received just under 20% of the votes. While a drop, these numbers indicate that a substantial percent of the public still supported the Democratic Forum, despite the economic hardships. However, the electoral coalition of the Free Democrats and FIDESZ received just under 21% and 19%, respectively; the two parties won control of many of the local governments, and Free Democrat MP and long-time dissident Gábor Demszky become mayor of Budapest.[11] The Democratic Forum was not the most supported party in September, but it was still supported by nearly a plurality of the public.

And then, in October, disaster struck for the Democratic Forum.

Late on the night of October 24—the day after the national holiday in celebration the 1956 Hungarian Revolution against the Russian occupation and its Stalinist regime—the government declared a 56% increase in gas prices. The timing, just before a weekend when a large percent of Budapest residents would vacation in the countryside, seemed to be a way to slip the enormous hike past public notice. It did, however, catch the attention of taxi drivers on the late shift. Information about the price hike spread among the Budapest taxi drivers across their radios and at gas pumps. A spontaneous, unplanned protest broke out. A large number of private taxi drivers convened outside parliament and demanded a meeting with government officials. The request was refused flatly. The drivers were told instead that their protest was illegal, since they had not been issued a license, and that they should disperse. (In response to taxi drivers yelling statements like "I won't be able to feed my family", one minister responded as television cameras rolled: "The government is afraid of no one.")

Instead of dispersing, the outraged drivers then began blocking the bridges between the Buda and Pest sides of the city. Within a day, the blockade had grown dramatically, and the protesters had blocked every bridge as well as the major roads into the city. Other groups joined the blockade, many apparently seeing it as a general protest against a government perceived responsible for worsening living conditions, but the taxi drivers kept their demands limited to insisting that the gas prices be reduced back to their original levels. They requested that the government meet them for negotiations. Instead of trying to soften the conflict, the Antall government responded that it would not negotiate with illegal protesters, and it threatened the taxi drivers with police intervention and arrest. At the same time, it mobilized a "counter-movement" by government supporters against the protesters—which, ironically, was also illegal.

Budapest immediately fell into shortages in food and other supplies. However, the protesters seemed to hold widespread public support. Despite its threats, the Antall government had its hands tied. The police refused to take action against the protesters, and President Göncz disallowed the deployment of the army. The Antall government was sharply criticized by the FIDESZ parliamentary delegation, and the Free Democrats went as far as to demand its resignation.[12]

The Taxi Blockade was resolved in three days, in time for traffic to begin on Monday morning. Petrol prices were increased by 35% instead of 56%, and future increases would be based more directly on market factors.

The Democratic Forum government was certainly unable to avoid increasing the price of gasoline. However, its handling of that price increase— announcing a 50% jump at night just before a long weekend—and its reaction to the protests that the announcement ignited were avoidable mistakes. The symbolism was damning for the Democratic Forum and its government. The Taxi Blockade began just after the holiday that commemorated the 1956 revolution. In 1956, the government's first response was to state that the protesters were acting illegally and that they should disperse; in 1990, the Democratic Forum government—the government of the party that promised a national spring cleaning of the former regime—reacted much the same way. The line "This is no longer the same country", probably coined by the economist and pundit László Lengyel, expressed what seemed to be the general reaction to the government's handling of this crisis. The government's response seemed to puncture Hungarian optimism towards the transformation and create the impression that politics had in fact not changed since the transformation.

According to the Szonda-Ipsos survey, the Democratic Forum was down to 15% support by January 1991. By May, its support was down to 11%, less than half its popular vote in the election a year before.[13] But, the influence of the Taxi Blockade was not limited to the mass politics field. With public support dropping, the intra-party issues provoked by the Democratic Forum–Free Democrat Pact suddenly surfaced. The internal rebellion of the populists was slowly beginning. On November 14, a few weeks after the Taxi Blockade, Founding Father Zoltán Bíró, the first party president, announced in a public letter to the Hungarian Democratic Forum's membership that he would step out of its presidium as well as the party. A month later, during the organization's fourth national meeting,

Founding Father and Democratic Forum Vice President Csaba Gy. Kiss sent in his resignation from the Presidium, stating that his work for the Democratic Forum would now be as a regular member. He noted that the party was losing its public support at the same time that it was becoming a "presidential regime."

During the same national meeting, another Founding Father, the populist writer Sándor Lezsák, gave a speech about the party's dropping support. He stated that for the Democratic Forum to thrive, it needed to remain "Hungarian", "democratic", and a "forum". Like the Kiss letter, Lezsák connected the Democratic Forum's loss of public support to the decline of the populists' internal position. It should be "Hungarian", in that it should promote the cultural initiatives of the populists. It should be "democratic", in that the party should not be controlled by one person, that is, the Prime Minister. And it should be a "forum", which is probably another reference to the need for internal democratic discussion.[14] It is interesting to note that, according to Lezsák, the Democratic Forum's dropping popularity was caused by the party's internal dynamics, not by the Taxi Blockade or the economic crisis.

Then, in February came the first direct, internal challenge to Antall's leadership. Fifty-two members of the Hungarian Democratic Forum's parliamentary faction announced that they wanted a vote of no confidence against faction leader Imre Kónya. Kónya was a close ally of Antall's. As the head of the Independent Lawyers' Forum, he was a key figure during the Opposition Roundtable and Trilateral Negotiations. He was also a negotiator during the meeting on the Democratic Forum–Free Democrat Pact. Kónya responded to the announcement by demanding that such a vote take place. He survived the challenge by a vote of 76 to 34. But, the highly public internal dissent and challenge was beginning within the party ranks.

**The Media War:**
Following the Taxi Blockade, Democratic Forum members of parliament began publicly quitting the party. The first to drop out, a week after the blockade, was Zoltán Király. Király was a nationally known figure. A member of the Hungarian Socialist Workers' Party, he had been a well-known television reporter from the city of Szeged. In the moderately more open electoral system of 1985, Király was nominated and then elected to parliament against the wishes of the party leadership, and he became a prominent nuisance to Kádár. Involved with the reform circles and the New March Front, he was thrown out of the Socialist party with Zoltán Bíró and others.[15] He ran as number ten on the Democratic Forum national list in 1990, only to publicly quit the party half a year later.

The second to drop, a few weeks later, was János Dénes, who had been a leader in the 1956 revolution and had been involved with opposition work since 1985. It was a bad beginning to a process that would get much worse. By the end of 1991, four more Democratic Forum MP's would become independents or join other parties.

In the post-Taxi Blockade period, Democratic Forum politics changed dramatically. The area in which it probably changed the most was in media politics. As had been discussed above, administration over the electronic media was an important area of the populist wing of the party, especially for István

Csurka, and Antall had negotiated that control away. After the blockade and the party's subsequent drop in public support, the populist wing became more willing to criticize Antall publicly. While there was a demonstration outside the Hungarian Radio Station just before the blockade, it was not a significantly important event. After the blockade, the demonstrations would become a central tool in the developing political struggles.

But there was a second way that the blockade had influenced Hungarian media politics. It was at this point that the Antall government seemed to realize the cost of the Pact.[16] By giving up administrative power, they had set free— others would claim, forfeiting to their main rivals, the Free Democrats—an elite group that could help or hurt their quest to maintain high public support. In this situation, the media was quite willing to broadcast actions, statements, and criticisms that were embarrassing to the government and Antall himself. Under these circumstances, they would have to lure the media into presenting the government and the Democratic Forum in the best light, using techniques that party leaders in countries with a longer tradition of professional, representative politics have become quite expert. The Antall group decided on another route: They began a highly public attempt to replace the heads of the television and radio stations with Democratic Forum loyalists.

Like many party battles, the media war took some time to develop. In the summer of 1990, the new presidents of the television and radio companies— Elemér Hankiss and Csaba Gombár, respectively—were proposed by Antall, supported by all six parliamentary parties, and approved by President Göncz.[17] They began to reorganize their respective companies with the intent to modernizing and westernizing them. They made a public point of refusing interference in appointments or programming policy by the government or any political party. The populists and others on the right who supported cultural policies became dissatisfied with the presidents rather quickly. The first demonstration outside the Hungarian Radio Station was during the October 23 holiday by activists, a day before the blockade; the organizers were associates of Csurka. The first government steps came later in 1990, when it cut financial support at the same time that broadcasting costs rose. Gombár went onto the radio to protest the move, claiming that the cuts were being made for political reasons. In July 1991, the Antall government initiated the appointment of six editors close to the Democratic Forum as vice-presidents of the companies. These vice-presidents, three for each company, would take administrative control over the electronic media. Göncz refused to accept the nominations, and an intense struggle began in the courts, parliament, and the news and print media. Large public demonstrations were held on both sides of the issue. The governing parties froze money to the stations and then created a new television station for Hungarians within and outside the nation's boarders, a station that would present news more favorable to the government. By the end of 1993, the Democratic Forum had won the stake for which it had fought; Hankiss and Gombár left their positions, the Democratic Forum appointees took charge, and these appointees reorganized the companies.[18]

But the cost of winning this one resource, administrative control over the electronic media, was high for the Democratic Forum. Had Antall simply maintained administrative control, he probably could have appointed whomever he wished with opposition complaint but no serious loss of support in any of the three party fields. He could have kept a consistent presentation while manipulating the administration behind the scenes.[19] Instead, Antall made that attempt to control the administration public and, in the process, dramatically switched positions. First, he handed administrative responsibility to Göncz, a Free Democrat. Then, he attacked Göncz for determining who would be presidents of these companies and publicly tried to circumvent his decisions. Had Antall simply maintained his administrative control with the claim of following "the law" or "democratic practices," he would not have been accused of a dictatorial attempt to control the media. But by switching positions, he produced a performance inconsistency, opening himself up to those charges and, it seems, alienating most Hungarian journalists.

### A "Few Thoughts" by István Csurka:

But this switching of positions damaged more than the Antall group's mass and elite political fields. It also had intra-party consequences. By effectively appointing Göncz and then attacking him for creating a biased electronic media, the Prime Minister opened himself up to the rather obvious charge that *he* had created this media biased against Hungarian cultural values. In more general terms, the Antall led Democratic Forum had promised a "national spring cleaning". He also presented himself as the head of a Christian-right coalition and played on patriotic themes, even going so far to claim that he would be the prime minister of all Hungarians (i.e., not just those that lived in Hungary but also those living in neighboring countries.) But, by admitting that he had lost control of the media to the liberals and by claiming that Communists were still in the bureaucracy and working to undermine his government, he opened himself to the charge that there had been no spring cleaning. If someone wanted challenge Antall from within the Democratic Forum, they could certainly claim that Antall had not lived up to either the original goals of the Lakitelek meetings or even his own promises.

István Csurka was certainly a person to take this move. First, he had been largely shut out of a government led by the party that he had helped build. Most painful, he was denied his greatest wish, to use the Hungarian media to reawaken traditional Hungarian values. Second, he had a large following in the rank-and-file and within the parliamentary faction. Third, he had other resources, notably his newspaper *Magyar Fórum [Hungarian Forum]*. Finally, the Antall led Democratic Forum was suffering low public support and internal discontent. Csurka certainly had an opportunity to retake control of the party and play a much greater role in Hungarian politics, and by August 1992, he was ready to challenge Antall.

Often when party politicians want to usurp the positions of the group in power, they begin building pockets of support at the same that they try to decentralize internal power. This process was discussed in Chapter 5: Grósz worked to undermine Kádár by building support within the government apparatus and among other key Socialist politicians at the same time that he tried to shift policy control away from the Politburo; and Pozsgay worked to undermine Grósz by building semi-autonomous party organizations at the same time that he challenged the legitimacy of the Grósz regime through the media. But Csurka was not trained as a party politician. He was trained as a writer. Csurka's move, instead of gradually shifting internal power away from Antall, was to write an essay. As it turned out, that essay would drop like a bomb.

The Csurka Tract, as it is often called, was published on August 20, 1992, in Csurka's newspaper, *Magyar Fórum*. The editorial, taking up eight full newspaper pages minus a few pictures, was titled: "A Few Thoughts on the Two Year Anniversary of the Regime Transformation in Regards to the Hungarian Democratic Forum's New Program." The piece began with a discussion about the goals set forth at the 1987 Lakitelek meeting, the meeting Antall did not attend. That was followed by the argument that the greatest mistake of the Democratic Forum and its government was that it did not finish the political transition immediately, as soon as it came to power. Instead, Csurka argued, Hungary continues to be controlled by Bolsheviks and liberals who, in turn, are connected to an international network of banks and other monetary interests. The reason, says Csurka, is because of the Democratic Forum–Free Democrat Pact. On the pact he wrote: "The goal was not the regime transformation but to secure the interests of the most important people who ruled continuously since 1945. In truth, only the nomenklatura won from the pact." He continued a few paragraphs later: "The government, following the law ratified by a majority in parliament, named three vice presidents for the Radio and Television Stations... The President refused to sign the appointment certificate because the vice presidents officially selected to step into office would take apart the illegally built administrative regime, which belongs to the government's adversaries and the nomenklatura securities built into the pact. Göncz said no because behind him stood the Communist, the reform Communist, the liberal, the radical nomenklatura, the Parisian, the New York, and the Tel Aviv network, and it gave him an order."[20]

Much of the essay is a diatribe against international bankers and the Alliance of Free Democrats. He repeatedly refers to Free Democrat politicians as "Bolsheviks." He mentions a speech from Free Democrat party president János Kis during the 1990 campaign in which Kis proposed a Democratic Forum-Free Democrat coalition government if the Democratic Forum got rid of its right wing, notably Csurka. Csurka points out that this was the same move of Stalinist Mátyás Rákosi towards the Smallholders Party in 1945, just before Rákosi began imprisoning and executing those politically on the right.[21]

But, the more obvious target of his attack was Antall, the man who had negotiated away control of the country to the Communists, the liberals, and the international network of bankers. Emphasizing that the government "needs its own press", he writes:

> *There is a minimum in the ambition for independence, first of all, that one must completely define the underlying goals for the internal politics and the nation, and failing that, if they also don't allow that, then one must inform the people. The government did not complete this minimum, and it did not even attempt to explain*

*why. It couldn't even have accomplish this, because for that it would need its own press and together they needed to inform. But, with the first wrong improvisation, it handed over the press and the media to its opposing powers. From then on there is the unending, constrained allusion that it cannot explain its goals, because the press is oppositional...* [22]

Csurka is inconsistent in his discussion of Antall, sometimes attacking and other times praising the Prime Minister. Csurka even called Antall among the great Hungarian statesmen, like Deák and Bethlen. The problem is obvious; Antall still holds a great deal of support within the party. Csurka's way around this problem is to point out that while Antall is a great leader, he is sick, and he is going to die soon. A sick man cannot lead a party and a nation through difficult times. There is a great deal of weakness, political naiveté, and gullibility within the Democratic Forum, Csurka admits, but this is why Antall needs to teach others the art of politics. [23]

One reason for the explosive reaction to Csurka's essay was his discussion of Jewish people. Csurka expressed concern over the inaccurate claims by some that the Hungarian Democratic Forum was anti-Semitic. He mentioned as an example a report in the *New York Times* the day after the first Lakitelek meeting. According to Csurka, it claimed that anti-Semites founded the new organization. How could the *Times* reach this incorrect conclusion after only one day? Csurka concluded that the liberal opposition (i.e., a group with a number of Jewish-Hungarian leaders, including Kis and Haraszti) must have passed these lies through its international connections with the banks and the press.

Csurka also presented an explanation as to how Jews helped stop Eisenhower from sending troops to assist the 1956 Hungarian Revolution against Russia. Tacitly rejecting the more common argument that Ike wanted to avoid a nuclear war, Csurka gave a different explanation:

*As Eisenhower stood before the difficult decision, with his opinion that the Suez Canal was a much more pressing crisis, about whether to intervene in what the Potsdam Treaty defined as a Soviet sphere of interest, the continuing bloodshed in the Hungarian Revolution, the leaders of the Jewish World Congress, based in New York, eased the decision: They brought it to his attention that in Budapest they are killing Jews.* [24]

**Crumbling from Inside:**

The Hungarian Democratic Forum now entered a full-scale party crisis. The jarring rhetoric of the Csurka Tract produced equally extreme reactions. On an elite politics level, it seemed to do nothing but damage the party. The international reaction to the Csurka Tract was overwhelmingly negative, mostly an outcry that the prominent Democratic Forum politician was promoting anti-Semitism. The tract was even condemned by the United States Congress. On a mass politics level, there was neither a clearly positive nor a clearly negative reaction. In the six months following its publication, aggregate support for the

Democratic Forum did not move significantly from 11%. But the most critical problem was intra-party. Not only did Csurka directly challenge Antall's leadership; he also set off a debate on issues about which the party was deeply divided.

Antall's response was measured. Csurka held a great deal of support in the party, and the Antall group feared that if Csurka presented a direct challenge or left the party, the majority of party supporters and faction members would follow him. In an interview a few days after the article was published, Antall referred to Csurka as a "good-hearted man," but rejected the notion that he was too sick to govern. In parliament about a week later, he distinguished himself from Csurka, saying that he cannot identify himself with the tract's many hurtful and incorrect statements. Antall's first reaction—probably the right one—was to gently disassociate himself from the tract, thereby avoiding the attacks against it without alienating the Csurka supporters.

However, Antall did not control the reaction of other Democratic Forum politicians. Exaggerated rhetoric was not new to the politicians of this party. But now, Democratic Forum politicians began using that rhetorical style against each other. In an article in the newspaper *Népszabadság* (or *People's Freedom*, the most widely read newspaper in Hungary, which many Democratic Forum members believed was a leftist publication,) Democratic Forum MP József Debreczeni wrote that Csurka's writing was completely Nazi ideology. In response, another prominent Democratic Forum member, Jenô Fónay, stated that anyone who condemns people as Fascists in 1992 must be a shameless Bolshevik agent. (He later apologized, pointing out that he is against both Fascism and bolshevism.) A majority within the Democratic Forum parliamentary faction also condemned Debreczeni's article, and Debreczeni was subsequently punished by the party's ethics committee.

At this point, the party began slipping into internal disarray. This stage of internal conflict would last until the summer of 1993, less than a year before the election. Within the Democratic Forum parliamentary group emerged two warring factions, a populist and a national-liberal wing, each forming its own association soon after the Csurka Tract was published. For the next year, Antall and his closest colleagues would try with little success to patch up the conflicts between these groups. Csurka was especially troublesome for the Antall government. He formed the Hungarian Road organization [in Hungarian, *Magyar Út*] which also can be translated more figuratively as the "Hungarian Way." Its point was that Hungary should follow a strictly Hungarian way through the transition instead of a foreign method imposed by outsiders, like Western bankers. He also began making a habit of publicly criticizing the Antall government as well as making statements that embarrassed that group. For example, Csurka began arguing publicly that Hungary had legal claim to territories now part of neighboring countries, statements that certainly could not help the Antall government's attempts to build working relationships with those neighbors and the West.

At this point, Antall was working desperately to keep his government afloat. His party and his parliamentary faction was falling apart beneath him, and as MP's quit the party, his majority receded closer and closer to fifty percent. To make problems even worse, his coalition partner, the Independent Smallholders'

Party, was also falling apart. Without a doubt, the Smallholders' Party was the party that entered parliament with the least collective political experience. While a few very old members had been involved in the 1945 party of a similar name, the vast majority had absolutely no political background. It was also the party with by far the least amount of higher education. Only about 5% of Smallholder MP's had "little doctorates"—a degree somewhere between the American masters degree and Ph.D.—far less than the other parties. Many of these MP were farmers or laborers of some sort. The problem with this, as Pierre Bourdieu points out, is that many of the most basic skills of politics, like debate and other areas of communication, are passed on through institutions of higher education.[25]

The Independent Smallholders' Party began falling into internal disarray already in 1991, with different groups within the party expelling each other and publicly invalidating each others decisions. In August, representatives of the Independent Smallholders' Party and the closely related National Smallholders' Party met to discuss combining. Instead of joining forces, the meeting slipped into a shouting match, and the National Smallholders' Party stormed out, publicly announcing that it would end all negotiations with the Independent Smallholders' Party. Two months later, the parliamentary faction and governing body, working independently, began expelling prominent members. Then, on November 4, the faction suspended party president István Torgyán's faction membership. Two days later, they demanded that Torgyán resign as party president. In response, Torgyán—who was accused of having worked as spy for the government during the previous regime—strengthened his hold of party's governing body.

By the end of the month, the party split. A small group of Smallholder MP's followed Torgyán out of the faction and the coalition. They subsequently won the court battle to retain the party name. The larger group remained in the coalition. But, even after the split, this faction continued to suffer internal turmoil. It divided further into multiple parties, each with the word "Smallholder" somewhere in its name. During the upcoming years, Antall repeatedly met with this group in an attempt to keep his government from collapsing. With great effort he succeeded, but in the 1994 elections, four Smallholder parties ran candidates on party lists.

The Smallholders MP's inability to maintain working relationships with each other made the crisis within the Democratic Forum even more acute. The government was in jeopardy of collapsing. It would seem that it was in no Democratic Forum politician's self-interest to have its government collapse before the term has ended. Yet, even as the possibility of a governmental collapse increased, the conflict grew more intense. The conflict finally came to a head in the summer of 1993. The party took another blunt move. On June 1, it publicly announced that six of its MP's, members of both the populist and national-liberal wings, would be expelled from the party's parliamentary faction, and several had their party memberships suspended. Csurka and Debreczeni were among those expelled from the party. This move was followed by many others quitting the party as well. In total, twenty Democratic Forum members of parliament quit the party that summer—less than a year before the election—to become independent or join another party. A large segment followed Csurka out of the party in mid-July. Csurka formed a new party, the Hungarian Justice and Life Party [*Magyar*

*Igazság és Élet Pártja*], which received recognition as a parliamentary faction in September 1993.

In the end, the Democratic Forum government survived intact until the end of the term, as Graph 5.1 shows. The price of internal conflict was almost the destruction of the government coalition, which would have been a disastrous loss in the elite politics field. In the mass politics field, support for the Democratic Forum hovered around 9% and 10% through most of 1993, as the conflict raged. With aggregate data, one can only speculate whether the highly public conflicts had helped keep the Democratic Forum at this low level. There is, however, one clear way in which the Democratic Forum's intra-party problems would translate into a poor performance in the mass politics field. The internal conflicts and decentralization of power opened the door for a new struggle for control of the party, a struggle that reached its height after Csurka and others had left. This internal struggle for power, coupled with the political inexperience of the party leadership, would make a unified campaign effort in 1994 virtually impossible. Low party competence, both in unifying a large political organization and in running an electoral campaign, would strike one last crushing blow to the Democratic Forum's chances to hold onto power. See Graph 5.1.

### The Rise of Sándor Lezsák:

On December 12, 1993, Prime Minister József Antall passed away at the age of sixty-one. The Minister of Interior, Péter Boross, was selected as the replacement by a joint meeting of the Democratic Forum's parliamentary faction and the party's national committee, which is the intra-party body that is both larger and less powerful than the presidium. While Boross would play an important role in the five months before the election, other members of the party leadership were quickly becoming more central. The first was Founding Father Lajos Für. A historian close to the populists, Für is credited with helping bring conservatives like Antall into the populist Hungarian Democratic Forum in 1988, and he subsequently played a peacemaker role between warring factions within the party. As the party struggled internally and the need for a peacemaker increased, Für rose in importance. The second figure was Antall supporter Tamás Szabó. Szabó, the manager of the upcoming 1994 parliamentary campaign, was made Minister Without Portfolio in March 1993. Effectively, he became the minister that headed privatization. The third and, as it will turn out, most important figure in the post-Antall period was Founding Father Sándor Lezsák.

Like Für, Lezsák had played a primary role in the Democratic Forum since the beginning. It was at Lezsák's country house in Lakitelek that the organization held its founding meetings in 1987 and 1988. By most accounts, an antagonism between Lezsák and Antall began very early, possibly because the young writer (accurately) saw the conservative historian as a serious challenge to his own position in the new organization. This conflict subsequently translated into the struggle between Lezsák and Szabó.

Unlike Antall, Lezsák's rise to power seemed unrelated to any competencies he might have brought the party. Lezsák had other resources in his favor. First, of the nine Democratic Forum founders, he was one of only three left in the party. Of the most prominent founders, only he and Für remained in the presidium: Bíró and Csengey left soon after the Taxi Blockade; Csoóri became head of the Hungarian World Organization, and Csurka created his own party. Lezsák could claim to be the head of the populist wing and the bearer of the Democratic Forum tradition.    Second, the internal conflicts produced reorganization that put Lezsák into important positions.    In 1993, Für quit the role of "administrative president"—effectively, the head of the presidium—because of his frustration over the failed negotiations between the populist and national liberal wings of the party.   The next person in line for that position was Lezsák. Third, Lezsák was a close ally of two other key Democratic Forum politicians: Prime Minister Boross and the treasurer.   Finally, the internal crisis and Antall's death decentralized power enough in the party that there was no clear successor to Antall.    There was no way for the Antall group to shut the door on this rising figure from the populist wing.[26]

The struggle for power between the Lezsák and Antall groups would continue into 1996, when the Democratic Forum split into two parties.   Lezsák won control over the Hungarian Democratic Forum, and a group including Iván Szabó, Tamás Szabó, Lajos Für, and Géza Jeszenszky formed a new party, the Hungarian Democratic People's Party.  Besides having roughly the same name and being unable to clarify the differences between the two parties, by 1996 it became clear to virtually everyone following Hungarian politics that new parties had virtually no chance of surviving.  Within a month, the new party disappeared from the political map: In the mass politics field, it had virtually no support; in the elite politics field, all the other parties abandoned it, probably because it had no significant public support.   In this way, by mid-1996, Lezsák became the party president and key player of the Hungarian Democratic Forum.

**Stumbling Through the 1994 Campaign:**
While the long-term effect of the internal conflicts was a party split— which was followed by a drop in public support for the Hungarian Democratic Forum and the disappearance of the new party—the immediate effect was that it helped undermine the party's ability to run an effective parliamentary campaign in 1994.  As the party that governed during an economic depression and unsettling social transformation, the Democratic Forum entered the campaign in a difficult position.  Low party competence increased those problems in two ways.  First, the internal power struggle was played out in a way that undermined the party's ability to put together a coherent campaign.   Both Lezsák (the head of the presidium) and Szabó (the campaign manager) tried to run the campaign, each using respective resources against the other.   Second, the party used campaign techniques that would not attract public support, apparently against the suggestion of its advisors.  An anonymous source within the campaign pointed out this second problem this way:

> *You should understand that the Democratic Forum politicians were armchair democrats; they understood democracy on an abstract level but weren't experienced in practical application. They learned much about campaign politics during the 1990 campaign.  However, the polling data showed that things had*

*changed dramatically by 1994... Lezsák was the campaign head
in 1990. After Antall got sick, he decided that he was going to
rush in and save the day. He and his group controlled the purse
strings. The campaign budget was around 8 million dollars.
One-sixth was spent on the electronic media; it should have been
more like half. Instead, the campaign did things like send flower
seeds and pens to prospective voters. The flower seeds didn't
even contain a campaign message—just the logo. Flower seeds
don't get you elected. I'm sure that Free Democrat supporters
happily put the seeds into their gardens and then voted against
us.*[27]

Indeed, the Hungarian Democratic Forum campaign flew in the face of the
political reality of an unpopular party governing over a depression. Its campaign
posters seemed to pretend that the public was not suffering from bad economic
circumstances. One poster showed five trees, one for each year from 1990 to
1994; the trees grew dramatically, with 1990 being the smallest and 1994 by far
the largest. In contrast, most Hungarians would probably have drawn the trees
withering; the Democratic Forum was taking credit for massive growth, which
certainly contradicted the reality of economically insecure people whose standard
of living had dropped. Another poster had a large picture of Boross, the candidate
for Prime Minister, with the line: "Thank you for the calm; it is the reward for
patience." It is unclear what calm the poster was referring to, since Hungary was
suffering from racing inflation, widespread unemployment, and conflict with
neighboring countries, not to mention being next door to the Yugoslavian civil
war.[28] The anonymous source gave another example, which has both mass and
elite politics implications:

*[Polls at the time] showed that the mood in the country was that
privatization was selling out the country to foreigners. There was
something to this thought, of course, but the reality of the
situation made it impossible to avoid. Lezsák decided to run an
ad titled: "Thank you for your trust" and listed foreign companies
that had bought privatized land... Keeping in mind perceptions at
the time, this move was suicidal. To make matters worse, they
misspelled the names of many of these companies. Then,
reporters called up the company headquarters to ask them if they
knew that the party was using their name for political gain. Shell
Oil in particular was extremely upset; they said that they had
been in Hungary long before the Democratic Forum had gotten
into power.*[29]

In the end, the Hungarian Democratic Forum received just fewer than 12%
of the list votes in the 1994 parliamentary elections. It dropped from 164 seats in
1990 to 38 seats after the 1994 election. There are many reasons for its defeat, not
the least being its governing over a depression. Low competence nonetheless
seemed to contribute to the problem. The use of jarring, extreme rhetoric; the
combative internal conflicts; the reaction to protesters in a way that echoed the

previous regime; and the presenting of campaign themes that made no sense in their political context: All these reflect a group in a new environment not sure of how to go about competing for political power.

**Graph 5.1**
**The Government Coalition's Slide Toward Collapse, 1990-94**

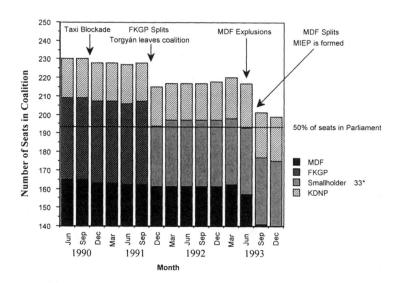

MDF – Hungarian Democratic Forum
FKGP – Independent Smallholders' Party
KDNP – Christian Democratic People's Party
MIEP – Hungarian Justice and Life Party

* "Smallholders 33" is the faction from the Independent Smallholders' Party (FKGP) that did not follow Torgyán out of the coalition but subsequently split into several more parties. This faction began with thirty-three members.

Sources: *Hungarian Political Yearbook, 1991*, pp. 498-517; *Hungarian Political Yearbook, 1992*, pp. 475-89; *Hungarian Political Yearbook, 1993*, pp. 432-40; *Hungarian Political Yearbook, 1994*, pp. 317-36;

# Notes:

[1] Malcolm Punnett and Gabriella Ilonszki (1994) "Leading Democracy: The Emergence of Party Leaders and Their Roles in the Hungarian Parties." *The Journal of Communist Studies and Transition Politics*, vol 10, no. 3, September. Terry Cox and Andy Furlong, eds. Special Issue: *Hungary: The Politics of Transition*, pp. 101-19. The quote is from page 113.

[2] By the time the new government formed, all the major parties promoted modernization and westernization, but they defined these terms differently. On one extreme, liberals supported following western countries as models; on the other, populists believed that modernization requires a return to traditional Hungarian values and sense of community. In the latter case, I believe, "westernization" and "modernization" were more rhetorical tools than seriously held goals.

[3] For further discussion on this issue, see Péter Hanák (1996) "The Anti-Capitalist Ideology of the Populists" in *Populism in Eastern Europe*, edited by Joseph Held (Boulder: East European Monographs), Distributed by Columbia University Press, pp. 145-61; also Miklós Lackó, "Populism in Hungary", *Populism in Eastern Europe*, pp. 107-28.

[4] Small, independent plots had become a prominent part of this economy during the Kádár period. But, their survival had been based on interdependence with the large cooperative and state farms and on excessively hard work by the owners. At this point, even the cooperatives and state farms were in deep trouble. The Kádár government had subsidized food prices, and the command economy had led to many costly investments for the farms. Following the transformation, the subsidies disappeared, and the high inflation and interest rates made investments into more efficient equipment extremely difficult. Production costs rose twice as fast as gross profits. By 1992, half of the Hungarian farm cooperatives were working in the red. Peter Agócs and Sándor Agócs, 1994, "The Change was but an Unfulfilled Promise: Agriculture and the Rural Population in Post–Communist Hungary", *East European Politics and Society*, 8 no. 1, pp. 32–57.

[5] Zoltán Bíró's interview on *Televízió A Hét [Television: The Week]*. See *Hungarian Political Yearbook*, 1991, p. 472.

[6] The lists are based on the recollection of János Kis. The critical point, that the content of the meeting was kept a secret from the Hungarian Democratic Forum presidium, is demonstrated by numerous other sources. Interview with János Kis.

[7] István Stumpf, "Evolution of Party Politics", In *Lawful Revolution in Hungary, 1989–94*, Edited by Béla Király. (Boulder: East European Monographs), Distributed by Columbia University Press, footnote 30 on p. 115; Andrew Arató, 1995, "Election, Coalition, and Constitution in Hungary," *The New Hungarian Quarterly*; István Kukorelli, 1994, "The Government and the President of the Republic: The Head of State in the Line of Five," In *Balance: The Hungarian Government*, Edited by Csaba Gombár et. al, 1990–1994, (Budapest: Korridor); Zoltán Farkas "The Antall Government's 'Success Story': Media Policy", In *Balance: The Hungarian Government*, Edited by Csaba Gombár et. al, 1990–1994, (Budapest: Korridor); "A Paktum; A Magyar Demokrata Forum és a Szabad Demokraták Szövetsége megállapodása", In *Magyarország Politikai Évkönyve, 1991*, Edited by Sándor Kurtán et. al, (Budapest: Economix), pp. 428–9.

[8] Interview with Haraszti.

[9] The debt was developed in the decades following Kádár's 1968 economic reforms, in which there was a generally recognized social compromise: On the one hand, the government permitted greater social freedoms and improved the standard of living; on the other, the population would not challenge the party's authority over the government and public institutions. The economic system was not particularly efficient, and

Hungarian production, for a slew of reasons, could rarely compete on Western markets. A significant portion of the improvements in living standards was therefore financed through foreign loans. For a detailed discussion on the development of these problems, see Nigel Swain, 1992, *Hungary; The Rise and Fall of Feasible Socialism*, (London: Verso).

[10] Zoltán Farkas, 1994, "The Antall Government's Economic Policy," In *Balance: The Hungarian Government, 1990–1994*, Edited by Csaba Gombár et. al, (Budapest: Korridor); Martin Tardos, 1995, "Change of Regime: Promising Development or Severe Crisis", In *Lawful Revolution in Hungary, 1978–94*, Edited by Béla Király, (Boulder: East European Monographs), Distributed by Columbia University Press.

[11] Tóka, "Parties and their Voters", pp. 136-7. The figures are based on list votes from settlements with over 10,000 inhabitants.

[12] Máté Szabó, 1992, "The Taxi Driver Demonstration in Hungary—Social Protest and Policy Change", In *Flying Blind; Emerging Democracies in East–Central Europe*, Edited by György Szoboszlai, (Budapest: Hungarian Political Science Association), pp. 357-81.

[13] http://www.szondaipsos.hu/partpref/

[14] *Hungarian Political Yearbook*, 1991, pp. 492.

[15] Tôkés, *Hungary's Negotiated Revolution*, pp. 204-5.

[16] Zoltán Farkas makes this point about the government's reaction to the blockade, though he believes that the Democratic Forum's loss in the local elections played a part as well. Regardless of whether one or both had influenced their thinking, it is clear that the government began changing its stance towards the electronic media late in 1990, right after the blockade. See Farkas, "The Antall Government's 'Success Story': Media Policy", p. 332.

[17] Zoltán Farkas states this as follows: "according to certain sources, both Elemér Hankiss and Csaba Gombár were proposed by József Antall as indeed he 'invented' Árpád Göncz for President of the Republic. Péter Tölgyessy claims to have handed over a list of several names to József Antall in the summer of 1990 and the Prime Minister picked Csaba Gombár from the list." Ibid, p. 332.

[18] Ibid, pp. 324-53

[19] Many claim that the Socialist–Free Democrat government (which took charge in 1994) followed this less overtly confrontational approach. During a period of intense media scrutiny over alleged fraud, the highly critical and very popular television news-magazine *Objective* was suddenly cancelled for "budgetary reasons." The opposition parties complained, but otherwise the cancellation had little impact on the Socialists' high levels of support.

[20] István Csurka, "Néhány gondolat a rendszerváltozás két esztendeje és az MDF új programja kapcsán" ["A Few Thoughts on the Two Year Anniversary of the Regime Transformation in Regards to MDF's New Program."] *Margyar Fórum*, August 20, 1992.

[21] Ibid.

[22] Ibid.

[23] Ibid.

[24] Ibid. The phrase "in Budapest they are killing Jews" is most likely based on the supposition that most Communists, including members of its secret police, are Jews. Killing a Communist would therefore be equivalent to killing a Jew: "in Budapest [Christian Hungarians] are killing [Communist] Jews."

[25] Richard Jenkins (1992) *Pierre Bourdieu*, (New York: Routledge), pp. 103-10, especially 108.

[26] *Hungarian Political Yearbook, 1994,* pp. 287-316, plus interview with anonymous source.

[27] Interview anonymous source.

[28] *Hungarian Political Yearbook, 1995,* pp. 72-81, 127-34.

[29] Interview anonymous source.

Chapter 6:

# Fluttering of the Free Democrats, 1990-1994

From a political science perspective, Hungarian politics in the 1990s presents a number of surprises. One surprise is the movement of public support from party to party in the 1991 to 1994 period. With the Hungarian Democratic Forum having had its public support cut in half by early 1991, and with the other two government coalition partners also struggling during this period, one would expect public support to switch to the opposition parties in parliament. One could also make some reasonable guesses at which opposition parties would gain from the Democratic Forum's losses. In the particular circumstances of Hungarian politics in the early 1990s, one might predict one of the following outcomes to the public abandoning the Democratic Forum:
1.  Public support might have shifted evenly to each opposition party in parliament: The Alliance of Free Democrats, the Federation of Young Democrats (FIDESZ), and the Hungarian Socialist Party;
2.  It might have shifted evenly to opposition parties not in the previous regime: the Free Democrats and FIDESZ;
3.  It might have shifted mostly to the main opposition party, the Free Democrats;
4.  Public support might have shifted back to the opposition party that had ruled before the transition, the Hungarian Socialist Party.

But, the movement of party support in 1990 and 1991 fits none of these patterns. As public support for the Democratic Forum dropped in this period, support for FIDESZ, the smallest opposition party, rose. At this point, support for the Free Democrats seemed to remain relatively stable. Then, support for the Free Democrats dropped as well, and FIDESZ support rose even farther. These changes are unexplainable from the standpoint of voters simply rejecting an unpopular government. In terms of the context alone—a three-party coalition governing over an economic decline and a difficult social restructuring—the rise of support for the smallest opposition party and fall in support for the main opposition party makes little sense.

The early problems of the Free Democrats and success of FIDESZ are also confusing if one looks at the distribution of resources—that is, party resources unrelated to competence. In 1990, the Free Democrats held ninety-four parliamentary seats (24% of the total) and was the main opposition party. In comparison, FIDESZ held only twenty-two seats, or 6% of the total. In the mass politics field, the Alliance of Free Democrats was the second most supported party, and much of the Hungarian public seemed to credit the Free Democrats for their extended, consistent stance against the Socialist regime; it received 21% of the list vote in 1990. FIDESZ received only 9%. By many accounts, the Free

149

Democrats had also developed strong ties with powerful western organizations; it would therefore be able to raise funds for campaigning and other activities. By the same accounts, FIDESZ had little financial support.[1] Finally, the Alliance of Free Democrats—once known as a party with an elite but no rank-and-file—had built a national party network that it could use for future campaigns. It now had both experts on policy issues and people to run a party operation. FIDESZ's network was smaller and far less organized. For example, while the Free Democrats ran candidates in all but two single seat districts, FIDESZ had run candidates in less than half of these races in 1990.

But, if competence at party politics is taken into consideration, an advantage for FIDESZ vis-à-vis the Alliance of Democrats might be found. The FIDESZ leadership was dominated by lawyers who were exposed to Western politics during early adulthood at the Bibó Collegium. They were also young, which meant that they had far less to unlearn as they entered this new political arena. While both parties were led by former dissidents, the Free Democrat leadership was much more experienced at dissident politics. Indeed, just as the populist writers had a tendency to write when they should have been building coalitions, the Free Democrat leadership would tend to revert to tactics from its hard-core dissident past. The critical problem for the Free Democrats from 1990 to 1992 was the transition from radical movement to party politics; it was, in a nutshell, the problem of replacing one type of competence for another. As will be show below, it was the lack of experience in party politics coupled with a tendency to reintroduce strategies of the democratic opposition that led to a crisis in the party, which in turn translated to a significant drop in public support.

### Party Competence and the Alliance of Free Democrats:

After entering the new parliament in 1990, the Free Democrat leadership faced a number of serious intra-party problems. The first was that they had virtually no background in or experience that was analogous to running a political party. Most of the people on the eleven-member administrative board had been "hard-core" members of the Budapest dissident community; all but one had some connection to the underground publication *Beszélô*, for example. In other words, the Free Democrat leadership had effectively been trained as intellectual subversives. They had a background as thinkers comfortable with the politics of intellectual debate, and their underground work included a great deal of writing. Until the very end, that intellectual energy was geared primarily towards undermining a regime's basis of power. Moving from this politics to party politics, including running a large bureaucratic organization, was a significant transition for this group.

Moreover, most of the Free Democrat politicians had virtually no political background whatever before 1989. Most had entered the organization just as the struggle to undermine Hungarian Communism had reached its energetic peak. Their political competencies were therefore built within a short, atypical political context. They had been attracted by the aggressive fight to topple the regime—the "radical" politics of the Free Democrats—and in early 1990 they were most familiar with that radicalism. They too had no time to develop the competencies that they would need for party politics.

This lack of experience in the pragmatics of party politics led to another problem. Power within the Alliance of Free Democrats was quite decentralized. The philosophers, sociologists, and writers in the party leadership recognized on an intellectual level the importance of building a hierarchical, bureaucratic organization, but they had difficulty translating that intellectual understanding into the practical, day-to-day running of the party. So, while János Kis was pushing through administrative changes, like having set agendas at administrative board meetings and creating more specific governing rules, the party as a whole was run through loose and decentralized decision-making processes. This lack of centralization meant that an unhappy membership could significantly hurt the leadership's political ambitions; it could even vote the party president out of power.[2]

So, on the one hand, the party leadership did not secure power into its own hands. Oddly, on the other hand, that leadership also did not take very good steps to appear democratic. The former dissidents in the party center did not look much like the rest of the party, including the parliamentary faction as a whole, which was much more diverse. Moreover, the center was heavily based in Budapest; of the ten administrative board members that ran for parliament in 1990, *all ten* ran as single-seat district candidates in Budapest—which is to say that there was not a single candidate on the board from outside the capital city.

This Budapest–country distinction within the Alliance of Free Democrats can be shown another way: 44% (14 out of 32) of the Free Democrat single-seat district candidates in Budapest were members of the democratic opposition; only 7% (10 out of 137) of the Free Democrat single-seat district candidates outside of Budapest had been members. Furthermore, those fourteen Budapest candidates were mostly major figures in the dissident opposition; the ten candidates outside Budapest were minor, peripheral figures largely unknown for their dissident activities.[3] The Free Democrat leadership allowed an identifiable distinction to emerge between its center, made up mostly of Budapest intellectuals from the democratic opposition, and the rest of its membership, a symbolic split that could help create an internal crisis for the Free Democrats.

**Political Theater and the Democratic Forum-Free Democrat Pact:**
If we understand "government" and "opposition" in terms of public perception, then the Alliance of Free Democrats blurred its advantageous role as the main opposition party within the first week of the new parliament.

The Free Democrats signed the pact with the Democratic Forum in reaction to two perceived problems. The first was in its elite politics. The Free Democrat leadership was concerned about moves by the populist wing of the Democratic Forum, especially Csurka's plan to retain government control over the media. In this field, the Free Democrats gained direct influence in certain policy areas through the pact. While it forfeited the veto power that it would have held in laws requiring a two-thirds majority, it was able to make its own candidate, Árpád Göncz, the President of the Republic. The pact also shifted control over the electronic media away from the conservative government and its populist wing to Göncz and a committee in which all six parties had equal influence.

151

The intra-party field was another reason that the Free Democrats entered the pact. The electoral loss to the Democratic Forum in 1990 produced an intra-party concern for the Free Democrat leadership. The party had been built rapidly on repeated successes over the previous half year, especially with the referendum campaign and then with the Danube-Gate scandal. The party even advertised itself as the one most capable of accomplishing feats with the slogan: "We know! We dare! We do!" The electoral loss had punctured a hole into the rank-and-file's euphoria. The party leadership feared that this loss might prompt internal dissent. With this deal, the Free Democrat defeat turned into a partial victory. The party had gained several important governmental resources, or at least had taken those resources out of the hands of its main opponents.[4]

But, in terms of public image, the pact had weakened the Free Democrats' ability to present a distinct role. The Democratic Forum could play the roles of government, and both FIDESZ and the Socialists could play the roles of opposition. But the Free Democrats were caught in an unclear role between the two. So, while the government could take credit for every change that the public might find positive, and while FIDESZ could capitalize on every problem the government had, the Free Democrats could take credit for almost nothing at the same time that it lost the legitimacy of complete separation from criticism. So, for example, every Free Democrat criticism of media policy could be countered by the argument that it, not the government, was responsible.

But, the pact was not a damning problem for the Free Democrats the way that it was for the Democratic Forum. The unhappy marriage did not cause a cause a split within the party. However, it did lead to other problems. It seemed to weaken the Free Democrats' public position vis-à-vis FIDESZ, which could be one reason why the latter gained support in the first six months of the new government while Free Democrat support remained steady. This inability to capitalize on the Democratic Forum's problems added to a growing internal perception that the leadership was making bad decisions and the party was underachieving. This intra-party perception would turn out to be far more important than the real extra-party problems that the Free Democrat leadership faced.

The Free Democrats weakened their public performance further, in comparison to FIDESZ, through its rhetoric style. Free Democrat politicians had a tendency to return to long-standing intellectual debates between the liberals and populists. Possibly the best example was a debate in parliament about the "Jewish question." While a Free Democrat MP was speaking about something unrelated, someone from the government coalition apparently yelled: "hordót a zsidóknak", which could be translated as: "He helped the Jews." The Free Democrat faction immediately reacted to this statement with anger, and parliament quickly moved into extended debate over issues related to Hungarian Jewry. This debate typified the developing conflicts between the Free Democrats and the government coalition. The issues of Hungarian Jews were closely related to the philosophical issues that divided the liberals and populists. But, any direct policy content was lost in the debate. By getting sucked into it, the Free Democrats and the government coalition were letting themselves appear detached from public concerns, which was entirely to the advantage of FIDESZ, which stayed clear of the issue. To make matters worse, after careful analysis, phonetic experts announced that the MP had not yelled "hordót a zsidóknak," but "hordót a szónoknak": "He helped the speaker."

### The Former Dissidents' "New" Strategy:

As 1990 progressed, the Free Democrats remained in a good mass politics position. While FIDESZ seemed to benefit the most from the government's problems, the Free Democrats did not lose much ground from May to October: During the parliamentary elections in May, the Free Democrats had won 21.4% of the list votes; during the local elections in September, it won 20.6%. FIDESZ, in comparison, had far more supporters in the local elections than during the parliamentary elections. It received 18.7% of the list vote in September, more than double the 9.0% of the list vote during the parliamentary election a mere six months earlier.[5] So, while the Free Democrats did not gain public support from the government coalition's early problems, it was still in a strong position in the mass politics field, likely stronger than the Federation of Young Democrats.

But, there was a fundamental problem for the Free Democrat leadership. There was dissatisfaction in the party, both among the MP's and through much of the organization, a sense that the party was not as successful as it could be. At the time that this organization expanded in late 1989 and early 1990, the party was forging ahead with repeated, dramatic successes as well as a clear political program. Now, the party that knew, dared, and did seemed to be making repeated mistakes. Even with the victories in local elections, there was a sense within the party that something had been lost, what Zoltán Ripp referred to as the "we didn't join *this* party" phenomenon.

The problem, it seems, was that the political context had changed but the leadership's political experiences had not. A year before, when the focus was on driving the final stake into the heart of Hungarian state socialism, this group of radical dissidents had brought applicable competencies to the struggle. They knew how to use a nationally televised signing of a negotiated agreement to further undermine a regime, and they knew how to further discredit that regime by showing proof that it was still spying on its citizens. But, once the new, multi-party field was established, that radicalism was no longer useful. The party leadership tried to shift its strategies to the new context, but now they were novices unable to take full advantage of circumstances that favored them.

The analysis of many party members was different. They argued that the party's problem was that it had abandoned its radical past and that the solution was to return to that radicalism. The leadership was inclined to follow this prognosis and return to strategies that had succeeded in the past, strategies with which the leadership was far more familiar.[6] Hungarian political scientist András Bozóki stated the problem in a similar way. He summarizes what will be discuss next as follows:

> *[The Alliance of Free Democrats] emerged from the Network [of Free Initiatives], and its leaders kept their "movement" attitude for a long time. The new party was successful as long as it could understand politics within the framework of a movement. The last*

> *chance for this was the Taxi Blockade. From this perspective, neither the regime opposition nor the announcement to take over the government were effective, because it could not arouse the public with a 'movement'. The political elite's slow professionalization and bureaucratization left less and less room for the previous critical, intellectual perspectives. The leadership's painful defeat made it clear that the situation had changed, and a significant part of the party's intellectual circle became disillusioned with politics.*[7]

The first indication of this return to earlier strategies came during the Taxi Blockade in late October. The Free Democrats' reaction was to demand that the government immediately step down. Free Democrat politicians also joined the demonstrators against the government. (In comparison, the FIDESZ leadership also harshly criticized the government's handling of the crisis, but they kept the criticism within the framework of a loyal opposition: They joined neither the protests nor the Free Democrats' demand for a resignation.) The Free Democrats' reaction was arguably appropriate for the circumstances: There was a spontaneous protest against the government, and that government immediately took a confrontational role against the protesters. However, in terms of multi-party politics, that harsh of a stand is usually successful only in a particular political context: When the public considers the government clearly in the wrong. In another setting, the audience might interpret the harsh stand as the opposition simply being power-hungry. It could undermine the party's claim to be working towards a collective good.

Then, in February 1991, the Free Democrats made a sudden and dramatic shift in its presentation. Admitting that the Democratic Forum-Free Democrat Pact was "a mistake", the Free Democrats took an even harsher stand against the government. During a two day meeting—and without the backdrop of civil protest or an equally extreme crisis—party president János Kis announced that the party was no longer the opposition to but the adversary of the Democratic Forum government. [In Hungarian, *"már nem ellenzéke, hanem ellenfele vagyunk a kormánynak"*.] He also announced that the Free Democrats were prepared to take over the government immediately.

The party's announcement that it was now the government's foe was prompted by intra-party and elite politics factors. On the intra-party level, there was the growing dissatisfaction with Free Democrat politics following the transition, the "we didn't join *this* party" feeling. On the elite politics level, there were signs that the Democratic Forum government might soon collapse.[8] However, the move produced no positive effects for the Alliance of Free Democrats: Its public support dropped; the intra-party discontent increased; and the government did not fall.

After announcing its adversarial relationship with the government, the party was out maneuvered by FIDESZ, which used the occasion to take a moderate (and "pragmatic") position focused on policy. In March, after the Free Democrats stated that they refused to debate the land compensation law any more, FIDESZ proposed that the six parties sit down in special meetings to work out there differences on major policy issues. Antall quickly announced his support for the idea with minor revisions, and each of the government coalition factions also stated their support. The Free Democrats were cornered into a no-win situation: It could either reverse its earlier stands by joining discussions on a topic it refused to discuss, creating a performance contradiction, or appear to be the only party unwilling to work out the country's problem. In either case, the party would undermine a critical component of its presentation: The appearance that it was promoting a collective good. The Free Democrats joined the negotiations with their proclaimed enemies; these negotiations fell apart by mid-May.

According to the Szonda Ipsos poll, public support for the Free Democrats dropped from 20% in January, 1991 to 16% in May 1991; if these figures are accurate (and not just the random fluctuation of sample data), the Free Democrats lost about one out of every five supporters. Over the same period, FIDESZ support rose from 27% to 39%; in May, 1991, it already had more than twice the public support of the any other party, with the Free Democrats coming in second. Free Democrat support would hover between 16% and 20% over the next half year months—though it would remain far behind FIDESZ—but the memberships' perception of failure in maintaining mass support would help promote the intra-party belief that the party was in trouble. The intra-party problem was not that the Free Democrats had dropped dramatically in public support since entering parliament but that FIDESZ seemed to be making most of the gains from the government coalition's problems.

Then, the Free Democrat leadership took another step reminiscent of its past. It formed the Democratic Charter, an organization with a symbolic reference to Charter 77 and a structure much like the Network of Free Initiatives. The Democratic Charter was a loosely structured network of people unified against what it defined as the Democratic Forum government's attempt to undermine the transition to democracy. The declaration was in three sections; the second and largest section was seventeen points, with each point beginning with the phrase "Democracy will exist when…" These points dealt with a variety of issues, all of them challenges to the Democratic Forum's governing coalition, but media politics was especially important on this list. The last two points dealt with freedom of the press:

> *16.     Democracy will exist when the radio and television will be guaranteed independence from the government, from the parties, and from local governments;*

> *17.     Democracy will exist when press freedom is not limited by state monopolization, or the weight of government dependent bank's financial policies, or the intimidation of reporters, or the current power would provide information to every legal press medium.[9]*

Like the Network of Free Initiatives, the Democratic Charter was an attempt to unify opposition against the government. The problem was that this opposition included both liberals and Socialists. The Free Democrat leadership could not continue to fight their old enemies while staging a new fight against a new foe. Free Democrat politicians would now fight against a right-wing dictatorship side by side with politicians from the Hungarian Socialist Party, the party the Free Democrats had accused of trying to undermine the transition to democracy not two years before. The Democratic Charter had no formal relationship with either the Alliance of Free Democrats or the Hungarian Socialist Party. Yet, its two leaders were prominent members of these parties: György Konrád was a well-known dissident writer from the democratic opposition with strong ties to the Free Democrat leadership; Iván Vitányi was a sociologist and a Socialist member of parliament. At the same time that many Socialist and Free Democrat politicians joined the Democratic Charter, few FIDESZ politicians joined. (The main exception was the liberal Gábor Fodor.) The Democratic Charter therefore gave off the image of being an Free Democrat–Socialist organization. It gave the strong impression that the Alliance of Free Democrats, the party of the hard-core anti-Communists, was now in bed with members of the former Socialist government—of all things, in an organization geared towards fighting dictatorship.[10]

On September 26, 1991 the Democratic Charter announced its existence with about 150 signatures. Two months later, on November 22, the former hard-core dissidents of the democratic opposition fell from power within the party. Péter Tölgyessy became the new party president, and most of the group connected to *Beszélő* left the administrative board and other key party positions. But, the former dissidents were not going to give up control of the party they built without a fight. The Alliance of Free Democrats would now dive into a full-scale internal crisis as several groups vied for power. For the first time, the Free Democrats would drop under 10% support, and many began wondering if the party would survive at all.

**The Tölgyessy Crisis:**

A party can fall into an internal crisis when one group makes a serious bid for power against the party leadership and when that intra-party struggle for power undermines the organization's external bids for power. By the end of 1991, the Alliance of Free Democrats was ripe for such a crisis. First, by most accounts, there was significant internal discontent over how the leadership was running the party. The Budapest intellectuals from the opposition movement became easy targets to blame for the party's perceived problems. Second, the power over electing the party president and board members was decentralized enough to make an internal coup possible. Third, the president and "godfather" of the party, János Kis, decided to retire from party politics and not seek reelection. Finally, there was a split in the Free Democrat leadership about a year before. Péter Tölgyessy, the only party leader not somehow affiliated with the democratic opposition, had been ousted from the leadership. Remaining in the party, he was now fighting the hard-core to win intra-party power.

Much like Antall in the Democratic Forum, Tölgyessy was a latecomer to Free Democrat politics. He joined as the Trilateral Negotiations were developing and was raised to head negotiator because of his legal background. He quickly gained prominence in the party and was soon a member of the administrative board. During the 1990 election, he was the first name on the Free Democrat national list and became its faction leader in parliament. That position provided

Tölgyessy a great deal of public exposure—especially since interest in politics was extremely high before the Taxi Blockade—which helped him develop his own mass and intra-party support. As in the Democratic Forum, the Free Democrat center brought an outsider within its ranks because that outsider possessed expertise valuable during the Opposition Roundtable. Once that individual rose high enough, a struggle for power broke out between the old guard and this new individual who the old guard had advanced.

Zoltán Ripp, who wrote a history of the Free Democrats, points out that the conflict between Tölgyessy and the other leaders was not ideological or policy based in the beginning. Instead, the administrative board wanted to maintain control over the parliamentary faction while Tölgyessy wanted to have greater freedom as faction leader.[11] In the terms of party politics, Tölgyessy was trying to create a new center of power in the parliamentary faction separate from the administrative board. The problem for Tölgyessy was that, unlike the Democratic Forum, most of the Free Democrat administrative board members were also members of parliament, and they held a great deal of power in that branch of the party as well. The party leadership was far too entrenched for a serious challenge at this point. That leadership handled Tölgyessy's attempt to win power by ousting him from his position, a sharp move that was visible and obvious to the public and rank-and-file. In October 1990, Iván Petô replaced Tölgyessy as faction head.

Ripp makes the claim that: "The party membership reacted with disbelief to the sudden, coup d'état like removal of Péter Tölgyessy as faction leader and his temporary replacement by Iván Petô." Ripp argues further that at first internal dissatisfaction against the leadership was slow to organize but that over time it founds its expression in Tölgyessy. It is, of course, impossible to know a membership's reaction or changing opinions without some quantitative evidence, which is rarely available on party organizations. Nonetheless, Ripp's claims are consistent with the intra-party events that followed. In December, a new administrative board was elected; Tölgyessy was not returned. Then, in January, Tölgyessy made a bid to retake the position of Free Democrat faction leader in parliament; Petô narrowly defeated him. As 1991 progressed, Tölgyessy became an open critic of the leadership and built intra-party support for himself by traveling around the country and speaking to Free Democrat branches in the countryside, where discontent seemed to be the highest. Finally, in late 1991, a real chance opened for him to challenge the former dissidents in the party center.

On September 30, János Kis sent a letter to Pál Juhász, the president of the Free Democrat National Committee—the larger and weaker of the two governing bodies—stating that he would not run again for party president. By most accounts, Kis had been becoming steadily less happy with the day-to-day work of running a party. A quiet, erudite man, he was not comfortable with the daily bureaucratic work and the endless interpersonal conflicts that came along with being a party president. Kis wanted to return to academic work.[12] The party center wanted to replace Kis with Alajos Dornbach, a Free Democrat MP associated with the former dissident movement: He had been part of a group called the 1956-ers, who were surviving leaders of the revolution, and he was involved with SZETA, the Organization to Help the Poor.[13] Two other Free Democrat politicians also submitted their names as candidates for Kis' old post: Imre Mécs, a former member of the democratic opposition who had run against Kis a year before, and Tölgyessy.

The problem for the party center was that it could not control the vote at the party congress. As the former dissidents and their allies had stumbled through their new roles as party leaders, Tölgyessy had built intra-party support for himself within the unhappy membership, especially within the Free Democrat branches outside Budapest. When the vote was taken during the two-day party meeting at the end of November, Tölgyessy was elected the first post-Kis president of the Alliance of Free Democrats.

The party immediately fell into crisis. During that meeting, Petô stepped down as head of the parliamentary faction, and much of the leadership refused to join the new administrative board. The new administrative board included only two members from the previous board: Mécs and Gabriella Béki. Béki was not part of the democratic opposition. Indeed, a majority of the new administrative board had no connection to the pre-1989 dissident community. Only four of this eleven member board had been in the opposition: the two losing candidates for president, Dornbach and Mécs; Ottila Solt, who had headed SZETA, the Organization to Help the Poor; and Pál Juhász, who had signed a 1979 Charter 77 petition and had written in *Beszélô* under the pseudonym "B.P."[14]

As the organization shifted into an intra-party crisis, its public support plummeted. As Graph 6.1 shows, in November 1991, the month of Tölgyessy's election, the Free Democrats were supported by 20% of likely voters. By February 1992, it fell to around 14%. By March, party support within this group was only 11%.[15] The crisis also influenced the parliamentary faction. After Petô stepped down as faction leader on December 2, 1991, the faction secretary József Gulyás stepped down from his position on December 3. Then, two other Free Democrat MP's quit the party to become independents: Zoltán Bertha on December 16, and Imre Barcza on December 30.[16] Three more would quit in 1992. Then, Alajos Dornbach quit the administrative board in a highly public protest against Tölgyessy not defending the Free Democrat parliamentary faction leader in a dispute with Prime Minister Antall. See Graph 6.1.

Meanwhile, internal power quickly slipped from Tölgyessy's fingers. Within a week, two camps formed within the party: the Liberal Circle (or *Szabadelvû Kör*), which focused on human rights issues, and the Liberal–Conservative Union, which promoted a Thatcher-style libertarianism. Together, the two groups included most of the key Free Democrat figures. They soon joined forces as the Liberal Coalition. The overriding goal of this coalition was to oust Tölgyessy from the party presidency.

Losing support of virtually all the key party members, most of whom were now in an intra-party alliance against him, and with the party under his "leadership" weakening on all fronts, Tölgyessy took steps that seemed to weaken his position even more. He began to make friendly overtures to the Democratic Forum government, a government that held low public support and was especially unpopular among Free Democrat members. He also tried to shift the party's ideologically to the right. Tölgyessy's response to the decentralization of intra-party power and the creation of new intra-party organizations was to create one himself: the *Polgári Demokrata Kör*, which could be translated as the Civic Democratic Circle. It was a signal that Tölgyessy wanted to move towards Antall as well as a more nationalistic ideology. It was an odd tactic, since anyone who supported such a move probably would not have been a member of the Free Democrats in the first place.

Finally, in November 1992, Tölgyessy fell from power. For the next election for party president there were two candidates: Petô, who was supported by the Liberal Coalition, and Tölgyessy. Petô's slogan was "Nincs két SZDSZ" (or "there aren't two Alliance of Free Democrats,") a clear shot at Tölgyessy's attempt to shift the party right ideologically. Petô also called for a return to the Free Democrats' previous success, an implication that Tölgyessy had caused the decline in party support. Petô defeated Tölgyessy easily with 64% of the vote. Tölgyessy was returned to the administrative board, where he served as a symbol of party unity but was in fact isolated and powerless.

**On the Road to "Modern," "Western" Politics:**

As the Liberal Coalition plotted Tölgyessy's demise, it also took critical steps towards making the Alliance of Free Democrats a more competitive party. First, intra-party power was shifted away from the hard-core, radical dissidents. This shift of the center away from the dissidents began during the Kis presidency, largely to the dismay of his friends from the opposition. As Kis told me:

> *[The] people with whom I worked together in* Beszélô *and who I was convinced were very good people, bright people, brave people, perhaps better than me, but absolutely not made for routine party politics, like Kôszeg and Ottila Solt. That was one conflict I had. The other was with Miklós Gáspár Tamás. Both Kôszeg and Tamás have written about this. Something like this also occurred between Miklós [Haraszti] and me too, except that he is an extremely, extremely good personality. He was more willing to understand, even though that was more against his personal interests than for others. Rajk was more willing to accept. Frankly, I came to the opinion that the only person from the hard-core opposition who was capable of becoming a leading politician in the new situation was Demszky. No one else.*[17]

This process of replacing the hard-core opposition began during Kis' tenure. In the second Administrative Board, elected in 1989, the hard-core dominated. In the third, there were only four of eleven members that were hard-core opposition: Haraszti, Kis, Mécs, and Rajk. However, this group, especially Kis, had a great deal of power over the party. The process completed itself after the Tölgyessy crisis ended. In the Administrative Board elected in 1992, only Mécs—the person who ran against Kis several times for party president—could have been considered a hard-core dissident.

At this point, the *Beszélô* group had completely stepped aside; it was replaced by peripheral members of the opposition. These "peripheral members" were either people who were quietly involved with the opposition but kept their jobs, often at the universities, or people who were sympathetic and friendly to the hard-core but not directly involved. Two examples from the former group were Iván Petô and Bálint Magyar; an example from the latter group was Péter Hack.[18] Magyar became the critical figure behind the scenes during and just after the Tölgyessy crisis.[19] While Kis was more an intellectual strategist, able to recognize long-term trends and their implications, Magyar was much more the tactician; as one source described it, Magyar was like a chess player who would think through the next fifteen moves.[20] He was the key strategist behind both Tölgyessy's demise and the revamping of the party. While Magyar was the person behind the ill-fated "We know! We dare! We do!" slogan in 1990,[21] he would become the head of a much more solid and consistent Free Democrat campaign in 1994.

Part of this party reorganization was a reversal of some previous strategies. Power became more centralized, and the leadership was stabilized. A notable example of this reorganization was the change in leadership rules. The terms for president and administrative board members was increased from one to two years. Following Tölgyessy's fall, there would not be another election for party president until after the 1994 parliamentary elections. Through this step, the party hoped to maintain more internal stability at the time when it would be competing for elected positions.

At the same time that power was centralized, the Alliance of Free Democrats took steps to appease the rank-and-file, especially those living outside of Budapest. A critical example of this was the advancement of another outsider, Gábor Kuncze, who had no ties to the democratic opposition or, it seems, the Free Democrats before 1990. Indeed, Kuncze was even more of an outsider than Tölgyessy. While he ran as a Free Democrat single-seat district candidate in 1990 and joined the party faction when the new parliament opened, he did not join the party itself until 1992. Kuncze was made head of the Free Democrat parliamentary faction in February of 1993, a few months after the Tölgyessy crisis was over. He then became the Free Democrat candidate for Prime Minister in 1994.[22]

The rise of Kuncze had both intra-party and mass politics implications. Unlike Petô, Magyar, Hack, and most of the Free Democrat leaders, Kuncze was neither born nor lived in Budapest. Kuncze also had a traditional Hungarian look, including a thick mustache. He was also well spoken and had a professional demeanor, which made him a good lead person in the party's attempt to regain public support.

With these internal changes also came a shift in the Free Democrat presentation. The new key word became "modernization." In Hungarian rhetoric, "modernization" can unify all the branches of liberalism. This is because in Hungary, to modernize effectively means to become more like Western Europe, and Hungarian liberalism is associated with the notion of "catching up with" or "joining" the West. British liberalism, human rights, and social democracy can all be seen as western ideals. Conversely, it is way to distinguish itself from both the populists and conservatives of the Hungarian Democratic Forum, who could be accused of wanting to return Hungary to an idealized and unattainable past. Moreover, in a Hungarian tradition dating back to at least the Kádár era, modernization is a way to promote the image of expertise—a valuable image at this point because many Hungarians seemed to believe that the Democratic Forum coalition was incapable of running a government. Finally, "modernization" was a way for the party to softly distance itself from its radical past without disowning it. Being the party for "modernization" was a better front than being the party of radicals determined to fight dictatorship, for sure, and since the shift was made when the party was already low in public support, the risks of this change to the party were minimal.

**The 1994 Free Democrat Parliamentary Campaign:**

The 1994 Free Democrat parliamentary campaign reflected this front of modernization. It was a dramatic change from 1990. The 1990 campaign was clever, showcasing the party's literate background. Slogans were often subtle references to Hungarian poetry, old movies, and even classical music, and they often had double-meanings and hidden jokes. But, this creative campaign lacked a clear focus. In 1994, the campaign focus was on trust. It was, by most accounts, less creative and certainly less entertaining. Moreover, it was markedly uniform, usually presenting a candidate—unlike the casual look of 1990, in a suit—in front of a simple blue background. By far the most exposure was given to Kuncze. Repeatedly, posters with the slogan "I trust him" showed Kuncze holding a baby, walking with his wife, talking with a worker, or simply sitting. It had a clear Western campaign style, and the professional look gave off an impression of a professional party.

Another aspect of this revamping of the Alliance of Free Democrats was its selection of parliamentary candidates. In 1990, the Free Democrats tried to create a well-defined system for selecting candidates, but in the end, it was rather arbitrary. In 1994, the method reflected the party's dual goals of presenting a strong image externally while it maintained internal control and harmony. As the designated "front man" and Prime Minister candidate, Kuncze was given spot number one. (Pető was made number one on the Budapest list and not put on the national list so that neither Kuncze nor Pető would be above the other on any list.) Number two was given to Gábor Fodor, who had quit FIDESZ in late 1993 and joined the Free Democrats in early 1994; he was given this high spot because he was a critical figure in Hungarian politics at that time.

After Kuncze and Fodor, intra-party considerations became more important, though at this time one's place in the network and one's public image tended to be relatively the same. These places were given first to Administrative Board members in order of how many votes they received to enter the board in 1992. (This system put Tölgyessy in spot number three, which had the added benefit of giving the appearance of party unity—a far better tactic than when they publicly ousted him as faction leader in 1990.) Following this group were members of the National Committee, the larger governing body, who wanted to run.[23]

Single seat candidates were selected through a technique that gave local party organizations much autonomy at the same time that the party center retained control over what mattered to it. The center wrote clear guidelines on what characteristics it was looking for in these candidates, and then it sent advertisements through the organization for candidates. The party also hired the employment firm Catro Sensor to create and administer a test for prospective candidates; this test included a combination of interviews and situation games. The prospective candidates were given point scores and a passing or failing grades. The local party unit then chose among those with a passing score.[24]

At this point, the Alliance of Free Democrats took all the steps it could to win back its previous good position. It handed control of the party from hard-core dissidents to people who seemed more capable of learning the new politics. This new leadership shifted the party front from radical liberalism to modernization, and it changed the rhetorical style to one consistent with that modernization front. It also reorganized and re-united the party towards winning governmental power. While the new leadership did not have the party background of the Socialists, it at least took the Alliance of Free Democrats off of its self-destructive path.

But while the Free Democrats would be in a better position in 1994 than it was in 1991 and 1992, it would make a decision that may have been even more costly in the long-run than the 1990 pact with the Hungarian Democratic Forum. The Free Democrats, the party that built its initial following by being the greatest opponents of the Socialist regime, moved steadily towards becoming the main ally of its former enemy. It would even go into a governing coalition with the Socialists in 1994. This was Antall's first major maneuver in 1990 when he transformed the Democratic Forum into a conservative party and defined the left as the Socialists, Free Democrats and Young Democrats, and it later became the strategy of the Young Democrats to push the Socialists and Free Democrats together. By making this alliance with the Socialists, first with the Democratic Charter and then eventually by joining its government, the Free Democrats produced three related mass politics problems. One, it blurred the Free Democrats' distinctiveness. As the former dissidents left—a necessary step—and as the party became less distinct from the Socialists, there became less reason for voters to support the Free Democrats. Two, it gave legitimacy to the Socialists. The biggest problem the Hungarian Socialist Party faced after the fall of the Berlin Wall was its history. By joining forces with its former arch-enemy, the Free Democrats it took significant steps towards disavowing that pre-1989 past. Since the Socialists and Free Democrats were close ideologically, once those distinctions were gone, the more powerful and experienced Socialists would become able to gradually squeeze out the Free Democrats.

Fluttering of the Free Democrats, 1990-1994

**Graph 6.1**
**Public Support for Alliance of Free Democrat, 1991-1994**

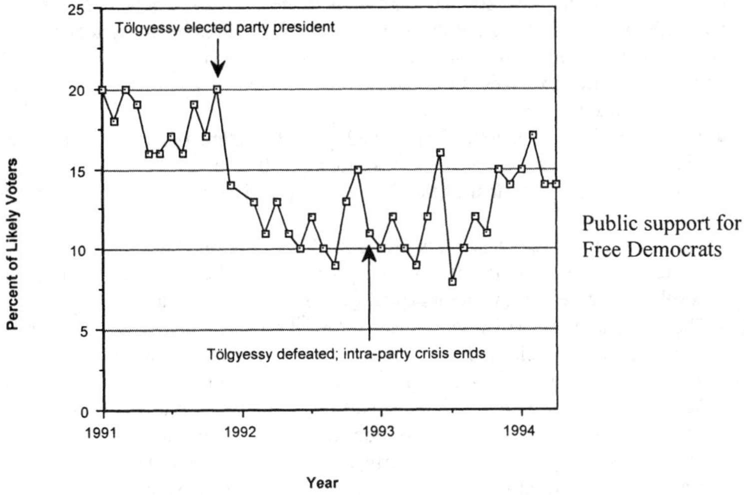

Public support for
Free Democrats

Public support is defined as the percent of likely voters who would vote for the Alliance of Free Democrats if the election were on the following Sunday.

Source: Szonda Ipsos, http://www.szondaipsos.hu/partpref/

# Notes:

[1] Because Hungarian disclosure laws are weak, there is virtually no way to determine what international organizations are funneling money to which parties. Nonetheless, there is a general sense among Hungarian intellectuals and my sources on the relationships between Hungarian parties and Western organizations. No source was capable or willing to give specific details, so none will be cited:

- The Hungarian Democratic Forum had gained western ties because in 1989 it was accurately seen as the electoral front-runner. It is argued that its western ties are generally weaker than that of the Alliance of Free Democrats and Hungarian Socialist Party;
- The Alliance of Free Democrats seemed to have developed ties through its many years in the radical opposition. It is also argued that the Free Democrats has been able to develop good ties with western capital because of its libertarian ideology;
- The Hungarian Socialist Party was believed to have developed ties with western organizations, especially those in former West Germany, during the Kádár era. Note that the Hungarian Socialist Party emerged from the reform wing of Hungarian Socialist Workers' Party, which tended to be more western-oriented, and that many of Hungarian Socialist Party's key politicians were from the foreign policy community. For example, Gyula Horn, the party president during this period, was the foreign minister that allowed East German tourists cross from Hungary to West Germany, the move that prompted the collapse of the Berlin Wall;
- The Federation of Young Democrats is believed to have had weaker ties to western organizations, though it clearly had a working relationship with West European liberal parties;
- The Christian Democratic People's Party's main western ties seemed to be other Christian Democratic parties;
- The Independent Smallholders' Party is believed to have had by far the weakest ties to western elites.

[2] See Malcolm Punnett and Gabriella Ilonszki. (1994) "Leading democracy: The emergence of party leaders and their roles in the Hungarian parties". *The Journal of Communist Studies and Transition Politics*, 10, no. 3. (Special Edition: ed. Terry Cox and Andy Furlong, *Hungary: The Politics of Transition*) pp. 101-19. Also interviews with Miklós Haraszti and Béla Légár.

[3] These figures were determined by comparing two lists: The Free Democrat candidate list from Table 1 of *Parliamentary Almanac* and the index of names in Csizmadia, *Documents*.

[4] Interview with Miklós Haraszti.

[5] Tóka, "Parties and their Voters", pp. 136-7.

[6] For discussion on intra-party dissatisfaction in the Alliance of Free Democrats, see Zoltán Ripp (1995) *Szabad Demokraták: Történeti Vázlat a Szabad Demokraták Szövetségének Politikájáról. [Free Democrats: A Historic Sketch of the Politics of the Alliance of Free Democrats.]* (Budapest: Politikatörténeti Alapitvány), pp. 85–102.

[7] András Bozóki (1997) "Mozgalmi–értelmiségi politika a rendszerváltás után: A Demokratikus Charta, *Politikaitudományi Szemle*, I ["Movement, intellectual politics after the regime transformation; the Democratic Charter", *Political Science Review*, Vol 1] p. 101. The translation is mine.

[8] At this point, the main threat to the government was the Independent Smallholders' Party, which was threatening to leave the coalition.

[9] The complete text of the declaration can be found in "Demokratikus Chartra" ["Democratic Charter"], *Hungarian Political Yearbook, 1992*, pp. 570–1.

[10] Bozóki, "The Democratic Charter", pp. 98-135.

[11] Ripp, p. 65-6.

[12] It appears that the "final straw" occurred when Solt Ottila, another former hard-core dissident, attacked Kis at an administrative board meeting. She criticized him for the decision to make the Free Democrats the "adversary" of the government and called him a bad party leader.

[13] *Parliamentary Almanac*, pp. 82-3.

[14] Ibid, pp. 176-7. Note that technically the administrative board has ten members; the eleventh, the president, is the de facto head of the board.

[15] Source: http://www.szondaipsos.hu/partpref/

[16] *Hungarian Political Yearbook*, 1992. p. 482.

[17] Interview with János Kis.

[18] This distinction between hard-core and peripheral members of the democratic opposition was presented to me by János Kis.

[19] This was determined by looking at the decision-making process, as it was described to me by Free Democrat informants. During interviews with Free Democrat politicians of that period, credit was repeatedly given to Magyar, not Petô, for important leadership decisions. I later double-checked this conclusion with a source who confirmed it on the condition that it be kept anonymous. This source informed me that while Petô was certainly very influential in the party, Magyar was always by his side during important meetings and was the more likely to determine the final outcome.

[20] Anonymous Alliance of Free Democrats source.

[21] Interview with Miklós Haraszti.

[22] *Parliamentary Almanac*, p. 241

[23] Interview with József Gulyás.

[24] Ibid.

Chapter 7:

# The Puzzling Resurgence
# of the Hungarian Socialist Party

One of the surprising developments of post-1989 politics in East-Central Europe was the remarkable turnaround of communist and socialist parties. Instead of simply disappearing or becoming small protest parties after being ousted by public vote, these successor parties gained traction in the new systems and often even gained significant public support.

Of all the cases, Hungary was the most dramatic. In 1990, during the first competitive elections for the Hungarian parliament in nearly half a century, the new parties collectively pushed the ruling Hungarian Socialist Party out of power. The Socialists were vilified as corroborators in János Kádár's soft dictatorship, the creators of Hungary's economic ills, and the bureaucrats of Soviet domination. Four years later, during the second competitive elections to parliament, the Socialists won an overwhelming victory over these new parties. Having won a majority of seats in a parliament with six parties, the Socialists went into coalition with the Alliance of Free Democrats, the party built by the radical, hard-core, anti-Communist dissidents. Since then, the Hungarian Socialist Party has retained a dominant position in Hungarian politics and is today one of the two strongest parties.

Why would Hungarians vote this vilified party back into power so soon after the triumphant fall of the Berlin Wall? Hungarian political scientists and pundits have given several answers. The most common, other than the relative competencies of the Socialist and new parties, are the following: (1) the "nostalgia theory;" (2) the "ideological shift" argument; (4) the argument that the Socialists had unfair resource advantages; and (4) the "media bias" explanation. The nostalgia theory—the argument that Hungarians wanted a return to the better days of Kádár's soft communism—is probably the most widely supported explanation. The media bias argument, on the other hand, was mostly promoted by pundits ideologically on the right, especially those who supported the Hungarian Democratic Forum.[1]

Few Hungarian thinkers would argue that only one of these factors led to the Socialists' electoral success. For example, Béla Király—a member of the Hungarian parliament from 1990 to 1994 who was also a sociologist in the United States—gave nine reasons for the Socialist revival, eight of which are listed below. (The ninth, the Hungarian electoral system, is only important because the two-stage election exaggerated the Socialist victory, causing the plurality of first round voter support to translate into a majority of parliamentary seats.)[2]

167

*Nostalgia for previous regime*:
➢ The desire of social security and the myth that it was "much better under Kádár."

*Party resources*:
➢ The nationwide Socialist party network, staffed by party professionals and apparatchiki;[3]
➢ The electoral alliance of the Hungarian Socialist Party and MSZOSZ, the national trade union;
➢ The Socialist support by the nouveau rich, consisting mostly of former apparatchiki;

*Media bias*:
➢ Socialist support by *Népszabadság*, the most popular daily in Hungary;
➢ The predominance of Socialist control over the county daily newspapers;

*Party competence*:
➢ The blunders of the Antall government, and the corruption it tolerated;
➢ The professionalism of the Socialist leadership in and out of parliament as well as the moderation of its left of center policies;


In his article "The reasons for the Defeat of the Right in Hungary," András Körösényi gave a related set of explanations.[4] He argued for three main reasons why the socialist-liberal coalition of the Hungarian Socialist Party and the Alliance of Free Democrats defeated the Hungarian Democratic Forum and it's allies in 1994. One, the relatively high standard of living prior to the transition and the subsequent inflation, unemployment, and general instability produced a nostalgia for the previous system. Two, after winning in 1990, the governing coalition shifted to a hard anti-Communist, conservative ideology which did not reflect the views of most of the Hungarian public. Finally, the governing parties made repeated mistakes because of their "inexperience and sheer incompetence."

Király, Körösényi, and other scholars on the region tend to emphasize some variant on the nostalgia theory while mentioning political competence but treating it as a less central cause. In contrast, Anna Grzymala-Busse put political skills at the center of her explanation. Studying the regeneration of the communist successor parties in Poland, the Czech Republic, Slovakia and Hungary, she argued that the success of each successor party was related its ability to transform itself to a more centralized and less membership-based party, while breaking with their discredited past. The ability to make this transformation was mostly a function of the skills of the party politicians. Grzymala-Busse argues further that those relative skills were a product of the evolution of each party institution. The communist party leaders in Poland and especially Hungary had more relevant skill than their Czech counterparts, for example, because these institutions based membership recruitment less on ideological zeal; they advanced members into leadership positions based more on technocratic competencies than steadfast party loyalty; and after 1956 the Polish and Hungarian parties engaged the public—and thereby gained related skills—more than in the Czech Republic after the Prague

Spring in 1968.[5] In brief, the Hungarian Socialist Party was able to gain such rapid success because its history led to party politicians who had competencies that made them better able to transform the party in ways that made it competitive in the new, representative system.

But, there is more to this remarkable Socialist revival than the economic and social dislocation of Hungarians or the political skills of the Socialists or the governing coalition. The shift in support to the Socialists came only *after* Hungarians rejected not only the government coalition but also two other new parties that had been widely supported: The Alliance of Free Democrats and the Federation of Young Democrats, or FIDESZ. Six months before the election, FIDESZ would have won easily. But, during the year leading up to the election, 80% to 85% of FIDESZ support evaporated. As Hungarians deserted FIDESZ, support for the Socialists rose. A key question is why the Young Democrats support nosedived in 1993 and 1994. One answer is that these former dissidents, who lacked much experience in party politics, made maneuvers that inadvertently subverted their public support.

This chapter presents the crux of the empirical argument in this book. Chapters 2 and 4 showed evidence that the Socialists entered the new political system with more relevant skills than the former dissidents. Chapter 5 and 6 showed how low party competence helped undermine the public support of both the Hungarian Democratic Forum and the Alliance of Free Democrats, and how this led to FIDESZ becoming by far the most widely supported party in 1991 and 1992. This chapter explores the final step in the Socialist revival, the collapse of FIDESZ support over twelve months in 1993 and 1994 and how that collapse led to the resurgence of the Socialists. The analysis will be done in three main steps. First, the chapter will review the movement of party support by the public during this period. Second, it will discuss the steps taken by the FIDESZ leadership that led to the collapse of its public support. Third, it will explore the strategic steps taken by the Socialists that made this resurgence possible.

**Shifting Party Support, 1990–1994:**

A critical argument of this chapter is that a prerequisite to the Socialist party revival in 1993 and 1994 was the public rejection of the newly formed parties, including those built by former dissidents. Specifically, the rise of public support for the Socialists came only after—and to some degree, as a direct consequence of—Hungarians deserting the Federation of Young Democrats. The purpose of this section is to establish this point in three steps. (1) The Socialist resurgence echoed the widespread desertion of FIDESZ. (2) The majority of Hungarians who deserted FIDESZ in 1993 and early 1994 voted for the Socialists. (3) The rise of support for the Socialists did not drive the desertion of FIDESZ.

The Socialist resurgence came in what could be considered the third of three stages in party support between the first two elections of the new republic. In the first stage, just after the 1990 election, the governing Hungarian Democratic Forum and the opposition Alliance of Free Democrats were the most supported parties. But, as discussed in Chapter 5, the Democratic Forum not only presided over a painful economic and social transition; it also made strategic decisions that undermined its public credibility, and that credibility seemed to be hurt further by its highly public intra-party war during this period. Similarly, as described in Chapter 6, the Alliance of Free Democrats reverted to its radical, dissident strategies in 1991, which hurt its public credibility as well as set of an intra-party war that crippled the organization for several years. This led to a second stage, in which overwhelming levels of support went to the Federation of Young Democrats. During this period from 1991 through 1992, FIDESZ often held three times the public support of any other party. At its height, it held 45% support among likely voters while the next strongest party held less than 15%. But this was followed by a third stage, in 1993 and early 1994, when support for FIDESZ virtually disappeared and the Socialists became the most supported party in Hungary.

The movement of public support from early 1992 to the election in May 1994 for FIDESZ and the Socialists is shown on Graph 7.1. Public support for FIDESZ rose over 40% in 1992 and remained between 38% and 45% over that year. Then, in January and February 1993 it dropped by 10%. It rose again to 45% in April but then began a rapid and relatively steadily plummet in the following year. FIDESZ support was dropping so fast that it was unclear if the party would even meet the 5% minimum list vote to reenter parliament after the next election. Szonda-Ipsos measured public support for FIDESZ among likely voters at 10% in April 1994.[6] In the first round of the parliamentary elections in May, it received 7% of the party list vote. See Graph 7.1.

Public support for the Hungarian Socialist Party followed exactly the opposite pattern. From January 1991 to December 1992, support for the Socialists remained relatively steadily, always above 5% and below 15%. Then, in January 1993 it began to climb. This climb seemed to mirror the decline of FIDESZ support during the same period. It even dipped in April 1993 when FIDESZ support rose again and then rose again as FIDESZ support plummeted. In April 1994, Szonda-Ipsos estimated that 37% of likely voters would vote for the Socialists.[7] In May, the Socialists received 33% of the party list vote.

Graphs 7.2a and 7.2b demonstrate both the electoral significance of this drop in support for FIDESZ as well as that the majority of likely voters who deserted FIDESZ in 1993 and early 1994 switched their support to the Socialists. These graphs are based on a panel study conducted by the Department of Political Science at the Central European University in Budapest, Hungary.[8] In September 1992, respondents were asked who they would vote for if the election occurred the following Sunday. Just after the 1994 election, the same respondents were asked whom they had voted for. See Graphs 7.2a and 7.2b.

Graph 7.2a shows the stability—or more accurately, the instability—of party support from 1992 to 1994. It demonstrates that only the Socialists held stable public support during this period. Of those who said in 1992 that they would vote for the Socialists, 87% actually did vote for them in 1994. In comparison, only 37% of those who in 1992 said that they would vote for the Alliance of Free Democrats did so in 1994. Similarly, only about half of those who said in 1992 that they would vote for the Hungarian Democratic Forum, Christian Democratic People's Party, or the Independent Smallholders' Party did vote for that party in 1994.

But the most extreme case was FIDESZ. Among Hungarians who said in 1992 that they would vote for the Young Democrats, a whopping 83% voted for another party in 1994. Moreover, *FIDESZ deserters* (i.e., those who supported FIDESZ in 1992 but voted for another party in 1994) made up a third (34%) of the entire Hungarian electorate. They were as large of a category as the percent of Hungarians who voted the Socialists back into power in 1994.

During the year and a half before the 1994 election, the Socialists were the big winners of Hungarians changing their minds about which party to support. As Graph 7.2b demonstrates, about half (52%) of FIDESZ deserters voted for the Socialists. A third (35%) voted for the Alliance of Free Democrats. Only about 6%, 2%, and 5% voted for the Democratic Forum, Christian Democrats, and Independent Smallholders, respectively. The CEU study also showed that while the Free Democrats also made significant gains among FIDESZ deserters, they also lost a significant percent of their 1992 supporters by 1994, and two-thirds of those who switched from the Free Democrats voted for the Socialists. So, while the Socialists made their greatest gains from FIDESZ deserters, they also capitalized from the Free Democrats inability to keep their own supporters loyal.

Any explanation of the Socialist resurgence must be able to explain this movement of party support. It cannot treat the Socialist rebound in isolation, nor can the analysis be limited to the Socialists and the government coalition. Instead, it should be able to explain why FIDESZ support rose in 1991 and 1992 and then plummeted suddenly in 1993 and 1994. It must also explain why former supporters of FIDESZ, the most radical and vehemently anti-Communist of all the dissident groups, decided to vote for the Socialists in 1994. As will be shown below, none of the standard explanations accomplish this.

*Explanation 1: Nostalgia for Socialism:*
The nostalgia theory, or the theory that Hungarians voted for the Socialists because they were disappointed by the transition to liberal democracy and wanted a return to the economic security of the previous regime, is probably the explanation most often given by political scientists and sociologists at Hungarian universities for the Socialist revival. Proponents of this theory point to two main pieces of evidence: (1) The standard of living dropped dramatically after the democratic transition. (2) Many Hungarians in 1994 believed that life had been better under the Socialist regime. (3) Those Hungarians who believed that life had been better under the previous regime tended to vote for the Hungarian Socialist Party.

Life in Hungary was relatively good during the decades that followed the 1956 revolution, and by the 1970s the governing Socialist party seemed to gain public support because of it. Hungarians had enjoyed relative prosperity through the 1970s and the early 1980s. As Graphs 7.3a and 7.3b show, there was virtually no unemployment for decades before the transition. Per capita income increased, on average, over 5% per year in the 1950s (though most of that increase occurred after Stalin's death in 1953 and especially after the 1956 revolution) and about 6% and 4% per year in the 1960s and 1970s, respectively. But, already in the early 1980s, these signs of developing prosperity were weakening. During the last three years of the regime, 1987 to 1989, real per capita income increased a mere 2%.

There were also the first, if tiny developments of unemployment. The once "happiest bunker in the camp"—as Hungary had been compared to its Warsaw Pact allies—was now feeling an economic pinch. It was under these conditions that the Hungarian Socialist Party, competing in an open election during economic stagnation, could muster only 10% of the vote. See Graphs 7.3a and 7.3b.

After the democratic transition, economic stagnation was quickly followed by economic decline. From 1990, when the Hungarian Democratic Forum government formed, through 1993, the last full year of that government, real per capita income dropped nearly 10% and real wages nearly 12%. During those four years the average annual rate of inflation (i.e., average yearly increase in the consumer price index) was 27%, with food prices doubling and fuel costs increasing by 170%.[9] While the unemployment rate was measured at half a percent in January, 1990, a few months before the new government took office, that measure was over 13% in January, 1994, a few months before the next election.

These declining economic figures seemed to correspond with another phenomenon. After a period of euphoria in 1990, many Hungarians became dissatisfied with democracy and believed that the post-1989 regime was worse than the Socialist regime. According to the Central European University survey of Hungarian voters in 1994, 59% of Hungarians were dissatisfied with democracy. Of those who were not satisfied, about half (49%) voted for the Socialists. In comparison, among those who were satisfied with democracy, a third (32%) voted for Socialists. Conversely, only 7% of Hungarians who were dissatisfied with democracy voted for the Hungarian Democratic Forum, while 21% of those who were satisfied voted for the Democratic Forum. Similarly, half of respondents (48%) believed that the post-1989 regime was worse than the pre-1989 regime. 21% thought that they were about the same and only 32% thought that the new regime was better. The relationship between comparing regimes and voting for the Socialists is stronger. Of those who thought that the post-1989 regime was worse, 62% voted for the Socialists and only 8% voted for the Democratic Forum. Conversely, of those who thought that the new regime was better, 15% supported the Socialists as compared to 26% who supported the Democratic Forum.[10]

There is, however, a significant problem with this evidence. While the nostalgia theory does an excellent job of explaining why many Hungarians voted for the Socialists instead of the Hungarian Democratic Forum, especially if one looks at only the 1990 and 1994 elections as snapshots, it does a much worse job of explaining the movement of the vote among six parties over that four year period. Notably, it cannot explain why there was widespread support for FIDESZ in 1992 and why that support evaporated in 1993 and early 1994.

One problem is that the economic data in fact does not correspond with the movement of party support. The significant economic decline occurred from 1990 to 1993, when FIDESZ, the most anti-Socialist and pro-small government of all the parties, became the most supported party, and FIDESZ support nosedived and Socialist support rose at the point when the economy had leveled off. Unemployment, which had jumped from virtually nothing to 13% from 1990 to 1993, remained steady at 13% from 1993 to 1994. Per capita income, which had dropped 10% from 1990 to 1993, rose 3% from 1993 to 1994. Similarly, real wages had dropped 12% from 1990 to 1993 but rose 7% from 1993 to 1994. If economic dislocation would have caused Hungarians to flock back to the Socialist party, that flocking should have occurred in the more painful 1991 and 1992, not in 1993 and 1994 when the situation was stabilizing.

Similarly, during the period when FIDESZ support dropped and Socialist support rose, satisfaction with democracy did not decline. Quite the opposite, satisfaction with democracy was rising at the same time that Hungarians were flocking to the Socialists. While 59% of Hungarians were dissatisfied with democracy in 1994, a whopping 78% were dissatisfied with democracy in 1992. Unfortunately, there was no question in the 1992 survey asking Hungarians to compare regimes, so there is no way to tell if the belief that life was better under Kádár increased or decreased as support for the Socialists rose.[11]

Beyond the problem that Socialist support rose while economic conditions were improving and satisfaction with democracy was rising, not dropping, the nostalgia theory cannot explain why an overwhelming plurality of Hungarians supported small government, British liberal FIDESZ in the first place. It also does not explain why that support evaporated unexpectedly in 1993 and early 1994. The latter point is shown in Graph 7.4. It shows the relationship between deserting FIDESZ between September 1992 and May 1994 and comparing the new regime against the pre-1989 regime in 1994. It is true that those who thought that the new regime was worse were more likely to switch support from FIDESZ to another party. Of those who believed that the new regime was worse, over 90% deserted FIDESZ, as compared to 88% of those who thought that the two regimes were about the same and 68% of those who thought that the new regime was better. But this is the difference between the overwhelming majority and the vast majority; nearly 70% of those who thought the new regime was better also abandoned FIDESZ. Dissatisfaction with the new regime was a factor that probably influenced decisions to abandon FIDESZ, but it was not the overriding reason. See Graph 7.4.

There is one other historic problem with the nostalgia theory. After the Socialist government took power in 1994, it did not reinstitute social welfare programs reminiscent of the Kádár era. Quite the opposite, privatization was accelerated, the cost of consumer goods continued to rise while wages stayed steady, and more parts of the social net were removed. Yet, the Socialists remained widely supported and came very close to winning the 1998 election. If the shift in party support was driven by nostalgia for the security of the Kádár era, then one would expect that this hope for security would have continued to shift the vote after 1994.

Thus, the answer seems to be that "nostalgia," generally understood, cannot be more than part of the answer. It cannot explain why in 1991 an overwhelming plurality of Hungarians rejected the Hungarian Democratic Forum and Alliance of Free Democrats in favor of the Young Democrats, the most radically anti-Socialist and pro-free market of the Hungarian parties at that time. Similarly, it cannot explain why most FIDESZ supporters deserted the party in 1993 and 1994.

*Explanation 2: Ideological Shift:*

A second explanation for the Socialist revival in 1994 is the ideological shift argument. There are two main versions of this explanation. The most common would probably be an ideological version of the nostalgia theory. Once Hungarians became aware of the economic pain that capitalism was causing them, they began to thirst for a return to state socialism or at least to support a large welfare state, like those in many Western European countries. A second version focuses on the ideological shift of parties. According to this version, after the Hungarian Democratic Forum and its coalition partners took power in 1990, they began to promote a cultural conservatism that did not reflect the views of most Hungarians. This led these Hungarians to reject the governing parties and support FIDESZ. Then, in 1993, FIDESZ suddenly shifted to the right as well. According to proponents of this argument, Hungarians on the left rejected FIDESZ and instead chose to vote for the only parties still on the left: the Socialists and the Free Democrats.

Table 7.1 gives a general sense of where Hungarians stood on ideological issues in 1992 and 1994. In both years, the Central European University Survey had asked Hungarians whether they definitely agree, rather agree, rather disagree, or strongly disagree with a battery of statements, many of them ideologically laced. This table summarizes the responses to six of these statements, except that the answers were collapsed to "agree" or "disagree" and coded as a more left or more right answer. (For example, agreeing with the statement "It should be the government's responsibility to provide a job for everyone who wants it" would be considered a more left answer. Conversely, agreeing with the statement "It would be harmful to the economy if the government tried to reduce income differences" was considered the more right answer.) See Table 7.1.

In studying Hungarian political ideology, it is helpful to distinguish between its economic and cultural dimensions. The first three statements measure economic ideology and are relatively self-explanatory. The second three statements probe cultural ideology and require interpretation. "Patriotism" was one of a set of related terms used by the Hungarian right to describe itself, and it regularly accused the parties on the left of lacking any sense of Hungarian identity, much less Hungarian patriotism. (In the case of the most right-wing Hungarians, the "communists" of the Hungarian Socialist Party and "Jews" of the Alliance of Free Democrats were considered to not even be Hungarians and therefore incapable of being patriotic or promoting the country's interest.) Conversely, the parties on the left tended to emphasize "westernization" and "modernization," and they also promoted themselves as the experts who would raise Hungary towards the level of Western Europe. "It is more important that a politician be a strong patriot than an expert" is therefore a way to determine where the respondent stood on this ideological distinction.

The final two statements also have implications that might not be self-evident. The abortion issue in Hungary is not strictly pro-life versus pro-choice, as it is defined in American politics. There is also an issue of birth rates and the decreasing number of Hungarians in East-Central Europe. This concern about depopulation and its perceived threat to ethnic Hungarians' role in Hungary proper and neighboring countries also makes abortion a cultural issue for Hungarians on the right.  Similarly, believing in God (that is, a Christian God) is an ethnic issue as much as it is a religious issue for right-wing Hungarians, some of whom do not consider non-Christian groups like Jews and Gypsies Hungarian.  Therefore, to agree that "Politicians who do not believe in God should not perform public functions" might be to believe that only ethnic Hungarians (defined partially in religious terms) should govern.

Table 7.1 may indicate that Hungarians tended to be closer ideologically to the parties on the left than those on the right.[12]  A majority—usually the vast majority—gave the answer more associated with the ideological left.  Probably the most revealing results come from the questions about providing jobs for everyone and whether patriotism is more important than expertise.  In 1994, 83% of respondents said that it was the government's responsibility to provide a job for everyone.  Similarly, only 28% believed that it was more important for a politician to be a patriot than an expert.  Thus, there is an initial reason to believe that Hungarians were more inclined to support parties on the left.

However, the table also clearly indicates that there was no ideological shift in Hungary during this period.  There is no difference greater than 3%.  For example, according to these statistics, 3% fewer Hungarians in 1994 than 1992 believed that government was responsible for providing everyone a job.  Similarly, according to the surveys, there was only a 1% difference between the percent of Hungarians in 1992 and 1994 who believed that it was more important for a politician to be patriotic than an expert.  Any difference between 1992 and 1994 can be easily explained as the random fluctuation of survey samples.  This changes are certainly not indications of an ideological shift that could have produced a 15% to 20% shift in the vote towards the Socialists.

The second version of the ideological shift argument focuses on the ideological shifts of parties, not voters.  In the end, the issue is the ideological shift of FIDESZ.  During the 1993 FIDESZ Party Congress, the newly elected party president, Viktór Orbán, made a speech in which he announced that FIDESZ was a party with a sense of "national responsibility," which could be seen as a sign that the party was shifting right in terms of cultural ideology.  This sign was then reinforced by a number of other symbolic steps that FIDESZ took over the next few months.  Then, later that year, several key liberal politicians of FIDESZ quit the party.  As FIDESZ showed signs of changing from a liberal to a patriotic ideology, support for the party declined at an incredible rate, and support for the Socialists and Free Democrats, the two parties on the left on cultural issues, increased.  Proponents of this ideological shift explanation argue that FIDESZ had represented Hungarians ideologically on the left (in terms of cultural issues) until 1993, and when it suddenly shifted to the right, these culturally liberal Hungarians deserted the party and supported the Socialists or the Free Democrats instead.

But this answer is also not consistent with the empirical evidence.  First, in 1992 FIDESZ was widely supported by Hungarians on the cultural left and right.  Among Hungarians who did not believe that it was more important for a politician to be a patriot than an expert (i.e., the ideologically left answer), 49% said that they would vote for FIDESZ if the election was the next Sunday.  Similarly, among Hungarians who did believe that it was more important for a politician to be a patriot than an expert (the ideologically right answer) 36% would have voted for FIDESZ. While there is a statistical difference between these two numbers, they also indicate that FIDESZ was the most supported party by Hungarians on the cultural right and left, since the next most supported party in each category held 16% support. Even among those who cared more about patriotism than expertise, FIDESZ held at least twice the support of each of its competitors.

Moreover, the desertion of FIDESZ for other parties is unrelated to cultural ideology. While 84% of 1992 FIDESZ supporters who did not believe that it was more important for a politician to be a patriot than an expert deserted the party by 1994, 90% of those who did believe that patriotism was more important also abandoned FIDESZ for another party. The differences between these two results was not statistically significant. In other words, 1992 FIDESZ supporters on the right were just as likely to desert the party after its ideological shift right as FIDESZ supporters on the left.

The relationship between FIDESZ desertion and the party's ideological shift shown in a more rigorous test in Graphs 7.5a through 7.5h. If the desertion of FIDESZ was caused by the party shifting away from most Hungarians' ideology, then one would expect an important difference in the public's perception of FIDESZ in 1992 and 1994. In 1992, one would expect Hungarians on the left to rate FIDESZ high and Hungarians on the right to rate the party low. Conversely, by the 1994 survey, one would expect the rating of FIDESZ by Hungarians on the left to fall and that rating by Hungarians on the right to rise. But, what actually happened in this period was quite different.

In the same surveys by the Central European University in 1992 and 1994 that asked Hungarians to agree or disagree with ideologically laced questions, Hungarians were also asked to rate each party on a scale from 1 to 7, with 1 meaning that the party "always opposes" their views and 7 meaning that the party "always expresses" their views. As it turned out, Hungarians virtually always voted for the party that they rated the highest. These party ratings and the answers to the ideologically laced statements were used to test the ideological shift argument as follows. (1) Using structural equation modeling, the answers to the six statements presented in Table 7.1 were reduced to two scales, one for cultural ideology and the other for economic ideology. (2) Using ordered logit, the rating of each party each year was predicted with four independent variables: cultural ideology, economic ideology, year of birth and gender. (3) Since the results of ordered logits are much more difficult to interpret than those of simple OLS regressions, these results are presented in graphical form Graphs 7.5a through 7.5h. Because FIDESZ shifted in cultural ideology, not economic ideology, the graphs focus on the relationship between ratings of parties and cultural ideology. (For a more exact description of the steps behind this quasi-experiment, see the Appendix.) See Graphs 7.5a through 7.5h.

The graphs show this relationship between party ratings and cultural ideology for each party each year. (Ratings of 1 or 2 were coded as "low ratings"; ratings of 3, 4, or 5 were coded as "middle ratings"; and ratings of 6 or 7 were coded as "high ratings". Economic ideology, age, and gender were held constant.) As one can see immediately, cultural ideology and the ratings of most parties each year are related. For example, only 10% of Hungarians scaled farthest to the left gave the Hungarian Democratic Forum a high rating in 1992 while 25% scaled farthest to the right gave that rating. Conversely, 51% of Hungarians scaled farthest to the left ideologically gave the Democratic Forum a low rating; only 28% of those scaled farthest to the right ideologically gave it a low rating. This pattern held in 1994. Of Hungarians farthest to the left, 18% gave the Democratic Forum a high rating and 31% gave it a low rating. As almost a mirror opposite, among Hungarians farthest to the right, 31% gave it a high rating and 18% gave it a low rating.

A similar pattern could be found for the Hungarian Socialist Party. In 1992, 29% of Hungarians farthest to the left rated the Socialists low while 53% of Hungarians farthest to the right gave it that rating. Conversely, 19% of those on the left rated the Socialists high while a mere 8% of those on the right gave it that rating. As with the Democratic Forum, the pattern persisted for the Socialists past the 1994 election. In May 1994, only 12% of those on the left gave it a low rating while 29% of those on the right gave it that rating. At the same time, a whopping 50% of those on the left gave it a high rating while only 26% of those on the right gave it that rating. So, while cultural ideology was not the only factor influencing how Hungarians rated these two parties (and whether they voted for one of them), it was certainly one factor.

However, the graphs show something completely different with the Young Democrats. In 1992, there is a clear relationship between cultural ideology and party support. For example, 49% of Hungarians scaled farthest to the left gave the Federation of Young Democrats a high rating in 1992 while 27% scaled farthest to the right gave it that rating. Conversely, 11% of Hungarians scaled farthest to the left ideologically gave FIDESZ a low rating; 26% of those scaled farthest to the right ideologically gave it a low rating. But, after FIDESZ's abrupt switch from left to right, the relationship disappeared. In 1994, there was barely a difference in ratings of FIDESZ by those on the left and right. 16% farthest to the left gave FIDESZ a high rating; 18% farthest to the right gave it the same rating. Statistically, there is no change. Similarly, FIDESZ was given a low rating by 24% of those farthest to the left and 28% of those farthest to the right. To the degree that there is statistically a slight change from left to right on this rating, it is in the wrong direction!

In other words, after FIDESZ changed the way it presented itself in 1993, something dramatic and unexpected happened. Instead of Hungarians on the left rejecting it and Hungarians on the right embracing it, by 1994 Hungarians on the left and right rejected FIDESZ at an equal level. Moreover, that rejection did not cause a widespread dislike of the party. Instead, most Hungarians seemed to become largely indifferent to the Young Democrats, with about 60% giving them a middle rating of 3, 4, or 5.

What makes this result especially interesting is that the FIDESZ 1994 graph is most like the Free Democrat graph in 1992. While there was a statistically significant relationship between cultural ideology and rating the Free Democrats in 1992, that relationship is clearly weaker than for other parties. 19% of those on the left gave the Free Democrats a high rating while 12% of those on the right gave it that rating. Conversely, 26% of those on the left and 36% on the right gave the Free Democrats a low rating. These similar results came in the midst of the Free Democrat party crisis, discussed in Chapter 6. The party president at the time, Peter Tölgyessy, attempted to make it into a "civic" party; he attempted to make the exact ideological shift that Orbán successfully took with FIDESZ in 1993. The other major factions with the party vehemently resisted this ideological change. For example, the main slogan of Ivan Petõ, the politician who defeated Tölgyessy in November 1992, was "there aren't two SZDSZ's," meaning that the only Free Democrat ideology was liberal.

Thus, FIDESZ's ideological shift in 1993 played a role in the party's near self-destruction and the revival of the Socialists. But, it had a different affect than what the proponents of the ideological shift argument contend. It was not a Hungarian rejection of FIDESZ for being ideologically on the right. To the contrary, it was the abrupt ideological shift itself that seemed to undermine the party's reputation among Hungarians of all ideological leanings. As will be argued below, it was a significant strategic mistake.

*Explanation 3: Manpower, Local Organization, and Money:*
    A third explanation of the Socialist victory is that the Hungarian Socialist Party had considerably more party resources than its competitors. Proponents of this argument claim that even though there was a transformation in the legal system, the Socialists held onto critical areas of political power. The Hungarians who could afford to buy privatized state property, they argue, were Socialists. Moreover, management of critical industries remained in the hands of Socialists. MSZOSZ (the National Confederation of Hungarian Trade Unions), which was the former state run trade union organization, went back into alliance with the Socialist before the 1994 election campaign started. And while the Hungarian Socialist Party lost its "party cells" in workplaces, its nationwide party structure remained intact. Proponents of this explanation believe that these resources, combined with a deep party structure, provided the Socialists with enough money, manpower, and organizational strength to defeat any opponent in an open election.

    There is probably no direct way to determine whether the Socialists or any other Hungarian party has advantages in these types of resources, because of the laxity of Hungarian campaign finance laws. One way around these problems is to focus on resource output. In this situation, output provides a better indication of party resources because it does not require party self-reporting, which will probably be biased if not outright falsified. Besides, output is a more appropriate indicator for the party resources argument than party resources themselves. The claim is not so much that the Socialists *raised* more money, for example, but that the party *spent* more money on the campaign. The question then becomes: Did Hungarian Socialist Party allocate significantly more resources on the 1994 parliamentary campaigns than its rivals?

    There are two main ways that the Socialists could have allocated greater resources than other parties. First, the Socialists could have spent more money on advertisement. But another aspect of this argument is that the Socialists had a deeper party organization. If this second argument was true, and if it affected the election, then the Socialists would have had a distinct advantage in single member districts. So, while a party with an underdeveloped party structure may have been able to run a single national campaign, only a party with a highly developed organizational structure could run hundreds of effective campaigns in single-member districts throughout the country.

The first conclusion can be tested by examining the results of Mediagnózis, an independent research organization that studied each party's use of paid advertisements during 1994 parliamentary campaign. Specifically, it counted the number of television and radio advertisements, small and giant posters, Budapest and county newspaper ads, and promotional shorts at movie theaters from March 1 to May 27, 1994. It then used these figures to estimate how much each party had spent on paid advertisements during this period. Its results are summarized in Graph 7.6. Mediagnózis found that FIDESZ had spent the most before the first round and that the Free Democrats spent the most between the first and second rounds. Overall, the Alliance of Free Democrats spent the most, around 178 million forints (around $1.78 million dollars by the dollar-forint exchange rate at the time.) FIDESZ was second with 163 million forints, and the Hungarian Democratic Forum was third with 141 million forints. In contrast, the Socialists spent around 38 million forints on advertisements, slightly less than one-fourth of what FIDESZ spent.[13] See Graph 7.6.

Having eliminated the possibility that the Socialists had outspent the other parties, the next question is whether a deeper party organization produced an electoral advantage for the Socialists in single-member district elections. If this argument is correct, then the Socialists would have done better in those single-member district races than nationally. Luckily, this prediction can be tested directly. In the first round of parliamentary elections, Hungarians cast two votes: one for the party, which translates into seats based on county and national party lists, and one for a candidate running for a single-member district seat. If the Socialists had a significant organizational advantage over other parties, that advantage would have translated into greater victories in the individual district elections. In other words, the Socialists' candidates for individual "mandates" would have run ahead of the Socialist party lists.

As Graph 7.7 shows, Socialist candidates for individual mandates did not run ahead of the Socialists' party lists. Quite the opposite, and ironically, of all the major parties, the Socialist individual mandate candidates dragged farthest behind their party's list vote. Nationally, Socialist individual mandate candidates received 2.7% fewer votes than the Socialist party lists (i.e., 31.3% - 34.0%). In comparison, it was the FIDESZ, Christian Democratic, and Democratic Forum individual candidates who tended to run ahead of the party lists during the 1994 first round. Again, as in the case of money, the Socialists may well have had a deeper and better-structured party organization. But, there is no evidence that a difference in organizational strength had any impact on the 1994 election. See Graph 7.7.

*Explanation 4: The Ex-Communist, Liberal Media:*

The party resources explanation is an argument about internal party resource. The media bias argument is about external resources, or the belief that the Socialists had retained control over a critical center of power. More specifically, Hungarian pundits and politicians on the right have argued that the Socialists had retained control over the print media while the Free Democrats gained control over Hungarian public television and radio. Proponents of this argument claim that biased reporting by a Socialist controlled print media helped fuel the Social revival in 1993 and 1994.

Béla Király presents a less partisan version of this argument within his nine reasons that the Socialist won in 1994. He focuses on the Socialists' connection to daily newspapers and rejects the argument that the Free Democrats controlled the electronic media. Király argues that two reasons for the Socialist victory are the "trustworthiness and professionalism of *Népszabadság*, the most popular daily, supporting, though nominally not belonging to, the [Hungarian Socialist Party]" and the "predominance of Socialist control of the counties' dailies." Király's discussion is worth quoting here precisely because he deals with the problems of the argument quite directly. He writes:

*Many of the positive epithets attached to the [Hungarian Socialist Party] have been applicable to the most popular daily, the Népszabadság, a paper with a world-wide system of reporters. The daily abandoned all ideological taboos. While in a professional way it was able to support the socialists' line, an objective presentation of the other side's views was not lacking either. First-rate, up-to-date information on foreign as well as domestic news, sophisticated style, moderate editorials altogether made it the most readable daily... Népszabadság has a solid status in the information business, a great asset for the socialists' cause.*

*[The] dailies of the counties also have been contributing substantially to the formation of public opinion. All the county dailies were, of course, under communist management and editorial administration prior to the change of regime... All the other counties' dailies [besides Pest County] survived with the help of Western capital investments. Western capital by and large considered the investment a business venture rather than a political influence-peddling operation. Thus... Western investors neither interfered with editorial policies nor with the personal affairs of the dailies. Since all these papers were managed and edited by experienced professionals, for investors it was practical to leave things as they were. That caused an immense gain for the [Hungarian Socialist Party]...*

Both the strengths and the problems with the media bias argument can be seen in Király's presentation. Proponents of this argument need to explain two oddities: How did communist control over news continue after privatization, when papers were bought by western capitalists, and why was readership highest for papers they claim were run by communist editors with a pro-Socialist bias? Király resolved these problems by emphasizing that these papers were run in an experienced and professional manner. His answer to the first issue is that *financial* control over daily newspapers went to western capitalists but *editorial* control remained in the hands of former communists who, Király implies, have personal loyalty to the Hungarian Socialist Party. In other words, the editors were peddling political influence while the owners were not looking. His answer to the second issue is that *Népszabadság* and the other formerly state run papers were able to retain the most readers because they had the most experienced and professional staff.

Graph 7.8 shows the relationship between what papers voters read and whether they voted for the Socialists in 1994. It indicates immediately the weakness of the media bias argument. One, for each paper regardless of its real or supposed political leanings, the Socialists received a plurality of votes by its readers. If the political bent of papers had any impact on the vote, it was certainly not enough to produce the 20% shift to the Socialists in 1993 and 1994. Two, for most papers, readers and non-readers were just as likely to vote for the Socialists; there is no statistically significant difference between reading and not reading that paper on the vote. This is notably true for the county dailies, read by half the voting public and which Király argued had promoted the Socialists. 43% of readers voted for the Socialists, as compared to 40% of non-readers; there is no statistically significant difference. See Graph 7.8.

The exceptions seem to be *Népszabadság* [roughly, the *People's Freedom*, which is the most widely read paper in Hungary] and *Népszava* [roughly, the *People's Word*, which was a Socialist party paper before the transition]. 57% of those who read *Népszabadság* voted for the Socialists, while only 35% of those who did not read this paper voted for the Socialists. Similarly, 55% of those who read and 40% of those who did not read *Népszava* voted for the Socialists, respectively. Of course, these relationships between newspaper readership and party support can go in two directions: The newspaper content can influence readers' perceptions of political parties, or political outlooks can influence both the perceptions of parties and choice of newspapers. Since only 10% of Hungarians read *Népszava,* the critical question becomes whether (a) political beliefs or other factors led Hungarians who were more inclined to vote Socialist to also read *Népszabadság* or (b) *Népszabadság* led some Hungarians to change their party support to the Socialists.

The Central European University panel study from 1992 to 1994 shows no evidence for the second possibility. Reading *Népszabadság* did not seem to lead people to change their support to the Socialists. First, there was no relationship between reading this paper and switching the party one supported. During the period of the Socialist resurgence, 58% of people who read this paper changed the party they supported, but 57% of those who did not read *Népszabadság* also switched from one party to another. Second, reading *Népszabadság* did not increase the likelihood that this group would switch their support to the Socialists. Specifically, among people who changed party support during this period, 48% of *Népszabadság* readers switched to the Socialists and 43% of those who did not read *Népszabadság* also switched to the Socialists. This difference was statistically insignificant.

Therefore, the Socialist resurgence cannot be even partially attributed to a Socialist control over the print media. Again, these tests cannot show whether *Népszabadság* or any other media outlet was providing biased reporting or commentary in favor of one or more political parties. But, it does show that if there was such a bias, that bias had no measurable impact on the vote.

## Party Competence and the Near Demise of the Federation of Young Democrats:

The movement of public support in the early 1990s that eventually led to the resurgence of the Hungarian Socialist Party so soon after the fall of the Berlin Wall therefore cannot be explained by these common arguments. The evidence for overwhelming Socialist party resources, either in terms of internal resources like money or organizational depth or support by former allies like the print media, is weak at best. A nostalgia for the security of state socialism may have influenced Hungarians' decision to vote for the Socialists, but it cannot explain the mass exodus from the Young Democrats over a few months in 1993 and 1994. Similarly, the ideological shift of FIDESZ did seem to have an impact on Hungarians' voting decision, but not in the way that proponents of the ideological shift explanation have contended.

But the answer to this puzzle seems to be contained in the previous discussion, especially Graphs 7.5a – 7.5h. The Federation of Young Hungarians was the most widely supported party in 1991 and especially 1992. A year away from an overwhelming electoral victory, the party made abrupt and unexpected changes in the way it presented itself, including suddenly switching from a more liberal to a more center-right ideology. After it made these changes, its support collapsed, with over 80% of its supporters deserting the party. The abrupt change in presentation, not a nostalgia for the Kádár era, drove the exodus from FIDESZ. The public rejection of FIDESZ in 1993 was a precursor to the Socialist revival, just as the public rejection of governing parties and the Alliance of Free Democrats in 1990 and 1991 was a precursor to the widespread support of the young, brash politicians of FIDESZ in 1991 and 1992.

But this leads to a question. Why would the Young Democrats make such an abrupt change in presentation while holding three times the support of other parties and seemingly guaranteed an overwhelming victory in one year? It would seem risky, even suicidal, to suddenly change the basis of a party's public support right before an election. The political scientists Anthony Downs would have referred to it as irrational. The answer, explored further below, seems to be that the former dissidents who ran the party simply did not recognize the problem. Both very young—FIDESZ leader Viktor Orbán would have become Prime Minister at twenty-nine had the party won the election—and lacking any party experience before the transition a few years before, the FIDESZ party leaders misdiagnosed small problems as reasons for radical change and severely underestimated the negative impact of an abrupt change in presentation.

### The Seeds of a Party Crisis:

The Democratic Forum-Free Democrat Pact and the Antall government coalition had put FIDESZ into an excellent position by 1991. FIDESZ was given the opportunity to present itself as the only true opposition party. Three of the parties—the Democratic Forum, the Christian Democrats, and the Independent Smallholders Party—belonged to the governing coalition and therefore would be associated with the country's economic problems. The Alliance of Free Democrats went into a governing pact that made disassociation from the government more difficult. And the Socialists came from the party that had governed during the Kádár era and was linked with the social and economic problems of the 1980s. In good times, it is tough to be the opposition. But, when the nation is going through a painful transformation, the opposition can stand completely separate from the government. It can disassociate itself from the country's problems as well as act as the group that stands against a government that it claims caused these problems.

FIDESZ also capitalized on the problems of other parties by presenting itself as the most pure and pragmatic. Unlike most of the other new parties, FIDESZ did not seem to have endless internal bickering; it did not seem to fall into arguments over personal or entirely ideological issues; and it did not seem to get involved in questionable deals. Different personal and professional experiences made it easier for FIDESZ politicians to play this role than it was for the politicians of the Democratic Forum and Alliance of Free Democrats. The FIDESZ politicians came of age in a generation that did not take the "old debates" between the ruralites and urbanites seriously. So, while some Democratic Forum and Free Democrat politicians had trouble avoiding what they considered fundamental controversies, FIDESZ politicians felt nothing at stake when they ignoring these discussions and focusing on more immediate issues. Moreover, since a majority of FIDESZ politicians were trained as lawyers in the late Kádár era, they tended to be well spoken with a clear and very direct rhetoric style.

However, FIDESZ did face some problems. One, many Hungarians had the impression that FIDESZ politicians were unprofessional and even unruly adolescents. Most FIDESZ MP's attended parliament in blue jeans, and the male politicians mostly wore long hair and rarely shaved. Two, FIDESZ politicians worried that their party was perceived to be the "Free Democrat youth organization." The two parties had a related history: Both emerged from the radical opposition; both refused to sign the agreement after the Trilateral Negotiations; they worked together on the referendum campaign and Danube-Gate; and each was defined as a liberal party in the new party system. Many FIDESZ politicians, including Orbán, feared that FIDESZ would lose its distinct image by being associated too closely to the Free Democrats. Three, having come from a loosely structured movement, the party remained loosely organized and had internal opposition against any development of a hierarchical party structure. Finally, within the party center—in this case, the party faction in parliament—a split began to develop between two opposing factions: the "Orbánites" and the "Fodorites".

While the conflict between the parliamentary faction and the opposition within the party organization was important, that importance can be easily exaggerated. The opposition wanted to maintain FIDESZ's movement characteristics, including keeping the organization decentralized. But, that opposition was much more a nuisance than a threat to the party center's power: It detracted from the external political work and helped make the FIDESZ administrative system inefficient. The key opposition leader, József Vas—a virtual unknown outside of FIDESZ—was no challenge to the dominant position of Orbán and the other party leaders that had entered parliament.  As Hungarian political scientist Zsolt Enyedi put it:

> *As a result of the general elections, the elite of that time went into parliament.  The center of power was relocated:  the parliamentary group replaced the Committee as the center.  The weight of the Committee was further diminished when, apart from four or five 'elders', young people unknown outside of FIDESZ gained places in this formally executive body.*[14]

The split within the party faction would turn out to become a much more serious problem.  The two key players in this split were Viktor Orbán, the de facto head of FIDESZ except when he was at Oxford on a fellowship, and Gábor Fodor, Orbán's roommate at the Bibó Collegium and the person who ran FIDESZ during Orbán's absence.  László Kövér, also from the Bibó Collegium and Orbán's other close friend, was another critical player.  Some have claimed that the split stems back to the collegium because of a personal conflict between Fodor and Kövér, but this appears to be a misreading of events.[15]   Another root might have been in late 1989, when Fodor had risen in prominence while Orbán was in England; Kövér asked Orbán to return because Fodor was, among other things, moving FIDESZ closer to the Free Democrats.  The party's relationship to the Free Democrats would be one of the critical issues defining the split.  However, after Orbán returned, there was no sign of a conflict for about a year.

The real split may have begun in January 1991 during a faction meeting in the town of Sopron.  Several MP's complained that there was not enough internal debate in the faction and that "some" FIDESZ politicians (i.e., Orbán and Kövér) were overconfident in their belief that the Young Democrats were much smarter than the other parties.  This lack of debate and self-criticism could be dangerous in critical times.  The meeting broke into a bitter argument.  The sides of this debate became the groups that would begin to polarize.  Fodor and his closest ally, Péter Molnár, were not among those who brought up the criticism, but they did support that side.  Many of the other FIDESZ MP's remained relatively neutral during this conflict and the polarization that followed; many did not pick a side until 1993.[16]

It is worth noting that the split at this time was not ideological in any definitive way.  Instead, it might be described as a tactical difference: The Orbánites emphasized the need to distinguish the party from the Free Democrats; the Fodorites emphasized that FIDESZ needs to work closely with the Free Democrats as its political partner.  Fodor and Molnár became members of the Democratic Charter, which was closely tied to the Free Democrats and the Socialists, for example, while Orbán and Kövér did not join.  But, in 1991, there was no civic or conservative wing in FIDESZ; it was entirely British liberalism.  Only later would that split become defined in strictly ideological terms.[17]

A critical problem for the Fodorites was that Fodor was hesitant to fight back.  As the conflict intensified, Fodor began attending fewer faction meetings, focusing his attention on his parliamentary committee work instead.   The Orbánites gradually won a solid majority within the faction; as the conflict developed, those trying to remain neutral eventually had to take a side, and many chose the Orbán–Kövér group.  The Orbánites were also benefited by the work of

János Áder, the MP who began running the FIDESZ administrative work after the referendum campaign. In 1990, the party center began building a second, more hierarchical and bureaucratic organizational structure on top of the decentralized federation that already existed. The overriding purpose of this new structure was to circumvent the intra-party opposition, to increase the efficiency of the party network, and to prepare the party for the 1994 campaign as well as to govern.[18] There was a second outcome of this reorganization: Because Áder ran the party office structure, he could appoint people loyal to the Orbánite side.

As 1992 progressed, a FIDESZ victory seemed ever more likely. But, the leadership, notably Orbán and Kövér, saw a number of problems that they believed needed to be fixed; they wanted to insure an electoral victory and to prepare to govern in 1994. It was then, at the height of FIDESZ popularity, that the Orbánites proposed a dramatic change in the FIDESZ organization and in the way that FIDESZ presented itself. Besides overhauling the party structure, Orbán and Kövér wanted to abandon two key aspects of FIDESZ's front: That it was an organization of young people, and that it was a liberal party.

*Exit Stage Right: The 1993 FIDESZ Party Congress:*

László Kövér, the primary author of the new party constitution, proposed three main changes to the old constitution. He proposed a complete reorganization of the party structure, making it into a hierarchical system led by a single president. That president was to be the front man and candidate for prime minister during the next election. Many of the groups through which the internal opposition functioned would be eliminated. He also proposed that FIDESZ be explicitly defined as a party, not as a movement. Finally, he proposed revisions to the constitution that would counter the image that FIDESZ was a youth organization. The meaning of "FIDESZ" would be changed: Instead of "Fiatal Demokraták Szövetsége" (literally, Federation of Young *Democrats*,) it would become "Fiatal Demokrácia Szövetsége" (literally, Federation of the Young *Democracy*.) The age ceiling of thirty-five would be eliminated, and an age minimum of sixteen would be instituted.[19]

While the name change was rejected and the congress revised many other points, the most critical changes were accepted. The party center, already holding significant power, further increased its control over the network. FIDESZ became a more efficient and hierarchical organizations, and the opposition led by Vas was eliminated. Orbán was elected party president. Since power became more centralized to the party president, his election constituted a shift in power to the Orbánites.

In his acceptance speech, Orbán defined FIDESZ as a "nemzeti elkötelezettségû" party, which roughly means a party having a sense of "national responsibility." In Hungarian political jargon, this statement was a clear signal that FIDESZ was taking an ideological step right on cultural issues. The critical term for FIDESZ became "polgár," which is often translated as "citizen" or "middle class." The use of this term also indicates a shift to the right, or more specifically, a shift towards the philosophy of Antall and his faction in the Democratic Forum and away from the liberalism of the Free Democrats.

To be even more specific, there are generally three Hungarian adjectives that might be associated with being liberal: "liberális," "szabadelvû," and "polgári." To some Hungarians, "liberális" has negative connotations. It implies that the person is an internationalist who does not care about defending Hungary or its culture. These Hungarians associate "liberális" with the worst aspects of capitalism, for example. "Szabadelvû" means almost the same thing, but its implications are different: It could be translated as "broadminded" or even more specifically as "freedom principled." While "liberális" people might cheat Hungary for their own benefit, according to this perspective, a "szabadelvû" person would not. Finally, "polgár" implies patriotism. It means "citizen" in a more French use of the term: citizenship with responsibility. It could imply the responsibility of a patriot towards Hungary and its culture. Similarly, polgár also means "middle class," but it could be seen as a reference to the pre-World War II, patriotic middle class that supported Admiral Horthy and its quest to win back the land that Hungary lost after World War I. In a political sense, then, the adjective polgári means "national-liberal", which does not imply the nationalism of some Hungarian populists but does imply the patriotism of József Antall.

Why would FIDESZ change its ideological self-definition at a time when it dominated the mass politics field? Several answers might be given. (1) FIDESZ needed to disassociate itself from the negative aspects of the term "liberális." (2) FIDESZ needed to distinguish itself from the Alliance of Free Democrats, partially because many Hungarians saw the Free Democrats as having the negative characteristics associated with liberalism. (3) FIDESZ was concerned about the rising power of the Hungarian Socialist Party and did not want to go into coalition with the ex-Communists, which the Free Democrats were clearly inclined to do. (4) The Orbán group wanted to redefine FIDESZ in such a way that the liberal Fodor would appear as an outsider.[20]

The problem with these explanations is that, from a strategic standpoint, they make no sense for the political context of early 1993. First of all, if the image of "liberális" was damaging the public's opinion about FIDESZ, that negative impression showed no influence on the party's public support, which was at 45% during the month when the congress was held. The same is true of the association of FIDESZ to the Alliance of Free Democrats. It is hard to see any damage the Free Democrats were doing to FIDESZ when the latter held a 30% lead over every other rival.

On the third point, the Socialists did not begin making serious strides towards catching up to FIDESZ in public support until *after* the congress. There was little threat at this time of the Hungarian Socialist Party challenging FIDESZ's domination.[21] Similarly, there was no indication in early 1993 that FIDESZ would be forced into a coalition with the Socialists. Instead, in early 1993 almost anyone would have predicted that FIDESZ would win an absolute majority of seats in 1994 and therefore be capable of determining the government coalition. Moreover, even if the FIDESZ leadership wanted to avoid going into coalition with the Socialists, it could have waited until after the election before announcing this decision; this internal decision required no significant change in its presentation.

Finally, neither Fodor nor his followers were a serious threat to Orbán's leadership at this time. By 1993, the Orbánites held all the critical intra-party resources. They held a majority vote in the parliamentary faction. They were about to win the party presidency. And they effectively controlled the party bureaucracy and the mechanisms for appointing or electing other important positions. It would seem that an ideological shift right to discredit Fodor and his allies—if this was their motivation—was absolutely unnecessary. Instead, the prudent step would have been to placate this minor group enough to keep the party appearing united as it prepared for the upcoming campaign.

Indeed, these arguments consistently miss the critical point: There was no serious threat to FIDESZ winning the election or the Orbánites holding control over the party. Regardless of the possible reasons, FIDESZ could have waited until after the election before making any decision that might have affected its public image. The change in FIDESZ presentation was not a product of circumstances; it was not forced onto the Young Democrats by a change in the context. Quite the opposite, it was a big decision probably made to fix problems that were comparably small and avoid dangers that might not have even existed. Because party politics was still new to the Orbánites, they probably did not realize that these decisions could have disastrous consequences and even put their political careers in jeopardy.

*FIDESZ Performance Errors and its Downward Shift of Support:*

Since entering parliament, FIDESZ had been presenting itself as young, liberal, pragmatic, and pure. The radical and alternative aspects of its presentation were not eliminated but put quietly to the side, such as when they began dressing less comfortably to parliamentary meetings and male MP's began shaving regularly. (Some, like Deutsch and Hegedüs, kept their long hair.) The combination of youth, pragmatism, and purity worked well together. It could be used to create a distinction between "older politicians" who did not seem to know what they were doing and "younger politicians" who looked for immediate, practical solutions to Hungary's problems and did not spend time on petty, internal fighting or get involved with secret or questionable deals. The liberalism put FIDESZ in a position to criticize the unpopular Democratic Forum government. In 1991, FIDESZ showed that it would not forfeit this distinction from the Democratic Forum easily. When the government looked as though it might collapse, FIDESZ announced that it would not join the Christian-right coalition.

During the period from January 1993 to May 1994, FIDESZ made not one but three changes in its performance that undermined this impression. In each case, these changes indicated that it was shifting away from liberalism and towards the unpopular Democratic Forum government. The first performance error occurred when FIDESZ was caught in a scandal with the Democratic Forum; the two parties used the allocation of a bogus party headquarters to funnel public money into their respective campaigns. The second occurred at the Fifth Congress, when Orbán announced that FIDESZ was a "civic" party. The third happened later in 1993, when its most prominent liberal politician, Gábor Fodor, quit the party. In each case, the performance change was followed by a significant drop in public support.

On January 11, 1993, the press informed the Hungarian public that the government had given the old officers' casino in Budapest to the Hungarian Democratic Forum and FIDESZ as their new party headquarters. The casino was an enormous building. While it was technically within the specifications for a publicly funded party headquarters, if divided in half, it was obviously not suitable for this purpose. Indeed, neither party used this allocated space as their respective party headquarters, nor did the Democratic Forum or FIDESZ move out of the headquarters that it already owned. Instead, the parties immediately sold the building to a Hungarian bank for 1.5 billion forints—over 15 million US dollars.

The image problem from this scandal was greater for FIDESZ than the Hungarian Democratic Forum. This was not the first scandal or accusation of corruption for the Democratic Forum. FIDESZ, on the other hand, was breaking new ground. While technically within the law, it was obviously misusing public funds, which certainly contradicts an image of purity. Moreover, it showed evidence that FIDESZ, the pure opposition to an unpopular government, was now working with that government's main party—on a shady deal, no less. FIDESZ had taken its first step towards shifting right.

FIDESZ's first big drop in public support occurred right after the scandal broke. Just before the scandal, in December, FIDESZ support was at 45%, around where it was hovering for the second half of 1992. In February 1993, Szonda-Ipsos recorded its level of support at 34%. FIDESZ seemed to have recovered from this drop relatively quickly. By April, support was back to 45%.

But, then, FIDESZ made its second performance change. In his acceptance speech at the Fifth Congress, Orbán made clear that FIDESZ was shifting right on cultural issues. This time, there would be no recovery: By June, FIDESZ support dropped to 33%. It would remain in the mid-thirties for several months. But, then, the conflict between the Orbánites and Fodorites came to a head.

The solidification of the Orbánites' control over FIDESZ took place quickly in April 1993. Orbán was elected party president on April 18 and thereby gained considerable administrative and symbolic power. A few days later, as expected, Áder was voted the administrative vice president, making this close ally of Orbán the formal head of the FIDESZ administration. The critical issue, as far as the Fodorists were concerned, was who would replace Orbán as faction leader. They proposed József Szájer, who they considered a compromise candidate between the two factions. The Orbánists were not interested in the compromise. They promoted Orbán's closest ally, Kövér, as the faction leader. Kövér won.[22]

It is unclear when the Alliance of Free Democrats first invited Fodor to switch parties or when the final agreement was reached. What is clear is that Fodor took his final stand in late October. He ran to become the head of the national committee, the larger but weaker FIDESZ governing body. The Orbánites promoted Szájer, who the Fodorists no longer considered a reasonable compromise. Using their significant influence through the new organizational structure, the Orbánists ran an aggressive campaign for Szájer and against Fodor. As Bill Lomax described these events:

*Gábor Fodor was one of the most popular politicians in Hungary and was more popular than Viktor Orbán, both in the party and in the country. Yet Fodor represented no challenge to Orbán leadership of FIDESZ and his presence in the party leadership was an invaluable electoral asset for the party. Viktor Orbán and his close supporters, however, chose to direct a vicious campaign against him and Fodor was defeated in the contest for the chairmanship.*[23]

Three days later, Fodor quit FIDESZ and gave up his seat in parliament. A popular politicians and a key member of FIDESZ throughout its history, his resignation was a severe blow to the party. Klára Ungár and Péter Molnár, two other prominent Fodorites, followed Fodor out of the party a few days later. The impact on FIDESZ's public image was devastating. By quitting politics—as it will turn out, temporarily—Fodor and his allies gave off the impression that they were victims; it appeared as if they were not seeking political advantage. To many Hungarians, on the other hand, Orbán and Kövér now seemed like power-hungry ogres, so determined to be in charge that they would push an old friend out of the party. Any image of purity or being above petty politics was shattered.

There was another problem with Fodor's highly public quitting. In the 1990 campaign, Fodor was used to represent FIDESZ's image as a liberal party. He was also the person with the closest ties to the Free Democrats, such as with his involvement in the Democratic Charter. Fodor's quitting reinforced the impression that FIDESZ had abandoned its liberal ideology and was moving towards the unpopular Hungarian Democratic Forum.

FIDESZ support, which leveled off around 29% during the early fall, now plunged. It continued to decline rapidly as the election neared. Yet, FIDESZ continued to race away from the front it presented at the height of its popularity. Having now shifted ideologically to the right and even having stated that it would go into coalition with the unpopular Hungarian Democratic Forum, FIDESZ no longer had a clear antagonist against which to act. The message became muffled: It tried to criticize the Democratic Forum government without attacking it too directly. In other cases, it presented itself through posters with longwinded writing and extensive lists of campaign promises; there was no ideological content or reference to another party.[24] On the other hand, it was rather clear in its attack against the Hungarian Socialist Party. While anti-communist rhetoric was consistent with the radical image of FIDESZ from the democracy movement, it seemed utterly inconsistent with the mood of Hungarians in 1994, who seemed much more concerned about replacing an unpopular center-right government.

The Young Democrats also worked hard to lose their image of youth. One of the primary slogans for FIDESZ in 1994 was: "The Orange had grown up!" (Orange was the FIDESZ party color, and the fruit was the party symbol.) This shift away from the youth image was also evident in its national and county lists, which were constructed mostly by Orbán and Áder. Older people were placed on spots six through ten on the national list to offset the image that FIDESZ was a youth party. (The lists were also made to reach another goal: to push the remaining Fodorites out of the party.)[25]

Then, late in the campaign, the campaign suddenly switched back to promoting its youth image, possibly because it realized very late that this image was one aspect of its former popularity. This may be the reason for one of FIDESZ's better known but not widely respected posters, which read: "If you are sick of the banana, choose the Orange!" "Sick of the banana"—in Hungarian, "unod a banánt"—is youth slang that means roughly the equivalent of "sick of the bull" in American English. It may have been a last ditch effort to win the vote of the last group willing to support FIDESZ.

According to people involved in both the 1990 and 1994 campaigns, the key difference between the two was that the 1994 campaign was significantly harder to run: Nothing seemed to work.[26] It lacked volunteer help, and it could not produce a clear campaign theme. In the end, the only reason that FIDESZ was not completely eliminated from Hungarian politics—that is, the only reason that FIDESZ did not fall under the 5% list vote needed to re-enter parliament—was because a percentage of young, unmarried people supported the party. Having effectively confused Hungarians about its ideology, FIDESZ did not seem to undermine its image of youth despite its efforts to appear "grown up," possibly because its leaders were still quite young and possibly because its name was still the Federation of *Young Democrats*. One can only speculate whether Kövér's proposed "Federation of the Young Democracy" would have more effectively convinced Hungarians that it was no longer a youth party, and whether that name change would have caused more FIDESZ supporters to abandon the party, possibly enough to drop its list vote in 1994 another 2% and under the 5% minimum needed to re-enter parliament and survive politically.

**The Third Resurrection of Béla Kun's Party:**
The history of the Hungarian Communist Party, as it was once called, is the tale of a party that shifted between obscurity and governmental power. It is an organization that has rebounded multiple times from seemingly complete disaster, a body that had been repeatedly beaten but never seemed to die. After the failed Hungarian communist revolution of 1919, the communists were forced underground for decades, only to reemerge as the ruling party with the help of the Red Army. In 1956, after the Hungarian Workers' Party collapsed, it renamed and revamped itself, becoming a powerful ruling party within a few years, again with the help of the Red Army. Then, by early 1994, even with the Soviet Union having collapsed and without the help of an army from the east, the offspring of Béla Kun's party began to once again scratch its way from under the tombstone. By, January, a few months before the next parliamentary elections, the Hungarian Socialist Party had surpassed the Young Democrats in popular support and seemed well on its way to once again take charge of the Hungarian government.

This resurrection of the Hungarian Socialist Party provides the last step in this analysis. I have shown so far that the three parties of inexperienced politicians made serious performance errors in the 1990 to 1994 period, and I have shown that significant drops in public support followed these errors. Now, I will show that Socialists' return to power is consistent with the argument that, as the most competent group at party politics, it eventually capitalized on other parties' mistakes. The following pieces of evidence will be provided. One, the Hungarian

Socialist Party did not have the same performance problems as the Democratic Forum, Free Democrats and Young Democrats; it maintained greater party unity and did not significantly contradict its own party image. Two, the rise in public support for the Socialists was tied directly to the drop in FIDESZ support.

*The Unity of Socialists:*

If one examines Hungarian party politics from 1990 to 1994, one becomes faced with a paradox. The recent history of the Hungarian Socialist Party would lead one to believe that it would contain the most ideological divisions of all the parties in the new parliament. Yet, it remained the most united during the first term of the new regime. The Hungarian Socialist Party emerged from a large, monopolistic organization that opened membership to people of most ideological orientations a quarter of a century before. While the new party was roughly made up of the reform wing of the old Hungarian Socialist Workers' Party, that reform wing was hardly a distinct group. The party was formed as a compromise between two platforms, and each of these platforms was an alliance among various groups. The party nonetheless held together as a united team, even after serious jockeying for power in 1990. On the other extreme was the Independent Smallholders' Party. This party was defined by a single issue: It argued for a radical re-privatization of land taken by the communist regime nearly a century before. It split into multiple, warring parties within two years of the 1990 election.

The unity of the Socialist party is also odd if one considers a second factor: The Socialists experienced an enormous political defeat in 1990. It was diminished from the party that monopolized Hungarian politics to a small opposition party in parliament that was routinely ostracized by the other party factions. In comparison, the most successful parties in 1990 were the Hungarian Democratic Forum and Alliance of Free Democrats. The Democratic Forum began experiencing internal strife within weeks after winning. Prominent members began publicly quitting the party and faction six months after the 1990 parliamentary elections; three years after that victory, the party split. The Alliance of Free Democrats lasted longer; its intra-party crisis began a year and a half after it became the largest opposition party in parliament. Indeed, the only party other than the Socialists to enter parliament in 1990 and not have a party unity crisis from 1990 to 1994 was the Christian Democratic People's Party. Its crisis began in 1996. Mostly because of that crisis, it did not return to parliament in 1998.

How does one explain this paradox, especially why the Socialist party would be so united when it was formed as an alliance of various factions? Hungarian political scientist László Vass provides the following answer: The notion that the Socialists were ideologically divided was a misinterpretation. The reason was that Socialist politicians were not ideologues; they were professional politicians. As professionals, they were driven by an ideology of winning power and running a government.[27] If one places this answer within the context of East-Central European politics immediately after the regime change, it makes complete sense. Many of the politicians of the new parties made decisions that were strategic blunders. One could make the argument that these politicians were driven more by their ideology than practical political considerations. In comparison, the

191

Socialists' steps always seemed to have strategic purpose and never seemed to be driven primarily by ideological considerations.

But, I would have to add one other point to this answer. From the available evidence, it appears that the politicians from new parties *thought* that they were making strategically wise moves. There are no indications that any of the performance changes discussed in this chapter and the previous two were done with the recognition that they might have negative or even disastrous effects. (For example, there is no evidence to show that Orbán and Kövér were consciously aware that their decision to change ideologically a year before an election would cause them to lose the election and nearly become eliminated politically.) Quite the opposite, these inexperienced party politicians seemed to believe that they were making positive and even wise decisions. To the degree that the leaders of new parties made decisions that did not mesh with the practicalities of party politics—and indeed, the mistakes were not always ideological in nature—they did so without recognizing that their decisions were strategic mistakes.

This does not mean that everything went smoothly for the Socialists after the transition. Quite the opposite, the crushing defeat produced a great deal of internal movement and disorder. As often happens after such a defeat, many members quit the party. As Patrick O'Neil pointed out, "many MSZMP [Hungarian Socialist Workers' Party] cadres who had clung to the new MSZP [Hungarian Socialist Party] deserted the party once the election made it clear that the old spoils system had truly come to an end."[28]

For our purposes, the more important shift was within the party center. In late 1989 and early 1990, the four most prominent Socialist party members were Imre Pozsgay (the popular reform politician; he became the faction head in the new parliament), Rezsô Nyers (the Kádárite who was the first party president of the Hungarian Socialist Party), Miklós Németh (the former Prime Minister), and Gyula Horn (the former Minister of Foreign Affairs.) Of these four, Horn was probably the least significant at that time. Accused of being in a *pufajkás* squad—the thugs who traveled the country to seek revenge on people who had crossed the party during the 1956 revolution—Horn allied himself to the reform communists late in the Kádár era. His most famous reform act was as the Hungarian Foreign Minister who permitted East German tourists to cross over to Austria, which led directly to the fall of the Berlin Wall. His closest ties among the key reformers were with Németh, who had been Foreign Minister before him, and Pozsgay. He was a member of Pozsgay's Central Committee sub-committee that concluded that 1956 was a popular uprising, for example. Horn advanced to his leadership position with the support of Németh and Pozsgay and against the wishes of Nyers.[29]

Within a year of the transformation, Horn secured intra-party power into his own hands. Németh did not even enter the new parliament. He instead accepted a job in Germany and left the country, putting him out of the picture. Then, in May, Horn was elected party president. Nyers was pushed completely out of the party leadership; he was not even returned to the presidium. (Nyers remained an Hungarian Socialist Party politician, even returning to parliament in 1994, but by then he was a minor and rather isolated figure in the party Horn dominated.) Finally, Pozsgay quit the party and the parliamentary faction in

November 1990. After the referendum campaign, Pozsgay steadily lost support on all sides. His old friends in the Democratic Forum completely disassociated themselves from him. His popularity with the public, already low in January 1990, dropped even lower by September. (Pozsgay's average score on feeling thermometers, in which respondents were asked to rate politicians from 0 to 100, was only 45 in September 1990; in comparison, Horn's average score was 75.)[30] Finally, his support within the party network seemed to decline as well; according to his own accounts, he was blamed for having negotiated too much away in 1989 and largely causing the Socialists' loss of power.[31] With these former leaders out of the way, and having secured both the roles of party president and symbolic head, Horn had taken charge of the party.

Once these intra-party conflicts were resolved in 1990—four years before the next parliamentary elections—the Socialist leadership became stable and remained so through the 1994 election. As Bill Lomax described:

> *Following these changes, the new leadership of the party remained stable and united, and has not had to face any direct challenges, although several platforms have been active within the party, amongst them the Union for a Social Democratic Hungarian Socialist Party, the Liberal Socialists, the Left Wing Unity platform, the Religious Socialists, and the Patriotic and Progressive Socialists. MSZP, however, probably more than any other Hungarian party, has come to behave much like modern democratic parties in the West, so that debates over policy and ideology have not so far caused it irretrievable damage or served to tear it apart.*[32]

Indeed, any intra-party problems that the Socialists had were front-loaded. They occurred over three years before the next election. To a lesser extent, the same was true of the Free Democrats; its crisis ended about a year and a half before the election. In comparison, the FIDESZ intra-party crisis occurred a few months before the election, and the Democratic Forum continued to have intra-party problems as the election approached. Nonetheless, by most accounts, the unity of the Hungarian Socialist was based on their many years of experience working in Kádár's party bureaucracy.

*The Socialists Party and the Mass Politics Field:*

It is hard to discuss the Hungarian Socialist Party's public presentation after its reorganization and before the 1994 campaign. The party stayed out of the limelight. It appears that the party's primary focus was to regain its legitimacy as a part of Hungarian politics. Many of these politicians had been prominent members of the previous government, including Central Committee members and department heads. After their 1990 defeat, the government and the opposition largely ignored them, and the public seemed to generally dislike them. There was probably no other reasonable strategy at this time than to gradually rebuild a positive image.

The party worked slowly to regain its legitimacy as a serious player on stage. One step in this direction was the Democratic Charter, which had Socialist

MP Iván Vitányi as one of its leaders. The Democratic Charter showed Socialist party members working with mainstream politicians. Moreover, these mainstream politicians were from the Alliance of Free Democrats and to a lesser extend FIDESZ, archenemies of the reform communists a few years before. Socialist politicians also presented themselves in the most professional manner possible. As Béla Király wrote about the Socialists:

> *The professionalism and moderation of the left-of-center policies of the MSZP leadership was impressive to watch. Never during the four years of the first post-communist parliament were they demagogic obstructionists; they rather behaved as a Western-type loyal opposition. In parliamentary committees as well as during plenary sessions of the legislature, they presented professionally prepared, moderate, practical, constructive proposals. Their parliamentary fraction operated in unison, representing a disciplined, well-informed, dignified body of statesmen, rather than unruly politicians. General appreciation and respect followed, contributing with this earned prestige to the political standing of MSZP.*[33]

MSZP, or the Hungarian Socialist Party, also maintained the highest level of consistency in its advertisements from 1990 to 1994. They were certainly not the best advertisements of either election. The 1990 FIDESZ campaign was certainly much more impressive, and its popular advertisements were probably one reason that a youth organization could win 9% of the party list vote, outdoing a number of parties that claimed long traditions in Hungarian politics. In 1994, while the Democratic Forum and FIDESZ campaigns could be described as disasters, the Free Democrat advertisements were well constructed with very consistent, positive themes. The Socialists' 1994 advertisements were somewhat less impressive than the professionalism of the Free Democrats' campaign. But, the Socialists held a consistent theme in both campaigns: security.

There were two reasons why a theme of security could work for the Socialists. The more obvious but probably less important reason was their history as a Socialist party and their new-found promotion of social democratic principles. With the other parties promoting some degree of economic liberalism in 1990, and with an economic crisis looming over the country, there were good reasons to present an image of promoting social welfare. A second reason was that Hungarians seemed to associate security with the expertise of those in charge. Since the 1960s, the Socialist party developed a reputation among Hungarians as an organization of experts, and during this period of understated ideology it even based much of its governing legitimacy on this impression. Similarly, when Grósz challenged Kádár for party power, his justification was also based on expertise: He presented himself as the head technocrat who was now questioning the decisions of the old party leadership. The Hungarian Socialist Party then adopted this image as well. It presented itself as a party run by Western oriented professionals who brought expertise to their jobs, and it implied that the defeated wing of the Hungarian Socialist Workers' Party were a group of hard-line communist ideologues. (Ironically, this was the wing that Grósz headed in 1989.)

# The Puzzling Resurgence of the Hungarian Socialist Party

That tradition of claiming security through expertise was then used in its battles against other parties on the new, multi-party politics. In 1990, a common Socialist slogan was "Válaszd a Biztos Jövôt!" or "Choose the Secure Future!" In 1994, the main slogan was "A Megbízható Megoldás," or "The Reliable Solution." (It is noteworthy that the key words in each slogan, "biztos" and "megbízható", are both built around the same root, "biz," or to have confidence in.) This theme was played further in 1994 with the secondary slogan, "Hogy a szakértelem kerüljön kormányra!" which could be translated as "For a government with expertise!"[34]

In other words, the Socialist mass politics strategy during the first years of the new regime was relatively passive. The party focused on rebuilding its legitimacy, both through consistent shows of moderation and professionalism and by slowly working its way back into the political mainstream. In political terms, it was damage control, a defensive strategy, not a forthright attempt to quickly regain power. Because of its widespread unpopularity as well as this defensive strategy, the Socialist revival so soon after the collapse of the Warsaw Pact was only possible if Hungarians first rejected the parties from the dissident movement. And as the evidence presented above shows, the rejection of the three main parties from the Hungarian dissident movement came immediately after each made fundamental strategic mistakes, though surely the Democratic Forum would have had difficulty maintaining support anyway while governing over a severe economic decline. The rise of support for FIDESZ came only after Hungarians abandoned the Hungarian Democratic Forum and Alliance of Free Democrats, and the Socialist revival came only after Hungarians of all ideological stripes deserted FIDESZ.

Most explanations of the Socialist revival see that rebirth as somehow Socialist driven. They often focus on the economic dislocation of the public or the organizational advantages the Socialists supposedly possessed. But these arguments not only misrepresent a critical aspect of the transition but also miss a fundamental issue in democratic transitions. From the perspective of dissident movements, these transitions come in two main steps: The collapse of the ruling elite, and its replacement by new political parties competing in free, fair elections. The problem for the Hungarian dissidents was that virtually overnight they went from nudging or cajoling the regime into reforming itself out of existence to attempting to run major political parties. The master strategists of the pre-transition stage became the fumbling neophytes in the post-transition stage. Had the parties that emerged from the dissident movement maintained consistent and united performances, then these parties may have achieved a goal presented during the transition by Hungary's most prominent dissident, János Kis: To keep the Socialists out of power for at least two decades after the fall of the Berlin Wall. The Socialist return to the central role in Hungarian politics was not a conspiracy or a sign of misguided thinking by the Hungarian public. It was the product of inexperience and low party competence by the dissidents turned party leaders.

**Graph 7.1**
**Support Among Likely Voters for FIDESZ and Socialists, 1992-1994**

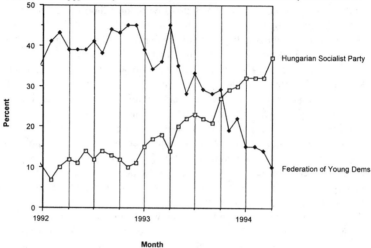

Source: Szonda Ipsos, http://www.szondaipsos.hu/partpref/.

# The Puzzling Resurgence of the Hungarian Socialist Party

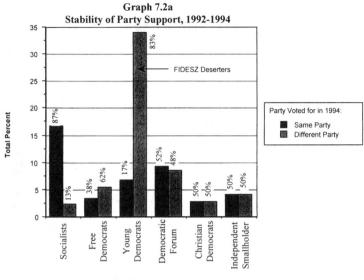

**Graph 7.2a**
**Stability of Party Support, 1992-1994**

Party Voted for in 1994:
- Same Party
- Different Party

FIDESZ Deserters

**Party Supported in 1992**

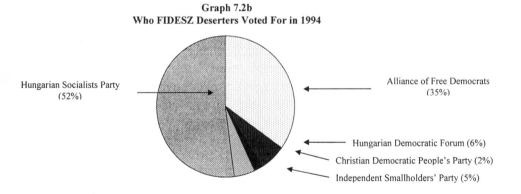

**Graph 7.2b**
**Who FIDESZ Deserters Voted For in 1994**

Hungarian Socialists Party
(52%)

Alliance of Free Democrats
(35%)

Hungarian Democratic Forum (6%)
Christian Democratic People's Party (2%)
Independent Smallholders' Party (5%)

Source: Central European University Survey (1992, 1994).

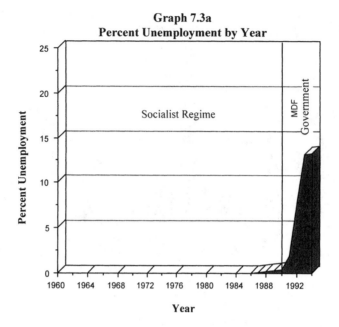

**Graph 7.3a**
**Percent Unemployment by Year**

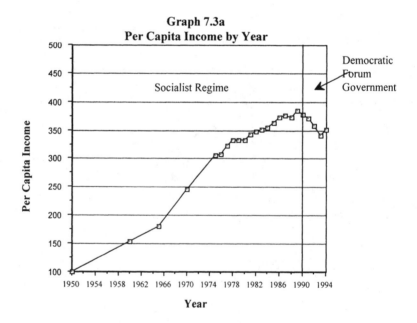

**Graph 7.3a**
**Per Capita Income by Year**

Sources: *Statistical Yearbook of Hungary, 1993*; *Statistical Yearbook of Hungary, 1995*[35]

**Graph 7.4**
**FIDESZ Desertion by Comparison of Regimes**

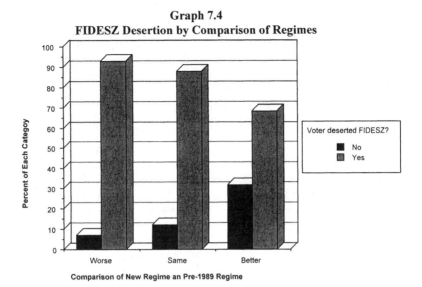

Source: Central European University Survey (1992, 1994).

199

**Table 7.1**
**Agreement or Disagreement with Ideological Statements, 1992 and 1994**

| | Percent giving "Left" Answer | |
| --- | --- | --- |
| | 1992 | 1994 |
| It should be the government's responsibility to provide a job for everyone who wants one. | 86% | 83% |
| It would be harmful to the economy if the government tried to reduce income differences. | 59% | 62% |
| The transfer of state-owned companies to private hands will help in solving the economic problems of our country. | 54% | 55% |
| It is more important that a politician be a strong patriot than an expert. | 71% | 72% |
| A woman should be allowed to have an abortion in the early weeks of pregnancy. | 87% | 87% |
| Politicians who do not believe in God should not perform public functions. | 81% | 84% |

For each statement, the respondent was asked to state whether he or she definitely agreed, rather agreed, rather disagreed, or strongly disagreed. These answers were collapsed into agree or disagree and then coded by whether they would be the answer associated with a more left-wing or right-wing ideology in Hungary.

Source: Central European University Survey (1992, 1994).

**September 1992**                    **May 1994**

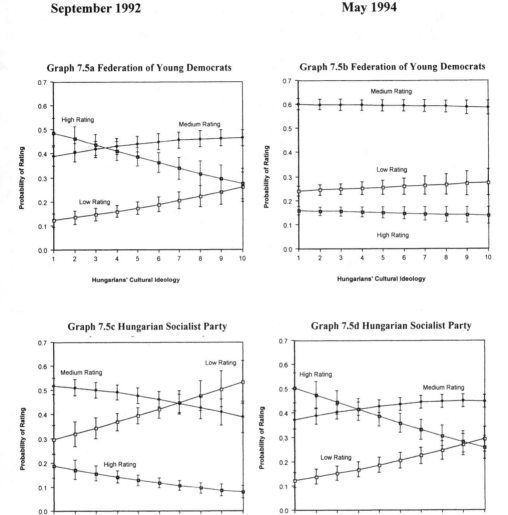

**Graphs 7.5a-7.5h: The Relationship between Party Ratings and Cultural Ideology**. For each level of cultural ideology from left to right, and with all else being equal, each graph shows the probability that a Hungarian would have given a party a low, medium, or high rating in 1992 or 1994. The graphs are based on surveys taken before or after the Federation of Young Democrats (the focus of this quasi-experiment) abruptly changed its cultural ideology in 1993. The graphs

suggest that after the Federation of Young Democrats shifted its cultural ideology, the relationship between voters' cultural ideology and their ratings of that party disappeared. Source: Central European University Survey (1992, 1994)

**September 1992**                                 **May 1994**

**Control (continued):**

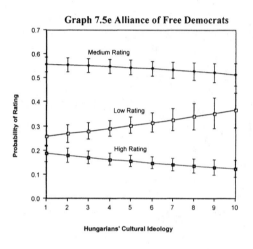

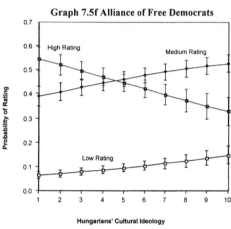

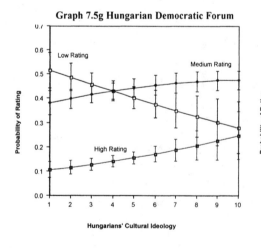

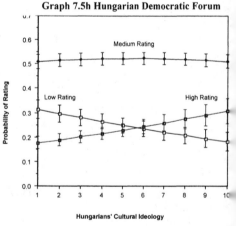

**Graph 7.6**
**Estimated 1994 Campaign Spending of Each Party**

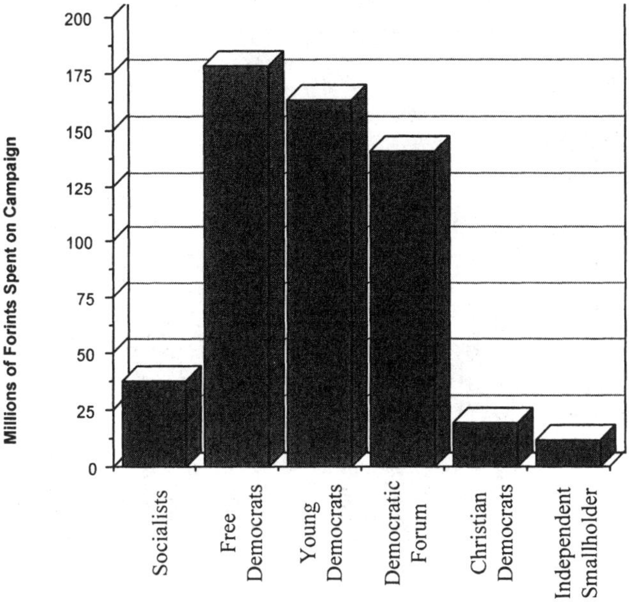

Source: Péter Matyac, "Az SZDSZ költött a legtöbbet reklámra" ["SZDSZ spent the most on advertisement"], *Népszabadság*. June 11, 1994, pp. 1, 4.

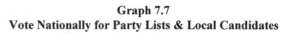

**Graph 7.7**
**Vote Nationally for Party Lists & Local Candidates**

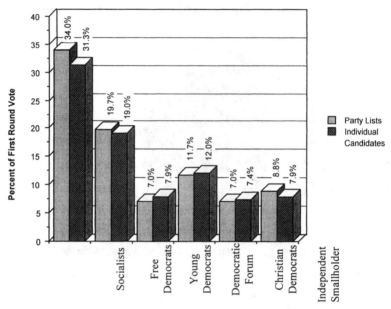

**Graph 7.8**
**Voting Socialist by Newspaper Readership**

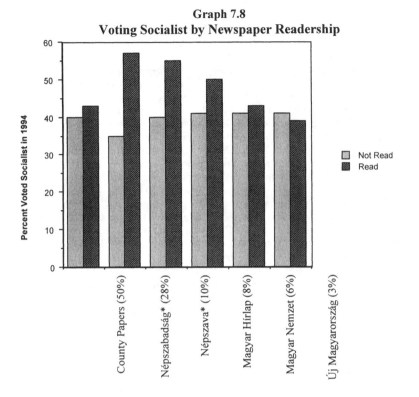

Number in parentheses shows the percent of likely voters who read that newspaper.

\* The relationship between whether the person read the newspaper and whether that person voted for the Hungarian Socialist Party in 1994 is significant at the .05 level.

# Notes:

1. This analysis is based partially on my having heard approximately half a dozen lectures on the Socialist victory by Hungarian university professors—like György Csepeli, head of the Sociology Department at Eötvös Loránd University, and János Kis, head of the Political Science Department at the Central European University—and other prominent Hungarian thinkers. Several of these lectures were given in New Brunswick, NJ, hosted by either Rutgers University or by the Hungarian Alumni Association.

2. Béla K. Király (1995) "Soft Dictatorship, Lawful Revolution, and the Socialists' Return to Power", in *Lawful Revolution in Hungary, 1989–94*. Edited by Béla Király. (Boulder: East European Monographs), Distributed by Columbia University Press, pp. 3–14.

3. This explanation could be categorized under "party competence" as well, since Király does discuss the professional experience of this network. However, the more important aspect of this explanation is that the Hungarian Socialist Party maintained its vast party structure after the transition, revising only the names of particular bodies and taking them out of the workplace. No other party had this well established party structure.

4. András Körösényi (1995) "The Reasons for the Defeat of the Right in Hungary," , trans. by Eszter Nadin with Johnathan Sunley, *East European Politics and Society*, 9, no. 1, pp. 179-94.

5. Anna M. Grzymala-Busse (2002), *Redeeming the Communist Past: The Regeneration of Communist Parties in East Central Europe*, (Cambridge: Cambridge University Press).

6. Szonda Ipsos, http://www.szondaipsos.hu/partpref/.

7. Ibid.

8. Central European University (1992), *The Development of Party Systems and Electoral Alignments in East Central Europe: The 1992 Survey in Hungary*. Machine readable data files. (Budapest: Department of Political Science, Central European University). Central European University (1994), *The Development of Party Systems and Electoral Alignments in East Central Europe: The 1994 Survey in Hungary*. Machine readable data files. (Budapest: Department of Political Science, Central European University). Both surveys are available from the Hungarian and the Slovenian social science data archives under the above title, and from the German archive (Zentralarchiv) in Cologne as "1992 Hungarian Election Study" and "1994 Hungarian Election Study".

9. Központi Statisztikai Hivatal [Central Statistical Office], 1995, *Magyar Statisztikai Évkönyv 1995 [Statistical Yearbook of Hungary, 1995]*, edited by Csák Liget, (Budapest: Regiszter Kiadó és Nyomda Kft), p. 314.

10. Central European University, *The 1994 Survey in Hungary*.

11. Central European University, *The 1992 Survey in Hungary; The 1994 Survey in Hungary*.

12. For a detailed discussion on the relationship between East-Central European parties and their supporters on these types of ideological questions, see Herbert Kitschelt, et. al (1999), *Post Communist Party Systems: Competition, Representation and Inter-Party Cooperation*, (Cambridge: Cambridge University Press), pp. 309-44.

13. Péter Matyac. "Az SZDSZ költött a legtöbbet reklámra" ["SZDSZ spent the most on advertisement"]. *Népszabadság*. June 11, 1994. p. 1, 4.

14. Zsolt Enyedi, "The Organizational Structure of FIDESZ", unpublished paper. This shift in power from the Committee to the parliamentary faction was also mentioned by István Hegedüs, a FIDESZ MP at that time, during my interview with him.

15. Three of my FIDESZ sources discussed the nature of this supposed personal conflict. Each argued that it was unrelated to the split.

[16] Interview with István Hegedüs.

[17] Supporters of Orbán argue that the FIDESZ leadership began shifting away from British liberalism when they concluded around 1992 that former Communists were the main beneficiaries of the transition because of their connections and wealth. Critics of Orbán argue that he and Kövér returned to the sharp anti-Communist rhetoric only after MSZP began catching up to FIDESZ in public support. Interviews with Sándor Holbok and István Hegedüs.

[18] Enyedi, "The Organizational Structure of FIDESZ".

[19] Ibid; Bill Lomax (1994) "Obstacles to the Development of Democratic Politics," in *The Journal of Communist Studies and Transition Politics*, Vol 10, no. 3. Special edition: *Hungary: The Politics of Transition*. edited by Terry Cox and Andy Furlong. pp. 93-5; *A Fiatal Demokrácia Szövetségének Alapszabálya. [Bylaws of the Federation of the Young Democracy]*, draft constitution at the Fifth Congress of the Federation of Young Democrats, Debrecen, April 16-18, 1993; *Módosító Indítványok az Alapszabály Tervezetézhez. [Proposed Amendments to the Draft Constitution]* Federation of Young Democrats, Fifth Congress, Debrecen, April 16-18, 1993.

[20] Sándor Holbok, who worked under Áder during the 1994 campaign, presented the first three explanations during my interview with him. These appear to be the most common explanations given by Orbán supporters. I added the fourth explanation. Interview with Holbok.

[21] István Hegedüs, a FIDESZ MP from 1990 to 1994, also makes the claim that FIDESZ politicians did not begin their hard anti-Communist rhetoric until *after* the Socialists began making real strides in public support. He also claims that during closed faction meetings before 1993, Orbán and Kövér spoke openly about possibly joining a coalition with the Socialists after the 1994 election. Interview with Hegedüs.

[22] István Hegedüs presented me with the Fodorite's interpretation of these events.

[23] Lomax, "Obstacles to...", pp. 94-5.

[24] See, as an example, the poster on page 81 in *Hungarian Political Yearbook, 1995*.

[25] Interview with Holbok. He specifically mentioned István Hegedüs and Zsusza Szelényi as two remaining Fodorites that they intended to eliminate by putting them low on lists.

[26] This statement is based on the interview with Holbok as well as informal discussions with FIDESZ staffers.

[27] László Vass is a professor of political science at the Budapest Economic University, and he worked as Pozsgay's assistant during the transition. I had the opportunity to ask Vass this question twice, the first time during a meeting in the parliament building, the second time at his office. He gave me this answer during the interview.

[28] Patrick O'Neal (1996). "Revolution from Within: Analysis, Transitions from Authoritarianism, and the Case of Hungary". *World Politics* 48: 579–603. The quote is from page 600.

[29] Tôkés, *Hungary's Negotiated Revolution*, p. 325.

[30] *Hungarian Political Yearbook, 1991*, p. 602.

[31] Imre Pozsgay (1988) *Koronatú és Tettstárs [Star Witness and Accomplice]*, (Budapest: Korona).

[32] Lomax, "Obstacles to...", pp. 88-9.

[33] Király, p. 10.

[34] *Hungarian Political Yearbook, 1991*, pp. 62-7; *Hungarian Political Yearbook, 1995*, pp. 72-81, 127-34.

[35] Per capita real income for each year was calculated in comparison to per capita real income in 1960. Registered unemployment was measured on January 1 of each year.

## Conclusion:

# Dissidents and the Dilemmas of Democratization

The Hungarian anti-Communist dissidents played a critical role in the country's democratization in 1990. While the Hungarian Socialist government would have probably taken steps towards democracy at this time in order to deal with debt problems and maneuver its way through shifting international circumstances, the ruling party was clearly attempted to produce democracy more in image than substance. But the Hungarian democratic opposition fought back, constructing initial steps towards civil society, uniting temporarily to create the Opposition Roundtable during the negotiations for transition, and forcing a referendum vote on a number of key issues. They then built political parties to challenge the Socialists and (temporarily) pushed them out of power.

But, after playing this central role, all but the youngest and a few other former dissidents were either eliminated from Hungarian political contention or largely marginalized. The hard-core dissidents who worked for decades to undermine the regime were quietly pushed to the side and sometimes even asked to leave the party they built, and the populist writers and Antall allies were either retired from party politics or defeated. The professional politicians of the Hungarian Socialist Party thrived after their revival in 1993 and 1994, despite their historical connection to the hated Soviet occupation. Similarly, the young lawyers of FIDESZ, who barely survived the 1994 election, recovered within a few years. The leadership around Orbán had reached a number of conclusions after the 1994 disaster, and one of the main lessons was that they need to build a party of professional politicians.

This elimination of most former dissidents is one predicted consequence of party competence. Dissidents face a serious and unfortunate dilemma during democratic transitions. They are often the key people who need to build new parties to compete in newly established free elections. As the people who stood in opposition to the regime, often over an extended period, they usually embody a symbolic role critical to that fundamental change. Moreover, while they would rarely have a background in party politics, the dissidents are among the very few people outside the regime with any political background, and during the first election they are often still acting as opposition groups attempting to finish changes that they had been struggling for over many years. The problem is that once the regime has in fact changed to democratic rules, many of these writers and intellectuals could become liabilities to the parties they founded. In times of stress, people tend to revert back to the competencies they know, and the tools of the dissident are not particularly applicable to multiparty politics.

209

A theory of party competence leads to the conclusion that most dissidents are unlikely to play the same critical roles after a democratic transition as they did before and during it. Some may be able to transform themselves into party politicians, and some may have gained so much stature during the dissident period that their symbolic roles overcome their competency limitations. But to survive, parties formed by dissidents are left with only a few options to deal with their low party competence. The dissidents and their allies can attempt to rapidly learn party politics. This can be a tall order, and its failure could have detrimental effects on the party and, depending on the circumstances, threaten the democratic transition itself. If the party or parties of dissidents fail, and if the only other parties are run by leaders of the former regime or by demagogues willing to take all steps necessary to secure their own power and glory, the marginalization or collapse of the dissident parties could help produce a de facto return to the previous regime or the rise of anti-democratic or extremist parties.

A second option would be to plan for their own replacement within the party organization. Even here, the dissidents may be facing few options. Most likely, the only people available with experience in party politics had been part of the previous regime. The best they can do is find people with backgrounds that are related to party politics and who seem capable of quickly learning this new approach to politics. They could then mimic, in an abbreviated form, the gatekeeping and training process that established political parties follow. Of course, this would ask dissidents to be extremely pragmatic and even embrace strategic steps that are hardly in their own interests. But it is specifically because they play such a central role to the democratic transition that dissidents may need to accept these limitations.

**Party Competence and Democracy:**

The theory presented in this book leads to another conclusion about the limits facing dissidents. The democracy for which they struggle and suffer is no utopia. First, a political elite will likely emerge, and that elite will probably include politicians from the previous regime. Second, that elite will not simply respond to public wishes in an attempt to win votes. Public control over their government, in any pure sense, is effectively impossible. Pragmatically speaking, the best the dissidents can hope for is a system in which the people at large have a significant (but certainly not complete) influence over policy and their basic rights are respected and protected by the government.

Part of the problem was expressed in its most stark form by Robert Michels early in the twentieth century. Following the sociology of his mentor and friend, Max Weber, he argued that modern democracies require political parties and that parties must be run by political professionals. Party politics is a specialized field that requires a particular expertise, he argued. However, Michels continued, that very expertise undermines modern democracy, if one understands democracy to mean that the people control their own government. This need for expertise produces a stratum of political leaders with competencies that the non-professional public as a whole cannot develop. Since the public can never develop these competencies, they become dependent on the political leaders to deal with technical issues and explain those issues to them, both of which dramatically shift power into the hands of a political elite.[1]

The need for specialized competencies—and a related phenomenon, political professionals—makes this stratum indispensable. It also provides the political elite as a group the skills to repel challenges to their privileged positions. While one faction of professionals may topple another, the elite structure itself must stay intact or, in extreme cases, be replaced by another elite structure. Even if political amateurs topple the old professionals, these neophytes must also become professionals to retain power. Either they develop related political competencies or others will usurp their positions.

The political competence difference between party politicians and the mass public is a primary reason why the public cannot retain control over its elected politicians. Just as the public is unlikely to gain more than a rudimentary understanding of medicine, they are unlikely to gain the experiences that would lead them to understand politics and policy. This is not an issue of native ability or whether the masses are putting enough effort into understanding politics. Instead, it is a product of division of labor. The complexity of political struggle and the technical nature of policy make it extremely unlikely that non-professionals can understand what parties, legislators, and organized interests are fighting over, that is, beyond the most basic level. Effectively, the public becomes dependent on others, usually the politicians themselves, to simplify policy debates for them.

Politicians can simplify these policy debates in such a way that they mislead the public. The symbolic nature of political theater makes it possible for politicians to build support for policy stands at the same time that they disguise the special interests behind those stands or how segments of the mass public could be hurt by those positions. Ethnic, class and other divisions within the mass public can be used to mask the organized interests behind policy proposals. Politicians can also find backdoor ways to shift social costs on particular segments of the mass public, including by claiming that they are stopping bureaucrats or lowering government waste. This is all possible not only because of the complexity of the policy process but also because the relationship between party action and social outcomes is not obvious. It is not always clear who is responsible for policy shifts that hurt the public, especially when the governing party actively works to hide its role or produce that confusion.

Moreover, the mass public is not the only group whose support parties need to maintain. Parties are equally dependent on elite organizations. If it needs to raise money to run campaigns and the party organization, and if the specific interest of a funding organization conflicts with the interest of most of the mass public, the interests of the mass public are not guaranteed to triumph. Quite the opposite, the party will likely try to support the interest of the organized group and sell that policy stand to the public. Similarly, foreign governments and international organizations often hold significant cards that major parties must take seriously. If a country runs into a debt crisis, for example, the governing parties often must reduce state spending and raise taxes regardless of how much pain it produces for the mass public. Similarly, if a dispute with neighboring countries affects a nation's relationship with other countries, governing parties must often take steps dictated by international politics irrespective of what the public may or may not want.

While the theory presented in this book conflicts with the utopian view that politicians obediently follow the wishes of the voting public, it also conflicts with the arguments that a power elite ignores the wishes of the mass public. A party can disguise policies that much of the mass public would dislike, but that party cannot take active and blatant steps that would outrage the public. Politicians can convince the people to support a war that would cost them money and lives by appealing to patriotism and other great symbols (e.g., making the world safe for democracy) as well as by accusing the enemy of barbarism. But it cannot simply go to war as it pleases. If much of the public begins to oppose the war, the governing party will be in great danger of being thrown out of power. As another example, a governing coalition can make a tax system more regressive by justifying changes with other names (e.g., sin tax or flat tax), but it cannot produce the type of overtly exploitative tax system common in feudal societies. And, while a mass democracy can create unfair criminal laws if those unjust characteristics are well masked, it cannot imprison people as it wills.

The level of mass influence over its government is not an absolute in this framework. A number of factors can influence how much the public actually influences policy. One factor is the degree to which the distribution of interests among elite groups relates to the distribution of interests among the mass public. In other words, what types of groups organize politically and lobby directly? If the capital becomes populated by lobbying organizations that collectively promote the interests of many segments of the general population (e.g., unions, religious groups, ethnic minorities, small farmers, etc.), then these segments of the population are more likely to have real influence on policy. Conversely, if the main lobbying organizations represent business interests and foreign governments, the public interest is less likely to influence government action.

A second issue is what resources elite organizations bring to parties. If organizations act as voices for segments of the population, if there are a wide variety of such organizations, and if these organizations do indeed influence the vote, then elite organizations will provide a very rough reflection of mass interests. However, when elite groups provide other resources for parties (as they normally do), then the relationship between the party and the public will be weakened. For example, if election laws allow high levels of campaign spending and make it easy for organizations to contribute large sums of money, then money becomes an important resource that can increase the influence of lobbying organizations. The organizations that can provide large sums of money—usually business groups—will normally become critical players in this process. The similarity or differences between the interests of these organizations and the mass public is therefore incidental.

Finally, a critical issue is how divided the political elite is. When the elite becomes divided over a particular issue, it is more likely to try to bring the mass public into its struggle. In other words, the side that appears to be losing the issue might attempt to build mass support for its position to gain an upper hand, or the side pushing for the change might try to build that support in anticipation of opposition. This is what E.E. Schattschneider had referred to as "socializing a conflict," or bringing new people into a conflict in order to shift the balance of power.[2] Conversely, if the political elite is largely united on a particular policy, it is unlikely to bring the mass public into the conflict regardless of where the public may stand on the issue. Instead, the specific debates will be kept more private among politicians and lobbyists while the mass public is often presented a horse-and-pony show to keep it from objecting. If most of the political elite has chosen to go to war, for example, then it will collectively take the theatrical moves to build public support and then pretend to heed the will of the people.

In other words, the rise of a stratum of professional politicians in representative democracies produces two problems for dissidents who are in the late stages of struggling for democratization. The first is that since they would probably build political parties, dissidents also have to prepare to either become professional politicians or, more likely, transfer control of these parties to people who can quickly develop the competencies that this form of political struggle requires. Second, depending on the particular circumstances, that stratum may become insulated from public demands. There are a number of mechanisms that help limit the second problem, and one of them is having a political elite divided against itself in a way that makes the struggle for public support especially acute.

**Party Competence and the Hungarian Party System:**
One of the most serious ways that this lack of division within the elite can occur is if one party gains a dominant position in the political system to the degree that the other parties become little more than weak or token opposition. Certainly, a single, dominant party that must run in free elections is hardly the same as a party that maintains control through force. That party still needs to maintain popular support, which keeps it from completely ignoring the needs of the mass public. But, since the system is not divided into clear teams, conflicts within the political elite are easier to keep out of the public discourse. The agenda is mostly set by that one party's leadership, for example. Corruption is also easier, as are quiet changes to the law that might otherwise produce a public backlash. In effect, there is no clear mechanism for socializing conflicts among politicians and lobbying organizations to the mass public.

In 1990, as the Hungarian dissidents were hardly concerned about this possibility. By February of that year, the Socialists were in a free fall, and the parties built by dissidents were primarily concerned about securing their own positions in the new government and pushing members of the former regime completely out of power. A goal of the hard-core dissidents who formed the Alliance of Free Democrats was to keep the Socialists out of power for at least twenty years. Instead, the Socialists started rebounding three years after the democratic transition and then won a plurality of votes and majority of seats in the 1994 parliamentary elections, a mere four years after being kicked out of power in a wave of pro-democracy euphoria.

The Socialists then remained a dominant party, and their strength vis-à-vis most of the new parties gradually grew in the decade that followed the 1994 revival. In 1998 parliamentary election, the Socialists were barely beaten by a center-right coalition of parties. Even then, the Socialists won a plurality of the list votes, 33%, which was roughly identical to their results in the 1994 election.

But, their electoral ally, the Alliance of Free Democrats, faired poorly, and the center-right coalition claimed a victory against the left coalition. During the second round of the election, when most of the single-member district seats tend to be determined, the center-right coalition won a significant victory, and the Socialists were forced into opposition. Four years later, in the 2002 parliamentary elections, the Socialist won a narrow victory. This time, the party of the former regime received 42% of the vote, which was yet again a plurality.

In sharp contrast, most of the parties built by dissidents and other party novices in 1989 and 1990 continued to have internal crises and flirt with elimination from Hungarian politics. By 2000, public support for the Alliance of Free Democrats, the party built by hard-core dissidents, was hovering around 5%. Once supported by around 20% of likely voters, the Free Democrats received 5.6% of the list vote in the 2002 elections, just barely squeaking past the 5% minimum vote needed to reenter parliament. The Hungarian Democratic Forum, the party formed by the populist writers that had been the first main governing party, split into two parties in 1996. The faction that left, made up of close allies to József Antall, the first prime minister of the new regime, formed a party that never gained popular support. This once central group quickly vanished from Hungarian politics. Another faction retained the Hungarian Democratic Forum name. In 1998, it received less than 3% of the list vote and was able to remain in parliament and Hungarian politics entirely because of help by another center-right party. The Christian Democratic People's Party, one of the government coalition parties from 1990 to 1994, began imploding in 1996. In 1998, the Christian Democrats received just over 2% of the list vote and disappeared from Hungarian politics. Finally, in the period before the 2002 election, the Independent Smallholders' Party imploded from a raging intra-party conflict. In the 2002 election, it received less than 1% of the party list vote and was eliminated.

The exception was FIDESZ, or the Federation of Young Democrats, the party built by young lawyers. The 1994 election was a devastating loss for the Young Democrat. Seemingly destined to easily win the election and lead the next government, it won barely enough list votes to re-enter parliament. A critical problem at this point, to add to FIDESZ's other problems, was an exodus of its staff. While the positions of the main party leaders, Viktór Orbán and László Kövér, were not seriously challenged at this point, the party shrunk significantly in size.[3] By the summer of 1994, FIDESZ had lost virtually all its support in all arenas.

However, the young FIDESZ leadership took their electoral disaster and near elimination from Hungarian politics as an opportunity to reevaluate strategies and finish reorganizing the party. First, the loss helped the leadership produce greater party unity. In 1993 and 1994, there were two main groups who left the party. Some were potential opponents to Orbán's leadership, including members of the internal opposition and the followers and allies of Gábor Fodor. (The last prominent Fodorites, István Hegedüs and Zsuzsa Szelényi, left the party in the summer of 1994, two days after the party congress, when they realized that they had no hope of influencing the organization.[4]) Others were pro-Orbán staffers who decided to seek other jobs after the FIDESZ defeat, thus cutting deeply into the organization's manpower. This group remained nominally loyal to the party and appeared willing to become active if the party rebounded.

The defeat also gave the party a chance to make another significant change. During the first year after the 1994 loss, FIDESZ completed its symbolic move to the center-right. It helped create the Civic Alliance, an electoral alliance with the Hungarian Democratic Forum and Christian Democratic People's Party, the other two center-right parties. It also changed its name, this time to FIDESZ–Hungarian Civic Party (in Hungarian, *FIDESZ–Magyar Polgári Párt*, with the acronym FIDESZ–MPP.) This was a particular good moment for a name change; having already lost virtually all its support anyway, and with the next election three years away, there was little chance that this move would have a lasting negative impact. Moreover, that name change indicated a more nuanced and thought through approach than the 1993 proposal for "Federation of the Young Democracy." By retaining "FIDESZ" in the name, the change was less jarring and retained the reference to its origin as a popular youth movement. Instead of seeming to dump its past, FIDESZ was attempting to synthesize that past with its ideological shift to the center right.

Finally, there were many signs that the FIDESZ leadership had learned hard lessons from its 1993 and 1994 period, and that these lessons would influence its future actions. The FIDESZ leadership became determined to not repeat the mistakes of 1993. Within the party, one commonly held explanation as to why FIDESZ lost in 1994 was that it was trying to fight on two fronts at once; it was criticizing the Democratic Forum government at the same time that it was attacking the Hungarian Socialist Party. Around 1996, FIDESZ saw opponents on both the left (the Socialists and Free Democrats) and the right (the Independent Smallholders' Party.) However, the FIDESZ leadership made a conscious decision not to attack the Smallholders' Party, since attacking both the Smallholders' Party and the Socialist government would confuse its message. [5]

Another example of this developing FIDESZ strategy was its idea to push Hungary towards a two party system. By pushing the system towards two parties, these large parties would then dominate Hungarian politics and gain greater security than the six parties in parliament. This appears to have been the primary motivation behind the Civic Alliance. By creating a campaign alliance in which FIDESZ, the Democratic Forum, and the Christian Democrats would run single district candidates together, the probability of winning these seats would increase dramatically, and each party would have a greater chance of surviving despite wild shifts in Hungarian party support. Moreover, the Civic Alliance would be the first step towards creating a larger, center-right party. By creating this party, they might then force the Socialists and Free Democrats into a single party, which would produce two dominant parties, one center-left and the other center-right. Both parties would be safe, and the center-right party would be in a good position to compete against the center-left party. As a FIDESZ strategist told me at the time:

> There are a number of reasons for our strategy to create a two-party system. The first is that when there are two parties, these parties have a fixed existence. There is no need to struggle to

survive, like you have to now in Hungary. Two, it forces [the Socialists of] MSZP and [the Free Democrats of] SZDSZ together. It is a good strategy for us to always keep away from SZDSZ. When we were allies with SZDSZ, they repeatedly fucked us, just like they fuck MSZP from behind now. Three, it will make it easier for us to get the upper hand on the right. If we work with [the Christian Democrats], they can pull in the older voters and we can pull in the younger voters.[6]

FIDESZ also took clear steps towards appearing like a professional party and a loyal opposition. Quite unlike the Smallholders' Party, which at the time acted as the a one-man show of József Torgyán, there was much variation in which FIDESZ MP's spoke in parliament, and their rhetoric was moderate though certainly critical of the government. Besides possibly helping rebuild FIDESZ reputation with the public, this style of loyal opposition created a way for FIDESZ to criticize the Socialist–Free Democrat coalition at the same time that it distanced itself from the more extreme Torgyán.

FIDESZ had stabilized itself by 1996, though its public support remained very low. But then, its closest allies began falling apart. In the Hungarian Democratic Forum, the conflict set off by the Democratic Forum-Free Democrat Pact of 1990 and made worse by the 1992 Csurka Tract continued to rage on into 1996. As that party split into two with very similar names—the new party called itself the Hungarian Democratic People's Party and seemed unable to explain why it split from the Hungarian Democratic Forum other than personal conflicts—public support for both wings plummeted. At the same time, internal conflict within the Christian Democratic People's Party was escalating. According to Hungarian political scientist Zsolt Enyedi, the intra-party conflict developed after the Christian Democrats fell from governmental power following the Socialist victory in 1994. The split was largely between the parliamentary faction, led by Tamás Isépy, and the party's National Committee, led by Gyôrgy Giczy. Isépy's group had benefited greatly from its relationship with Antall and the Democratic Forum and continued to have the stronger position in the elite politics field; besides its role in parliament, for example, it also had the stronger relationship with other European Christian Democratic parties. In comparison, Giczy's group had greater control over the party apparatus and had more support by the rank-and-file.[7] By the 1998 election, the party had effectively collapsed; Isépy and some of his colleagues ran as FIDESZ candidates.[8]

The Socialist resurrection of 1993 and the FIDESZ revival of 1996 show a similar pattern. In the former case, the Socialists began climbing in public support only after support for new parties, notably FIDESZ, plummeted, and these drops in support had always followed intra-party crises. In the same way, it was during the intense leadership battle within the Christian Democratic People's Party in 1996 and a few months after the Democratic Forum split into two parties that FIDESZ began its rise in public support. In October 1996, as support for the other two center-right parties dropped, FIDESZ support jumped to 19%. A month later, it rose again to 22%. During the first round of the 1998 election, FIDESZ received just under 30% of the party list vote. The Christian Democrats disappeared, and the Democratic Forum would have been eliminated had it not gone into an electoral alliance with FIDESZ.

In the 1998 election, FIDESZ became the main governing party, even though the Socialists won more party lists votes (33%.) It accomplished this through an electoral alliance with the Independent Smallholders' Party, which received 13% of that vote. Declaring themselves the victors of the first-round, FIDESZ was able to win a much larger number of single-member seats in the second round and thereby gained enough seats in parliament to form a government.

The ascent of FIDESZ on the political right then continued around 2000. That ascent followed a similar pattern to its revival in 1996. Again, another new party took self-destructive steps, and again FIDESZ capitalized on its demise. This time, it was the Independent Smallholders' Party, which during the first few years of the new regime performed arguably the most spectacular implosion of all the parties, splitting into five by the 1994 election. The 2001 crisis was triggered by allegations of corruption, including bribery, against József Torgyán, the party president and Minister of Agriculture. Torgyán was forced to resign as minister in February. By May, the party split into two warring camps, one backing Torgyán and the other determined to oust him. Each held its own party convention and elected its own leader of the party. The party's disciplinary committee, allied with Torgyán, expelled six prominent Smallholder MP's for speaking out against Torgyán. The anti-Torgyán group, in response, voted to have Torgyán removed from the party faction. To add absurdity to self-annihilation, in the midst of the conflict, Torgyán claimed that underworld figures associated with his opponents in the party were intending to assassinate him, a claim that Hungarian politicians responded to with mostly bewilderment. As the party slipped into this highly public intra-organizational war, its public support effectively evaporated. In the 2002 election, the Independent Smallholders' Party received less than 1% of the party list vote and disappeared.

As the Independent Smallholders' Party collapsed, the stranglehold over Hungarian politics by the Hungarian Socialist Party and FIDESZ tightened. In the 2002 parliamentary election, the Socialists received 42% of the vote and FIDESZ, running together with the Democratic Forum but in fact holding most of the candidacies, received 41%. The only other party to pass the 5% minimum threshold was the Alliance of Free Democrats, which barely survived with 5.6% of the list vote. In other words, the two strongest parties constructed by the Hungarian dissident movement, one by the Budapest radicals and the other by the populist writers, face probable political extinction in 2006. To make matters worse for them, the Democratic Forum, which decided to distance itself from FIDESZ after the 2002 election, fell into yet another intra-party crisis in late 2004 and split once again. Sándor Lezsák, the writer who hosted the founding meeting of the organization at his Lakitelek home in 1987, was the last of the Democratic Forum founding fathers to quit the organization. Lezsák became an independent member of Parliament with his allies. At the same time, FIDESZ took yet another step towards a complete takeover of the Hungarian right, changing its name yet again after the 2002 defeat to FIDESZ—Hungarian Civic Alliance (in Hungarian, Hungarian, *FIDESZ–Magyar Polgári Szövetség)*, which could also be translated as

Hungarian Civic Union. It is a clear indication that FIDESZ plans to unify the Hungarian center-right and the less extreme right-wing under its organizational umbrella. A decade after their nearly disastrous defeat in 1994, the Young Democrats are within striking distance of becoming the only significant party on the Hungarian political right.

It is no surprise, considering the backgrounds and histories of the other parties, that Hungarian politics evolved to become dominated by a party of Socialist politicians with decades of party experience and a party built by young lawyers. FIDESZ was the least institutionalized of all the parties to enter parliament in 1990, since it assembled an entirely now organization. In comparison, both the Democratic Forum and Free Democrats had longer histories and built themselves onto other organizations, including churches and local clubs. Similarly, the Christian Democrats and the Independent Smallholders were the revamped versions of pre-Stalinist era parties. But even in 1990 it was clear that the young lawyers in charge of this radically anti-communist organization were more capable of learning the new, democratic politics. They made significant strategic errors, notably their sudden shift in ideology and effective expulsion of an extremely popular politician in 1993, but they learned rapidly from those mistakes. Note, as one clear example, that name changes after 1993 were carefully orchestrated and occurred only after electoral defeats and years before another election. From a competence perspective, it is also no surprise that from the beginning of the new regime in 1990, the evolution of the party system was driven to a large extent by new parties undermining their own public credibility through rapid shifts in presentation and highly public intra-party wars.

But a disturbing question emerges. In 1994, FIDESZ came within 2% of the vote of being eliminated from Hungarian politics, and since its support was dropping extremely fast—80% to 85% percent of its supporters deserted the party in the months before the election, and its public support continued to drop after the election—its elimination from Hungarian politics was a real possibility. What would have happened in Hungarian politics had FIDESZ disappeared? The other moderate right parties, the Hungarian Democratic Forum and the Christian Democratic People's Party, effectively collapsed due to internal strife by 1998, and the Democratic Forum survived only because of its electoral relationship with FIDESZ. The more right-wing, Independent Smallholders' Party collapsed from internal conflict by 2002. Political outcomes can seem inevitable, even deterministic, but in the Hungarian case it is clearly to a large degree luck that FIDESZ survived politically past 1994. Had it dropped further in support—for example, had it been more effective in abandoning its popular youth image in 1994—what party other than FIDESZ would been able to effectively challenge the Socialists?

The question can be posed another way: Had FIDESZ been eliminated, who would Hungarians on the center-right vote for? They certainly would not support the liberal Alliance of Free Democrats, and every center-right party would likely have imploded by the 2002 election. This would leave them with two options: They could support the Socialists, or they could vote for a more right wing party, possibly the Hungarian Justice and Life Party, which opposed joining NATO and the European Union and supports expanding the Hungarian border into

Rumania, Serbia and Slovakia. In other words, because of the inability of new Hungarian parties, especially those on the right, to develop enough competence at party politics to sustain public support, Hungary could easily have drifted back to a situation in which the Socialists became the overwhelmingly dominant party with only token opposition from smaller parties and possibly more radical groups. In this way, Hungary could easily have taken significant steps back to towards the Kádár era and close to the goals of Imre Pozsgay and Károly Grósz, the leaders of the Hungarian Socialist Workers' Party who in 1989 worked to create a democracy more in style than in substance. Or, without real alternatives, disenchanted Hungarians may have shifted their support to more right-wing parties.

This, in sum, is the problem explored in this book that dissidents and others face as they try to build a new democratic system. Like the Hungarian dissidents, they may be inclined to focus on changing the procedures, building civil society, and removing members of the previous regime. But besides that, for the next decade and beyond, they have to build party organizations that are sustainable and are able to maintain public support after the euphoria has evaporated. This is not simply an issue of building solid institutional structures. The promoters of democracy have to devise a strategy for building party competence within their organizations, so that these parties can maintain their public support—and by extension, the new regime will be more likely to keep its public legitimacy—and a stable multiparty system will develop. A likely step would be the dissidents forfeiting their roles to others more capable of developing these skills, and almost definitely a stable group of professional party politicians would have to rise to positions of power. A stratum of political professionals is hardly ideal and contains its own set of limitations and dangers. But, the alternative to that stratum is significantly worse.

# Notes:

[1] Robert Michels. 1962. *Political Parties; A Sociological Study of the Oligarchical Tendencies of Modern Democracy*, Trans. by Eden and Cedar Paul, (New York: The Free Press).

[2] E.E. Schattschneider (1960) *The Semisovereign People; A Realist's View of Democracy in America*, (New York: Holt, Rinehart and Winston), pp. 1-19.

[3] Interview, Sándor Holbok.

[4] Interview, István Hegedüs.

[5] Interview, Sándor Holbok. I have heard this explanation from several FIDESZ politicians and activists, though never by anyone outside the party. While it is doubtful that FIDESZ lost in 1994 because it campaigned against both the Socialists and the Democratic Forum, the explanation does indicate that FIDESZ strategists had learned the importance of clear, consistent messages.

[6] Ibid. The two party strategy was also described to me by an anonymous source.

[7] Zsolt Enyedi (1996) "Organizing a Subcultural Party in Eastern Europe: The Case of the Christian Democrats", *Political Parties*, vol. 3, pp. 377-96.

[8] Isépy ran as number seventeen on the FIDESZ national list. Other prominent Christian Democratic politicians were also on this party list: Mihály Varga, László Surján, and János Latorcia were numbers six, nineteen, and twenty, respectively.

# Appendix:

# Statistical Analysis of FIDESZ Defeat

The quasi-experiment on how FIDESZ's abrupt switch of its cultural ideology influenced its public support was conducted on data from the Central European University Surveys of 1992 and 1994. Specifically, the same ordered logit model was estimated eight times, once for the rating of each party discussed in the book (FIDESZ, the Hungarian Socialist Party, the Hungarian Democrat Forum, and the Alliance of Free Democrats) in each of two years, 1992 and 1994. (The tests were also run for the other two parties in Parliament at the time, but the results are not included for the sake of brevity.) The research design is presented in Figure A.1.

The dependent variable was the rating of each party from one to seven. The respondent was asked, "How much do the following organizations express or oppose your views and interests?"[1] A "7" denotes that the party expresses their views and interests well and "1" means that the party strongly opposes their views and interests. (In 1992, these were questions Q10a through Q10f, while in 1994, they were HPQ10a through HPQ10f.)

The main independent variable was cultural ideology, and the other independent variables were economic ideology, year of birth, and gender. The ideology variables were created from six variables based on respondent reactions to statements. The respondents were read each statement and then asked if they "definitely agree", "rather agree", "rather disagree", or "definitely disagree". The statements were as follows:

- "It should be the government's responsibility to provide a job for everyone who wants one." (Q16c in 1992 and HPQ16c in 1994);
- "It is harmful for the economy if the government tries to reduce income differences between rich and poor." (Q16d in 1992 and HPQ16d in 1994);
- "The transfer of state-owned companies to private hands will help very much in solving the economic problems of our country." (Q16f in 1992 and HPQ16f in 1994);
- "Politicians who do not believe in God should not perform public functions." (Q16h in 1992 and HPQ16h in 1994);
- "A woman should be allowed to have an abortion in the early weeks of pregnancy, if she decides so." (Q16n in 1992 and HPQ16n in 1994);
- "It is more important that a politician be a strong patriot than that he/she be an expert." (Q16o in 1992 and HPQ16o in 1994);[2]

221

The statistics were run in several steps. First, missing data problems were resolved by using a multiple imputation technique developed by Gary King and his colleagues at Harvard University.[3] For each data set (i.e., 1992 and 1994), the fourteen variables mentioned above plus six dichotomous vote variables were loaded into Amelia, the software developed by these researchers, at once. Each of these dichotomous vote variables was created from Q6a in 1992 ("If the election were this Sunday, which party list would you vote for?") and HPQ6a in 1994 ("Which party list did you vote for?"). If the respondent said that he/she would vote or had voted for the particular party (for example, FIDESZ), then the particular dichotomy (e.g., the FIDESZ vote dichotomy) would be coded as "1". If the respondent said that he/she would vote or had voted for another party, the particular dichotomy was coded as "0". If he/she claimed not to vote, it was loaded as a missing value. Each variable was forced to remain ordinal except year of birth. Five imputed datasets were created.

Second, a LISREL was run on the Amelia output to measure underlying cultural and economic ideology. 16c, 16h, 16n, and 16o were loaded onto the cultural ideology factor. 16c, 16d, and 16f were loaded onto the economic ideology factor. These factors were then used as independent variables in the ordered logits.

The twelve ordered logits mentioned above were then run, and statistical simulations of the results were created. All the independent variables except cultural ideology were held constant at their means.[4]

**Figure A.1**
**Research Design:**
**How an Abrupt Ideological Change Influences Party Ratings**

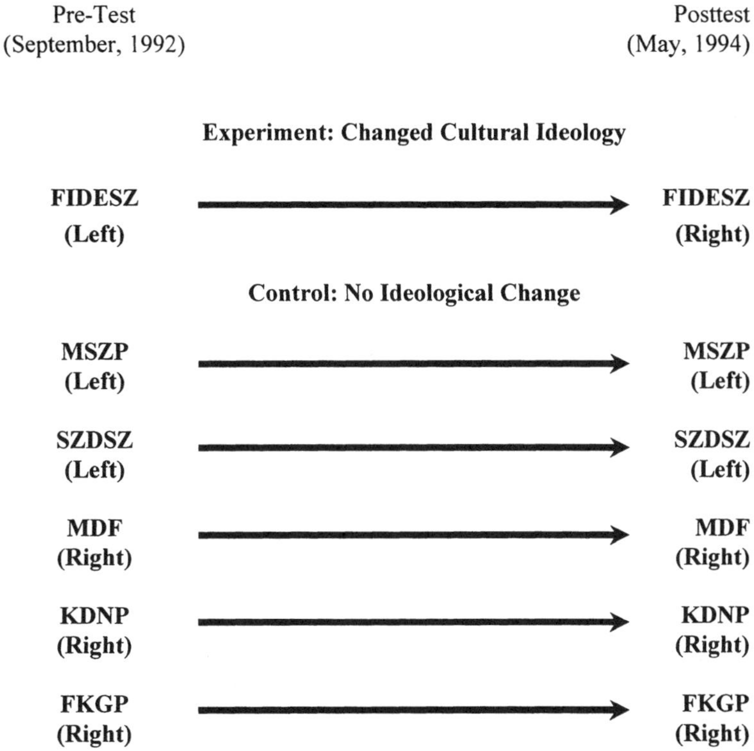

| Pre-Test | Posttest |
|---|---|
| (September, 1992) | (May, 1994) |

**Experiment: Changed Cultural Ideology**

**FIDESZ**                ⟶         **FIDESZ**
**(Left)**                                **(Right)**

**Control: No Ideological Change**

**MSZP**       ⟶       **MSZP**
**(Left)**                   **(Left)**

**SZDSZ**       ⟶       **SZDSZ**
**(Left)**                   **(Left)**

**MDF**       ⟶       **MDF**
**(Right)**                   **(Right)**

**KDNP**       ⟶       **KDNP**
**(Right)**                   **(Right)**

**FKGP**       ⟶       **FKGP**
**(Right)**                   **(Right)**

# Notes:

[1] The wording presented here were taken from "The Central European University's 1994 Hungarian Election Study: English translation of the questionnaires", which was provided by Gábor Tóka, the main investigator.

[2] Ibid.

[3] King, Gary. et. al (2001), "Analyzing Incomplete Political Science Data: An Alternative Algorithm for Multiple Imputation," *American Political Science Review*: 95, 1, pp. 49-69.

[4] Gary King, Michael Tomz, and Jason Wittenberg (2000) "Making the Most of Statistical Analyses: Improving Interpretation and Presentation", *American Journal of Political Science*, Vol. 44, No. 2 (April): 341-355. A current version of Clarify software is available at http://GKing.Harvard.Edu.

# Bibliography

Aczel, Tamas and Tibor Meray. 1959. *The Revolt of the Mind: A Case History of Intellectual Resistance Behind the Iron Curtain.* New York: Praeger.

Ágh, Attila. 1990. *A Századvég Gyermekei. Az Államszocializmus Összeomlása a Nyolcvanas Években. [The Children of the Century's End: The Collapse of State Socialism in the 1980s.]* Budapest: Közgazdasági és Jogi Könyvkiadó.

————, ed. 1994. *The Emergence of East Central European Parliaments: The First Steps.* Budapest: Hungarian Centre of Democratic Studies Foundation.

————. 1994. "The Paradoxes of Transition: The External and Internal Overload of the Transition Process." In Terry Cox and Andy Furlong, eds. *Hungary: The Politics of Transition.* Special edition to *The Journal of Communist Studies and Transition Politics,* 10. pp. 15-34.

————. 1995. "Partial Consolidation of the East-Central European Parties; the Case of the Hungarian Socialist Party." *Party Politics,* vol. 1, no 4. pp. 491–514.

————. 1997. "Defeat and Success as Promoters of Party Change; the Hungarian Socialist Party after two Abrupt Changes." (Research note.) *Party Politics,* vol. 3, no 3. pp. 427-44.

Agócs, Peter and Sándor Agócs. 1994. "The Change was but an Unfulfilled Promise: Agriculture and the Rural Population in Post-Communist Hungary." *East European Politics and Society*, vol. 8, no. 1. pp. 32-57.

Agócs, Sándor, ed. 1991. *Lakitelek 1987, A Magyarság Esélyei; A Tanácskozás Hiteles Jegyzôkönyve. [Lakitelek 1987, The Chances for Hungarianism; The Authentic Minutes of the Conference.]* Budapest: Püski.

Balogh, Sándor and Lajos Izsák. 1977. *Pártok és Pártprogramok Magyarországon: 1944–1948.* Budapest: Tankönyvkiadó.

Berglund, Sten and Jan Ake Dellenbrant, eds. 1991. *The New Democracies in Eastern Europe; Party Systems and Political Cleavages: Second Edition.* Brookfield, VT: Edward Elgar Publishing Company.

Bibó, István. 1991. *Democracy, Revolution, Self-Determination; Selected Writings.* Károly Nagy, ed. András Boros–Kazai, trans. Boulder: East European Monographs. Distributed by Columbia University Press.

———. 1994. *Demokratikus Magyarország; Válogatás Bibó István Tanulmányaiból.[Democratic Hungary; Selections from the Essays of István Bibó.]* Budapest: Magvetô Könyvkiadó.

Bihari, Mihály and Béla Pokol. 1992. *Politológia. [Political Science.]* Budapest: Universitas.

Bihari, Mihály. 1996. "Az Állampárt Végorái; Egy Pártkongresszus Szociológiája" ["The Government Party's Last Hours; The Sociology of a Party Congress."] in Mihály Bihari, *Magyar Politika, 1945–1995: A Magyar Politikai Rendszer Történetének Fôbb Szakaszai a Második Világháború Után. [Hungarian Politics, 1945-1995: The Most Important Stages of the Hungarian Political System's History after the Second World War].* Budapest: Korona. pp. 85-95.

Bourdieu, Pierre. 1977 [1972]. *Outline of a Theory of Practice*. Cambridge: Cambridge University Press.

———. 1984 [1979]. *Distinction; A Social Critique of the Judgement of Taste*. Cambridge: Harvard University Press.

———. 1988 [1984]. *Homo Academicvs*. Stanford: Stanford University Press.

———. 1990 [1980]. *The Logic of Practice*. Stanford: Stanford University Press.

———. 1990. *In Other Words: Essays Towards a Reflexive Sociology*. Matthew Adamson, trans. Stanford: Stanford University Press.

———. 1991. *Language and Symbolic Power*. John B. Thompson, ed. Cambridge: Harvard University Press.

———. 1993. *The Field of Cultural Production; Essays on Art and Literature*. Randal Johnson, ed. New York: Columbia University Press.

Bourdieu, Pierre and Loïc J. D. Wacquant. 1992. *An Invitation to Reflexive Sociology*. Chicago: University of Chicago Press.

Bozóki, András, ed. 1992. *Tiszta lappal: a FIDESZ a magyar politikában, 1988–1991 [With a clean slate: FIDESZ in Hungarian politics, 1988–1991.]* Budapest: FIDESZ Press.

———. 1993. "Hungary's Road to Systemic Change: The Opposition Roundtable." Jozsef Borocz, trans. *East European Politics and Society,* vol. 7, no. 2. pp. 276-308.

———. 1994. "Party Formation and Constitutional Change in Hungary." In Terry Cox and Andy Furlong, eds. *Hungary: The Politics of Transition*. Special edition to *The Journal of Communist Studies and Transition Politics*, 10. pp. 35-55.

————, ed. 1994. *Democratic Legitimacy in Post-Communist Societies.*
Budapest:
T-Twins.

————. 1997. "Mozgalmi–értelmiségi politika a rendszerváltás után: A
Demokratikus Charta. ["Movement and intellectual politics after the
regime change: The Democratic Charter"] *Politikatudományi
Szemle* 1997. I. szám. pp. 98–135.

Bozóki, András, András Körösényi, and George Schöpflin, eds. 1992. *Post-
Communist Transition; Emerging Pluralism in Hungary.* New York:
St. Martin's Press.

Brown, J.F. 1988. *Eastern Europe and Communist* Rule. Durham: Duke.

Bruszt, László and David Stark. 1992. "Remaking the Political Field in
Hungary: From the Politics of Confrontation to the Politics of
Competition." In Ivo Banac, ed. *Eastern Europe in Revolution.*
Ithaca: Cornell University Press.

Bugajski, Janusz and Maxine Pollack. 1989. *East European Fault Lines;
Dissent, Opposition, and Social Activism.* Westview Special Studies
on the Soviet Union and Eastern Europe. Boulder: Westview Press.

Calhoun, Craig, Edward LiPuma, and Moishe Postone, eds. 1993. *Bourdieu:
Critical Perspectives.* Chicago: University of Chicago Press.

Central European University. 1992. *The Development of Party Systems and
Electoral Alignments in East Central Europe: The 1992 Survey in
Hungary. Machine readable data files.* Budapest: Department of
Political Science, Central European University.

————. 1994. *The Development of Party Systems and Electoral Alignments
in East Central Europe: The 1994 Survey in Hungary. Machine
readable data files.* Budapest: Department of Political Science,
Central European University.

# Bibliography

Connor, Walter D. 1997. "Social Change and Stability in Eastern Europe." *Problems of Communism*, vol. 26, no. 6 (November–December). pp. 16-32.

Cox, Terry and Andy Furlong. 1994. "Political Transition in Hungary: An Overview." In Terry Cox and Andy Furlong, eds. *Hungary: The Politics of Transition.* Special edition to *The Journal of Communist Studies and Transition Politics*, 10. pp. 1-12.

Cox, Terry and László Vass. 1994. "Civil Society and Interest Representation in Hungarian Political Development." In Terry Cox and Andy Furlong, eds. *Hungary: The Politics of Transition.* Special edition to *The Journal of Communist Studies and Transition Politics*, 10. pp. 153-79.

Csepeli, György and Antal Örkény. 1992. *Ideology and Political Beliefs in Hungary; The Twilight of State Socialism.* Brian McLean and Julianna Parti, trans. New York: Pinter.

Csicsery, George Paul. 1990. "The Siege of Nógrádi Street, Budapest, 1989." In William M. Brinton and Alan Rinzler, ed. *Without Force or Lies; Voices from the Revolution of Central Europe in 1989–90.* San Francisco: Mercury House.

Csizmadia, Ervin. 1995. *A Magyar Demokratikus Ellenzék (1968–1988): Dokumentumok [The Hungarian Democratic Opposition, 1968–1988: Documents.]* Budapest, T-Twins Kiadó.

———. 1995. *A Magyar Demokratikus Ellenzék (1968-1988): Interjúk [The Hungarian Democratic Opposition, 1968-1988: Interviews]* Budapest, T-Twins Kiadó.

———. 1995. *A Magyar Demokratikus Ellenzék (1968-1988): Monográfia [The Hungarian Democratic Opposition, 1968-1988: Monograph.]* Budapest, T-Twins Kiadó.

Deák, Isván. 1995. "A Fatal Compromise? The Debate over Collaboration and Resistance in Hungary." *East European Politics and Society*, vol. 9, no. 2, Spring. pp. 209–33.

Donáth, Ferenc, et al., eds. 1980. *Bibó Emlékkönyv [Bibó Memorial Book]* Budapest: Samizdat.

Downs, Anthony. 1957. *An Economic Theory of Democracy*. New York: Harper & Row, Publishers.

Drew, Paul and Anthony Wootton, eds. 1988. *Ervin Goffman; Exploring the Interaction Order*. Boston: Northeastern University Press.

Dús, Ágnes, ed. 1993. *Magyarország Miniszterelnökei: 1848 - 1990*. Budapest: Cégér.

Duverger, Maurice. 1954 [1951]. *Political Parties; Their Organization and Activity in the Modern State*. Barbara North and Robert North, trans. New York: John Wiley & Son, Inc.

Enyedi, Zsolt. 1996. "Organizing a Subcultural Party in Eastern Europe: The Case of the Christian Democrats." *Political Parties*, vol. 3, pp. 377-96.

Enyedi, Zsolt and Magdolna Balazs. 1996. "Hungarian Case Studies: The Alliance of Free Democrats and the Alliance of Young Democrats." in Paul Lewis, ed. *Party Structure and Organization in East-Central Europe*. Brookfield, VT: Edward Edgar, Publisher. pp. 43-65.

Epstien, Leon D. 1967. *Political Parties in Western Democracies*. New York: Frederick A. Praeger, Publishers.

Ekiert, Grzegorz. 1996. *The State Against Society; Political Crises and Their Aftermath in East Central Europe*. Princeton: Princeton University Press.

FIDESZ Documents. *FIDESZ; Az Elsô Száz Nap. [FIDESZ: The First One Hundred Days.]*

———. 1991. *Federation of Young Democrats.*

———. 1993. *A Fiatal Demokrácia Szövetségének Alapszabálya. [Bylaws of the Federation of the Young Democracy.]* (draft constitution.) Federation of Young Democrats, Debrecen, April 16-18, 1993

———. 1993. *Módosító Indítványok az Alapszabály Tervezetézhez. [Proposed Amendments to the Draft Constitution]* Federation of Young Democrats, Fifth Congress, Debrecen, April 16-18, 1993.

Gati, Charles. 1989. "Reforming Communist Systems: Lessons from the Hungarian Experience." In William E. Griffith, ed. *Central and Eastern Europe: The Opening Curtain?* Boulder: Westview. pp. 218–40.

Gerô, András. 1995. *Modern Hungarian Society in the Making: The Unfinished Experience.* James Patterson and Enikô Koncz, trans. Budapest: Central European University Press.

Gombár, Csaba, et al. 1994. *Kormány a Mérlegen: 1990–1994. [The Hungarian Government on Balance.]* Budapest: Politikai Kutatások Központja.

Grzymala-Busse, Anna M. 2002, *Redeeming the Communist Past: The Regeneration of Communist Parties in East Central Europe,* Cambridge: Cambridge University Press.

Hanák, Péter, ed. 1988. *One Thousand Years: A Concise History of Hungary.* Zsuzsa Béres, trans. Budapest: Corvina.

Held, Joseph, ed. 1992. *The Columbia History of Eastern Europe in the Twentieth Century.* New York: Columbia.

———, ed. 1996. *Populism in Eastern Europe.* Boulder: East European Monographs. Distributed by Columbia University Press.

Horváth, Agnes.1998. "Tricking into the Position of the Outcast: A Case Study in the Emergence and Effects of Communist Power" *Political Psychology*, vol. 19, no. 2. pp. 331–2.

Janda, Kenneth. 1980. *Political Parties: A Cross-National Survey.* New York: Free Press.

Janos, Andrew C. 1982. *The Politics of Backwardness in Hungary, 1825–1945.* Princeton: Princeton University Press.

Jenkins, Richard. 1992. *Pierre Bourdieu.* New York: Routledge.

Joseph, John E. and Talbot J. Taylor. 1990. *Ideologies of Language.* New York: Routledge.

Kéri, László, ed. 1994. *Orbán Viktor. [Viktor Orbán]* Budapest: Századvég Kiadó.

Key, V.O. 1964. *Politics, Parties, and Pressure Groups*, 5th ed. New York: Crowell.

King, Gary, et al. 2000. "Making the Most of Statistical Analyses: Improving Interpretation and Presentation", *American Journal of Political Science*, 44: 341-355.

King, Gary, et al. 2001. "Analyzing Incomplete Political Science Data: An Alternative Algorithm for Multiple Imputation," *American Political Science Review*, 95: 49-69.

Király, Béla, ed. 1995. *Lawful Revolution in Hungary, 1989–1994.* Boulder: East European Monographs. Distributed by Columbia University Press.

Kis, János, et al. 1987. "Társadalmi Szerzôdés, a Politikai Kibontakozás Feltételei" ["Social Contract: Conditions of Overcoming the Political Deadlock"] *Beszélô*, no. 20.

———. 1989. *Politics in Hungary: For a Democratic Alternative.* Boulder: East European Monographs. Distributed by Columbia University Press.

# Bibliography

Kiss, József, ed. 1992. *Az 1990-ben Megválasztott Országgyûlés Almanachja [The Almanac of the Parliament Elected in 1990.]* Budapest: Jelenkutató Alapítvány.

Kiss, Yudit. 1994. "Privatization Paradoxes in East Central Europe." *East European Politics and Society*, vol. 8, no. 1, Winter. pp. 122–52.

Kitschelt, Herbert. 1992. "The Formation of Party Systems in East Central Europe." *Politics and Society*, vol. 20, no. 1, March. pp. 7–50.

_____. 1993. "Comparative Historical Research and Rational Choice Theory: The Case of Transitions to Democracy." (Review Essay.) *Theory and Society*, vol. 22. pp. 413–27.

_____. 1995. "Formation of Party Cleavages in Post-Communist Democracies; Theoretical Propositions." *Party Politics*, vol. 1, no 4. pp. 447–72.

Kitschelt, Herbert, et al. 1999. *Post-Communist Party Systems: Competition, Representation, and Inter-Party Cooperation.* Cambridge: Cambridge University Press.

Knoke, David and James H. Kuklinski. 1982. *Network Analysis*. Series: Quantitative Applications in the Social Sciences, no. 28–001. Newbury Park, CA: Sage.

Konrád, George. 1995. *The Melancholy of Rebirth: Essays from Post-Communist Central Europe, 1989–1994.* Michael Henry Heim, trans. San Diego: Harcourt Brace.

Kornai, János. 1991. "The Hungarian Reform Process: Visions, Hopes, and Reality." In Ferenc Fehér and Andrew Arato, eds. *Crisis and Reform in Eastern Europe.* New Brunswick: Transaction. pp. 27-98.

_____. 1993. *Útkeresés. [Searching for a Road.]* Budapest: Századvég Kiadó.

233

Körösényi, András. 1995. "The Reasons for the Defeat of the Right." (notes and comments.) Eszter Nadin with Johnathan Sunley, trans. In *East European Politics and Society,* vol. 9, no. 1. pp. 179-94.

Kovács, Zoltán. 1993. "The Geography of Hungarian Parliamentary Elections 1990." In John O'Loughlin and Herman van der Wusten *The New Political Geography of Eastern Europe.* London: Belhaven. pp. 255-73.

Kovrig, Bennet. 1979. *Communism in Hungary: From Kun to Kádár.* Stanford: Hoover Institution Press.

Központi Statisztikai Hivatal [Central Statistical Office.] 1993. *Magyar Statisztikai Évkönyv 1993 [Statistical Yearbook of Hungary, 1993.]* Csák Liget, ed. Komárom: Komáromi Nyomda és Kiadó Kft.

———. 1995. *Magyar Statisztikai Évkönyv 1995 [Statistical Yearbook of Hungary, 1995.]* Csák Liget, ed. Budapest: Regiszter Kiadó és Nyomda Kft.

Kubik, Jan.1994. *The Power of Symbols Against the Symbols of Power; The Rise of Solidarity and the Fall of State Socialism in Poland.* University Park, PA: Pennsylvania State University Press.

Lawson, Key. 1976. *The Comparative Study of Political Parties.* New York: St. Martin's.

Lengyel, László. 1996. *A Rendszerváltó Elit Tündöklése és Bukása. [The Glittering and Downfall of the Transformation Elite.]* Budapest: Helikon.

Lomax, Bill. 1994. "Obstacles to the Development of Democratic Politics." In Terry Cox and Andy Furlong, eds. *Hungary: The Politics of Transition.* Special edition to *The Journal of Communist Studies and Transition Politics*, 10. pp. 81-100.

Luca, Gábor et. al, eds. 1994. *Parliamenti Választások 1994 [The 1994 Parliamentary Elections.]* Budapest: Osiris–Századég.

Bibliography

Mahr, Alison and John Nagle. 1995. "Resurrection of the Successor Parties and Democratization in East-Central Europe." *Communist and Post-Communist Studies,* vol. 28, no. 4. pp. 394–408.

Mair, Peter. 1994. "Party Organizations: From Civil Society to the State". In *How Parties Organize: Change and Adaptation in Western Europe.* Richard S. Katz and Peter Mair, eds. London: Sage. pp. 1-22.

Márkus, György. 1991. "Pártok és Törésvonalak" ["Parties and Cleavages"] *Társadalomtudományi Szemle [Social Science Review],* no. 1–2. pp. 89–91.

Michels, Robert. 1962. *Political Parties; A Sociological Study of Oligarchical Tendencies of Modern Democracy.* Eden and Cedar Paul, trans. New York: The Free Press.

Michnik, Adam. 1985. "A New Evolutionism." In Adam Michnik, *Letters From Prison and Other Essays.* Berkeley: University of California Press. pp. 135–48.

Moldován, Tamás, ed. 1990. *Szabadon Választott; Parliamenti Almanach 1990 [Freely Elected; Parliamentary Almanac of 1990.]* Budapest: Idegenforgalmi Propaganda és Kiadó.

Molnár, Miklós. 1979. "The Communist Party of Hungary." In Stephen Fischer–Galati, ed. *The Communist Parties of Eastern Europe.* New York: Columbia University Press.

Mommsen, Wolfgang J. 1989. *The Political and Social Theory of Max Weber; Collected Essays.* Chicago: The University of Chicago Press.

O'Neal, Patrick. 1996. "Revolution from Within: Analysis, Transitions from Authoritarianism, and the Case of Hungary". *World Politics* 48: 579–603.

Ostrogorski, Moisei. 1964. *Democracy and the Organization of Political Parties; Volume II: The United States.* Martin Lipset, ed. New Brunswick: Transaction Press.

Paczolay, Péter. 1993. "The New Hungarian Constitutional State: Challenges and Perspectives." In A. E. Dick Howard, ed. *Constitution Making in Eastern Europe.* Baltimore: Woodrow Wilson. pp. 21–55.

Pamlényi, Ervin, ed. 1975. *A History of Hungary.* Budapest: Zrínyi.

Panebianco, Angelo. 1988. *Political Parties: Organization and Power.* Cambridge: Cambridge University Press.

Pokol Béla. 1994. *A Magyar Parlamentarizmus. [The Hungarian Parliamentarianism.]* Budapest: Cserépfalvi Kiadása.

Pomper, Gerald M. 1992. *Passions and Interests: Political Party Concepts of American Democracy.* Lawrence, KS: University Press of Kansas.

Pozsgay, Imre. 1988. *Koronatú és Tettstárs [Star Witness and Accomplice.]* Budapest: Korona.

———. 1993. *1989; Politikús–pálya a pártállamban és a rendszerváltásban. [1989; Political Career in a Party State and During a Regime Change.]* Budapest: Püszki.

Punnett, Malcolm and Gabriella Ilonszki. 1994. "Leading Democracy: The Emergence of Party Leaders and Their Roles in the Hungarian Parties." In Terry Cox and Andy Furlong, eds. *Hungary: The Politics of Transition.* Special edition to *The Journal of Communist Studies and Transition Politics*, 10. pp. 101-19.

Putnam, Robert D. 1993. *Making Democracy Work; Civic Traditions in Modern Italy.* Princeton: Princeton University Press.

Révész, Sándor. 1995. *Antall József Távolról [Joseph Antall from a Distance]* Budapest: Sík Kiadó.

———. 1997. *Aczél és Korunk [Aczél and Our Times]* Budapest: Sík Kiadó.

# Bibliography

Ripp, Zoltán. 1995. *Szabad Demokraták: Történeti Vázlat a Szabad Demokraták Szövetségének politikájáról. [Free Democrats: A Historic Sketch of the Politics of the Alliance of Free Democrats.]* Budapest: Politikatörténeti Alapitvány.

Rothschild, Joseph. 1989. *Return to Diversity; A Political History of East Central Europe Since World War II.* New York: Oxford University Press.

Sándor, Kurtán, Péter Sándor, and László Vass, eds. 1991. *Magyarország Politikai Évkönyve, 1991. [Hungarian Political Yearbook, 1991.]* Budapest: Ökonómia Alapítvány – Economix Rt.

————. 1992. *Magyarország Politikai Évkönyve, 1992. [Hungarian Political Yearbook, 1992.]* Budapest: Demokrácia Kutatások Magyar Központja Alapítvány – Economix Rt.

————. 1993. *Magyarország Politikai Évkönyve, 1993. [Hungarian Political Yearbook, 1993.]* Budapest: Demokrácia Kutatások Magyar Központja Alapítvány – Economix Rt.

————. 1994. *Magyarország Politikai Évkönyve, 1994. [Hungarian Political Yearbook, 1994.]* Budapest: Demokrácia Kutatások Magyar Központja Alapítvány – Economix Rt.

————. 1995. *Magyarország Politikai Évkönyve, 1995. [Hungarian Political Yearbook, 1995.]* Budapest: Demokrácia Kutatások Magyar Központja Alapítvány – Economix Rt.

————. 1996. *Magyarország Politikai Évkönyve, 1996. [Hungarian Political Yearbook, 1996.]* Budapest: Demokrácia Kutatások Magyar Központja Alapítvány – Economix Rt.

————. 1997. *Magyarország Politikai Évkönyve, 1997. [Hungarian Political Yearbook, 1997.]* Budapest: Demokrácia Kutatások Magyar Központja Alapítvány – Economix Rt.

_____. 1998. *Magyarország Politikai Évkönyve, 1998. [Hungarian Political Yearbook, 1998.]* Budapest: Demokrácia Kutatások Magyar Központja Alapítvány – Economix Rt.

Sartori, Giovanni. 1976. *Parties and Party Systems; A Framework for Analysis: Volume I.* New York: Cambridge University Press.

Schöpflin, George. 1979. "Opposition and Para–Opposition: Critical Currents in Hungary, 1968–78." In Rudolf L. Tôkés, ed. *Opposition in Eastern Europe.* Baltimore: Johns Hopkins University Press.

Schöpflin, George, et. al. 1988. "Leadership Change and Crisis in Hungary." *Problems of Communism*, vol 37, September-October. pp. 28-31.

Stark, David and László Bruszt. 1998. *Postsocialist Pathways: Transforming Politics and Property in East Central Europe.* Cambridge: Cambridge University Press,

Sugar, Peter, Péter Hanák, and Tibor Frank, eds. 1990. *A History of Hungary.* Bloomington: Indiana University Press.

Swain, Nigel. 1992. *Hungary: The Rise and Fall of Feasible Socialism.* New York: Verso.

Sykes, Patricia Lee. 1988. *Losing From the Inside; The Cost of Conflict in the British Social Democratic Party.* New Brunswick: Transaction Books.

Szabó, Máté. 1992. "The Taxi Driver Demonstration in Hungary – Social Protest and Policy Change." In György Szoboszlai, ed. *Flying Blind - Emerging Democracies in East-Central Europe.* Budapest: Hungarian Political Science Association. pp. 357-81.

Szacki, Jerzy. 1994. *Liberalism after Communism.* Chester A. Kisiel, trans. Budapest: Central European University Press.

Szarvas, László. 1994. In Terry Cox and Andy Furlong, eds. *Hungary: The Politics of Transition.* Special edition to *The Journal of Communist Studies and Transition Politics*, 10. pp. 120-36.

# Bibliography

Szeleny, Anna. 1994. "Constructing the Discourse of Transformation: Hungary, 1979–82." *East European Politics and Society*, vol. 8, no. 3, Fall. pp. 439–66.

Szoboszlai, György, ed. 1989. *Pártok és Rendszerek; A Magyar Politikatudományi Társaság Évkönyve, 1989. [Parties and Regimes; The 1989 Yearbook of the Hungarian Political Science Society]*. Budapest: Magyar Politikatudományi Társaság.

————, ed. 1990. *Parliamenti Választások 1990: Politikai Szociológiai Körkép [The 1990 Parliamentary Elections: Social Political Panorama.]* Budapest: MTA.

Tamas, Bernard Ivan. 1998. "Parties on Stage: Evaluating the Performance of Hungarian Parties," In Gabor Toka and Zsolt Enyedi, eds.*The 1994 Elections to the Hungarian National Assembly*. Berlin: Sigma.

Tamás, Miklós Gáspár. 1994. *Másvilág; Politikai Esszék. [Another World: Political Essays.]* Budapest: Új Mandátum Könyvkiadó.

Tóka, Gábor. 1994. "Pártok és választóik 1990-ben és 1994-ben". ["Parties and Their Voters in 1990 and 1994"]. *Társadalmi Riport 1994*. Rudolf Andorka, et. al., eds. (Budapest: TARKI) pp. 395-75.

————, ed. 1995. *The 1990 Election to the Hungarian National Assembly: Analysis, Documents, and Data*. Berlin: Sigma.

Tôkés, Rudolf L., ed. 1979. *Opposition in Eastern Europe*. Baltimore: Johns Hopkins University Press.

————. 1996. *Hungary's Negotiated Revolution; Economic Reform, Social Change, and Political Succession*. Cambridge: Cambridge University Press.

————. 1997. "Party Politics and Political Participation in Post-Communist Hungary. In Karen Dawisha and Bruce Parrott, eds. *The Consolidation of Democracy in East-Central Europe*. Cambridge: Cambridge University Press. pp. 109-49.

Waller, Michael. 1995. "Adaptation of the Former Communist Parties of East–Central Europe; a Case for Social Democracy?" *Party Politics*, vol. 1, no. 4. pp. 473-90.

Ware, Alan. 1987. *Citizens, Parties and the State; A Reappraisal.* Princeton: Princeton University Press.

Weber, Max. 1946. *From Max Weber: Essays in Sociology.* H. H. Gerth and C. Wright Mills, eds. New York: Oxford University Press.

―――. 1978 [1918-20]. *Economy and Society; An Outline of Interpretive Sociology.* Guenther Roth and Claus Wittich, eds. Berkeley: University of California Press.

White, Stephen, Judy Batt, and Paul Lewis, eds. 1993. *Developments in East European Politics*. Durham, Duke University Press.

Wyman, Matthew, et al. 1995. "The Place of 'Party' in Post-Communist Europe." *Party Politics,* 1: 535–48.

# Author Biography

Bernard Ivan Tamas is an assistant professor of Politics and Government at Illinois State University. He received his Ph.D. from Rutgers University in 1999. With the aid of a Fulbright Fellowship to the Central European University in Budapest, Hungary and other grants, Professor Tamas conducted his dissertation research on the political parties that had emerged from the pre-1989 Hungarian democracy movement. Dr. Tamas was a postdoctoral fellow at the Harvard-MIT Data Center, a visiting scholar at Harvard's Center for Basic Research in the Social Sciences, and a visiting professor at both Brandeis University and Williams College. His scholarship focuses on political methodology as well as minor or emerging political parties. This is his second book.